MASTER JACQUES

Master Jacques

The Enigma of Jacques Anquetil

RICHARD YATES

Foreword by Phil Liggett

To Vi

First published in Great Britain in 2001 by
Mousehold Press
Victoria Cottage
Constitution Opening
Norwich, NR3 4BD

in association with

Sport & Publicity
75 Fitzjohns Avenue
Hampstead
London, NW3 6PD

Cover design by Jayne Odell
Cover photograph: Photosport International

ISBN 1 874739 18 8

Printed in Great Britain by Watkiss Studios Ltd, Biggleswade

CONTENTS

Author's Acknowledgements

I would like to express my thanks to Janine Anquetil, Vin Denson, Jacques Seray and Richard Allchin for their help with this book.

Publishers' Acknowledgements

For their invaluable help in the production of this book the publishers would like to thank Roger St Pierre, John Pierce, Luke Evans, and Phil Liggett.

Picture Credits

The publishers would like to thank the following for providing the illustrations listed below:
Photosport International: p. 96, p. 108, p. 168, p. 173, p. 192;
Roger St Pierre: p. 118, p. 124, p. 140, p. 144, p. 153.

Publishers' Note

I was just twelve years old when I first became really interested in cycle-racing. I read every magazine I could get my hands on and there, in what seemed to me to be the fabulous world of continental racing, certain names kept reappearing: there was Tom Simpson, of course – being British, and the great Rik Van Looy and the wonderful Spanish climber, Federico Bahamontes, both in their latter years, but still top stars, and a host of others, including Rudi Altig, Raymond Poulidor, and the usual crop of Italians who were going to replace Fausto Coppi. And there was also a certain Jacques Anquetil – even his name was magical. He rode like a king and often behaved like one. Despite his fame, he was something of an enigma in the cycling world, even then, but you could be sure of one thing – if he was riding one of the big tours his name would light up the start list and, more often than not, would figure in final results, frequently as the winner.

Later, came other big stars – Merckx, of course, and Hinault, Induráin, Lemond and Armstrong, all of them multiple-Tour de France winners – but somehow it has always seemed to me that Anquetil was in a class of his own. He may not have dominated his rivals so completely as they were to do, but who else showed such a calculating commitment and such willingness to suffer in the pursuit of victory? We should never forget that Jacques Anquetil was the first rider to win the Tour de France five times and, for that, he will be for ever remembered in the record books.

What the record books will not show, however, is the agony he would put himself through, and the dedication to achieve that success while, at the same time, giving free reign to his love of the 'good life'. No rider could get away with that nowadays – late nights, partying on the eve of important races, and so on: there is not a team manager who would tolerate it … for long! Even so, if Jacques Anquetil were racing today, you feel sure that somehow he would still manage to do it 'his way'.

Anquetil is often referred to as 'the natural'. In some ways this is a slightly ironic title, given his freely admitted willingness to using stimulants, albeit in a very controlled way. Yet, without doubt, he was one of the most naturally gifted racing cyclists of all time. This was never more apparent than when riding in his speciality – the individual time trial. His aerodynamic position was a joy to behold, his cadence and pedalling style surely a gift from the gods.

Known best as a stage-racer, it is often overlooked just what a great one-day rider he was whenever he had something to prove, to the public or, more importantly, to himself. He could probably have won any single-day race on the calender and, although he only won three classics, he did so with enough panache as to leave little doubt as to just what a great champion he was. However, Jacques Anquetil answered to one man and one man only, and that was Jacques Anquetil, and more often than not he considered it a waste of preparation and effort to dedicate himself to the classics. How lucky that was for the classics specialists.

Anquetil's career came to be shaped by his intense rivalry with Raymond Poulidor, and one of the ironies in his life was his lack of popularity in France, even at the height of his career. He was respected and admired, while Poulidor was adored. Towards the end of his racing career, however, he did begin to win the hearts of the French public with exploits that could not be ignored, not even by Poulidor's most partisan supporters.

It was only after he retired that he gained the popularity his racing achievements had never fully brought him. With his dignity and honesty Anquetil became a national treasure; his characteristic courage and humour when he found himself facing cancer eventually brought him the love of a nation that he so dearly wished for.

In the world of cycling and international sport there have been very few champions held in such high regard, and there are many enthusiasts who, even now, still find themselves missing Master Jacques. I am proud to say I am one of them. What a sensation he would be today – handsome, mysterious and such amazing natural talent – but still something of an enigma.

This book is about Jacques Anquetil the man as much as it is about Jacques Anquetil the racing cyclist. It is, we hope, a fitting tribute to a fine man, and a fantastic athlete whose legend, along with our memories, will never, ever die.

Richard Allchin
for the Publishers

Foreword

Jacques Anquetil had it all: the looks of a film star; the determination to win, with the talent to back it up; and the apparent belligerent confidence that all champions seem to possess. In reality he was a shy man who wanted success and was afraid of life.

Maître Jacques, a name given him after his domination of the 1961 Tour de France in which he led from the first day to the last, was indeed the big boss of his period. He was also a fatalist and felt compelled to live his life to the full, afraid that if he shut his eyes he may never wake up again.

At 23 he won his first Tour de France. He did it in arrogant style after demanding his own team for the three-week race so that he could ride as a rival to the then French hero, Louison Bobet. He won the third stage into his home town of Rouen then, on stage five, in the Belgian city of Charleroi, Anquetil pulled on his first *maillot jaune*. He lost the lead, regained it, and by Paris he was the winner by almost a quarter of an hour. Bobet, who disliked Anquetil and everything the young talent represented, had been reported to be very motivated for a fourth Tour win, but he never rode the race. Instead, French team manager, Marcel Bidot, put his faith in a young blood who did not let him down.

Anquetil, a proud Norman, died at 53, living the later years of his life in a château near Rouen, where he would roam the grounds at night watching the wildfowl migrate, the wild boar eat, or just staring at the stars. He was afraid to miss a single minute of life for he knew it would end soon enough. When his father died at 56 Anquetil said: 'I will never live to that age.'

His team-mates, when ordered to the château to stay on the eve of a race, dreaded the occasion. Why? Because Jacques would make them drink fine wine or champagne, and play cards until sleep forced its way upon them. Anquetil, the champion, could live his life through 24 hours, but his less-gifted team-mates could not.

Stories of Anquetil dancing on tables and gambling into the night during stages of the Tour of Italy are true. The very next day, while wearing the leader's pink jersey, he would fall behind the pack, be sick, and then return, only to win the day and the race! No, Maître Jacques was no ordinary man. There was only one Jacques Anquetil.

We all knew that when, at nineteen and riding as an Independent for the L'Auto Cycle Sottevillais, he won the most coveted time trial in the world – the Grand Prix des Nations. Annihilated would be a better word, since he left the top names among the professionals so far behind. He would win the Nations eight more times, never losing the race on which he first built his reputation.

At the time, the Tour de France could wait, as Jacques set his sights on the World Hour Record held by the greatest of all champions, and Anquetil's hero, Italy's Fausto Coppi. In 1956, at the second attempt, he went 288 metres farther than Coppi had done and, before his career ended in 1969, he went farther than new record holder, Roger Rivière, as he pedalled an unheard of gear ratio of 52x13 to cover 47 kilometres 493 metres against Rivière's 47 kilometres 346 metres. However, this record would never be ratified after Anquetil refused to submit to a drugs test, feeling it was below the dignity of a professional athlete.

His elegance and general aloofness did not endear him to his French public, and when another Frenchman, Raymond Poulidor, came along, whose image of a country peasant proved more acceptable, then it was he, rather than Anquetil, who quickly became the people's champion.

The pair locked in battle wherever they rode and Anquetil almost always won. It was a matter of honour to Jacques and it meant that Poulidor became known as the eternal second, losing a momentous Tour de France to Anquetil in 1964 by just 55 seconds after 4,504 kilometres of bitter struggle.

One achievement that will never be repeated came in 1965 when Anquetil won the prestigious Criterium du Dauphiné stage-race for a third successive year. This race, held in the high Alps and Provence, was hard enough, but the idea that Anquetil should then go straight to Bordeaux and start the longest race of all, the Bordeaux–Paris, seemed ridiculous.

The Bordeaux–Paris is sadly no longer held, but on average a dozen or so riders took part in the 600-kilometre race to Paris, most of which was behind small motor cycles called Dernys.

Anquetil, using a private aeroplane loaned by his great admirer, French President Charles de Gaulle, flew from Nîmes to Bordeaux, being massaged on the way. He just had time for a meal before the start and then the race left Bordeaux at midnight. By 7 a.m. Anquetil had abandoned, but after being insulted beyond belief by team manager Raphaël Géminiani, he took his bike and started again. It was a dour struggle which ended in solitary victory after he broke clear of two others, including Britain's Tom Simpson, with twelve kilometres left to the Parc des Princes stadium. At the finish Anquetil did a rare thing in public: he cried, realising that his victory in Paris was one of the finest athletic performances ever recorded by a cyclist.

I was privileged to meet Jacques Anquetil during many Tours de France, when he came along as a radio reporter after his retirement from racing. The image of his big, barrel chest puffing out as he explained a point was there for all to see.

He was a champion without equal – he was Jacques Anquetil – and when told he needed an urgent operation for stomach cancer his reply was typical: 'The operation must wait until after the Tour de France is over.' Jacques died in November of the same year, leaving this world as he came in: a champion the like of which we will never see again.

Phil Liggett
Hertfordshire, 2001

Picture reproduced by kind permission of Jeremy Mallard,
from his limited-edition print 'Jacques Anquetil'
© Jeremy Mallard

Author's Introduction

Exactly who and what Jacques Anquetil was remains one of the great enigmas in the history of cycle-racing. At first sight he seems to have been something of a Jekyll and Hyde character, as, indeed, were so many other great champions: once on a bike the gentle Fausto Coppi was transformed into a merciless dominator; the quiet, unassuming Rik Van Looy became utterly intimidating; the casual, relaxed Eddy Merckx was obsessed with winning everything and anything. Anquetil, however, was different. Yes, he could at times be selfish towards his own team-mates, but he did not have that desire to crush and humiliate his rivals.

Jacques was at his best during the solitary effort of the time trial when, if need be, he could dig deep into his considerable reserves. He could produce such tremendous performances, even when he was not on form, that most people are still willing to concede that he was the greatest time-trialist ever, but his extraordinary bravery seemed to go unnoticed. Because he was so stylish a rider his courage was barely appreciated.

Newsreel film shows Anquetil on the Puy de Dôme during the 1964 Tour de France after he had been dropped by Poulidor, close to the finish of the climb. He was suffering so much that he was hardly conscious, yet still his pedalling remained smooth – even when driving himself to this extremity he still he looked stylish. And the result of this stupendous effort was to be booed by sections of the crowd. Anquetil was always baffled by the hostility directed towards him by some fans; he never could understand why Poulidor, who achieved so much less, was so much more popular.

If Raymond Poulidor was the people's choice, Anquetil was the one who produced the results – the first man ever to win five Tours de France. Yet, even here, the enigma remains: he could have done more, most especially in the one-day classics. There is little doubt that his record could have been as good as Coppi's, but it wasn't. Too often he seemed to have lacked motivation and to have been ready with his excuses even before the race.

Despite all appearances to the contrary, Anquetil was a deeply shy man. Charming and seemingly relaxed in public, he had a horror of crowds in general and strangers in particular. Here again, he was misunderstood – his shyness often being taken for indifference or haughtiness. Similarly, his lack of hypocrisy on the subject of drug use in cycling was misrepresented.

Perhaps the fact that he successfully managed to keep so much of his life private is one reason why he never inspired the kind of affection that Poulidor did. So, in spite of the hundreds of interviews he gave, and the thousands of photographs that were taken of him, he remains the least understood of any of the great cycling champions.

While much of his life will remain private, this book is an enquiry into his character as well as a record of his career. Some questions may be answered in these pages, others not, and yet more questions may arise. Judge him if you will, for I cannot.

Richard Yates

PART ONE – THE PRINCE

Chapter One

Jacques Anquetil's life spanned one of the most remarkable periods in French history. He was born into a country which, despite its enormous class divisions and crushing rural poverty, was still among the most powerful in Europe, claiming the biggest army on the continent, if not in the world. But its self-confidence was about to be eroded from within.

On the very day of Anquetil's birth a scandal emerged, the repercussions of which would weaken the country at a time when she most needed to be strong. The newspapers had exposed a certain big-time swindler, Stavisky, the son of a Russian Jewish immigrant, who had close connections with influential politicians and senior police officers. He was found dying in a chalet near Chamonix and the police story of suicide was believed by no one. The public was convinced that Stavisky had been eliminated in order to save the skins of the corrupt politicians.

A month after the affair at Chamonix, several extreme right-wing organisations staged a big protest in Paris to express their disapproval of the corrupt French Parliament – demonstrations come naturally to the French and it has been suggested that in doing so they are subconsciously reliving the French Revolution. It was only the determined efforts of the French police that prevented the mob getting their hands on the members of Parliament and tearing them limb from limb. The night came to an end with many injuries and several deaths, and the turmoil was to continue for many years to come.

In 1940 France suffered her worst defeat ever when the Germans overran the country in six weeks. Occupation by the enemy of one half of the country was as humiliating as the French puppet, collaborationist administration of the other half of the country.

The humiliation and despair of the defeat in 1940 was followed, in the early post-war years, by political strife: the country was brought virtually to a standstill by a series of strikes and the threats of a Communist takeover. On top of that, the seemingly unworkable new Fourth Republic embarked on a couple of shameful, deeply unpopular, and ultimately unsuccessful colonial wars in South East Asia and North Africa.

It was finally France's old wartime hero, General de Gaulle, who established political and economic stability, and General de Gaulle was one of Anquetil's greatest fans.

When Jacques died in 1987 he left a country in which poverty and fierce class distinction had been largely eliminated, a country which had regained its self-respect and had re-emerged as one of the leaders among European nations. General de Gaulle readily acknowledged how much Jacques had contributed to the new prestige and glory of the nation. It is no exaggeration to say that Jacques Anquetil was part of the French renaissance.

When Jacques was born at a clinic in Rouen on the 8th January 1934 he was a beautiful baby with blond hair and blue eyes. His paternal grandfather had been killed in the trenches in the First World War and his mother had been an orphan from the age of two. She had been brought up by nuns in an orphanage, so she naturally had strong religious beliefs which she passed on to her children. Jacques himself had only one sibling, Philippe, born in 1937, but she had no less than nine and one of her brothers was married to her husband Ernest's sister.

Ernest and Marie Anquetil lived in a house on the outskirts of Rouen, and Jacques' father was a builder; indeed his work was so respected that most considered him to be a master builder. Ernest Anquetil had always been mad keen on cycle-racing but, with his father already dead, and having seen two of her sons die from congestion of the lungs, his mother had no great desire to see the health of a third son put at risk, so she warned her son that if ever he brought a racing bike to the house she would slash the tyres.

Ernest was mortified by his mother's intransigence, but continued to believe that she was wrong, and so he bought his son Jacques a bicycle at the age of four. Marie did not want the stabilisers removed, but her husband insisted. After hours of patient instruction, little Jacques still could not maintain his balance and kept ending up in the ditch. Eventually, Ernest gave up in despair and put the bike in the cellar. The following day, when his father was away, a determined Jacques brought the bike up again and would not give up until he could ride it properly. On his father's return he triumphantly demonstrated his newly acquired skill.

With the outbreak of war in 1939 Ernest was conscripted back into the army and did not return home until the following August. Building work was by now extremely scarce and the only jobs on offer were for constructing fortifications for the German army. Ernest would sooner have died than work for the enemy, so with the help of some relations the family bought a small farm just outside Rouen. In fact, they moved a mere six kilometres to the hamlet of Le Bourguet which was itself just a stone's throw from the small town of Quincampoix. They were certainly in the country, but only just.

With the wartime food shortages it was, without doubt, a good move to make and, small though the farm was, it was certainly more than the subsistence farming that the majority of French peasants practised. The little enterprise specialised in strawberries, although large quantities of apples were grown as well. Ernest Anquetil pushed his handcart to Rouen at 3.30 a.m. and sold his produce in the market. He eventually managed to acquire more land and even expanded his production to the extent that he was obliged to take on workers to do the picking, and a small truck to transport the crop.

For the six-year-old Jacques it was like moving to paradise. There were trees to be climbed, birds' nests to be discovered, apples to be picked, butterflies, insects, fields to play in – everything. He went to school in Quincampoix and came home for lunch; this meant a total of six kilometres a day to be either walked or run. The little local school, where even the teacher wore clogs, usually saw Jacques at the top of the class with his best subject being mathematics and his worst, literature. It was a period when all of the children outside of the towns went to a village school. Normally, the unaided teacher was obliged to educate all the local children, of all ages, in a single class of perhaps as many as 50 pupils. But, nevertheless, most of them left with a certificate to prove that they had reached the required standard.

Anquetil's home in Quincampoix

Jacques saw his fair share of trouble. The parish priest was furious with him when he discovered that it was Jacques who had put stones in the lock of the church door. Like all children he was fascinated by the amount of abandoned war material that could be found, but his father took great care to explain the importance of not touching unexploded shells. With his cousin Marcel Bidault he went boating on a pond in an aircraft fuel tank cut in half. He fell in once and returned home soaked to the skin. His mother rapidly put dry clothes on him and hid the wet ones. If his father had found out he would have made him kneel on a log for half an hour and, if he had cried out in pain, he would have been beaten as well.

Jacques always had a very high regard for his father who had always tried to instil in him the pride of doing a job well. Ernest was clearly the master of the house and although he had a heart of gold, he did have rather an unfortunate side to his character. When he had drunk too much, and this could mean as little as three glasses of wine, he could become violent and dangerous. Once he threatened to take a knife to Jacques' legs to make sure that he never raced again. The young Anquetil was well used to such things and usually, on such occasions, went to hide at his Aunt Albertine's house. A few years later, Jacques drove to his parents' house to show them his new car. Ernest was in one of his drunken rages, and went off to find an axe and a can of petrol in order to destroy it.

Alcohol was regarded more as a staple diet than a luxury and it inevitably led to a high incidence of alcoholism with the lives of whole families being ruined. One day Jacques' mother refused to take any more of her violent and domineering husband. She left the house and rented a small flat in Paris. No amount of pleading from anyone could persuade her to return.

As the war was coming to an end Jacques wanted a bike that would fit him, but the harvest had been very poor and there was little money for luxuries. He offered to pick the strawberries and then the apples so that his father employed one less person. This was done and, at the age of eleven, Jacques finally had a new bike which fitted him: a light blue Stella with fat tyres. After a couple of years he sold this 'first communion' bike for 4,000 francs and bought a racing bike cheaply from a friend. At the age of thirteen he attempted to ride to Dieppe, some 50 kilometres away, but gave up after 40 kilometres.

Just after the war the school-leaving age was fourteen so, by 1948, the decision had to be taken as to which profession he would enter. His parents wanted something better for him than the job of *agriculteur*, so he was enroled at a technical college in Rouen for three years to learn the trade of metal-worker and designer. At the college in Sotteville, on the southern outskirts of Rouen, most people found him secretive and shy, but he made some good friends. They went to the cinema together, rode their bicycles to the sea at Dieppe or perhaps went swimming in the River Seine to the south of Rouen. Jacques was fascinated to see, on the other side of the river, the big expensive mansions with their lawns coming down to the water and a boat moored inside the boat-house. This was an entirely different world to his tiny house with two rooms and a kitchen, no electricity, and a hayloft upstairs which could only be reached by a ladder. His father's passion for roses and the well-trimmed hedge made the house look attractive enough, but Jacques wanted something better when he grew up, but he knew he would never get it by working at a normal job.

During the week he stayed at Sotteville with Madame David who fed him very well. She received payment in the form of food from the Anquetil farm, delivered by Jacques himself on Saturday mornings.

His closest friend was Maurice Dieulois whose father had finished second in the military sprint championship before the war and became the President of the A C Sottevillais after it, but was now too busy with his combined grocery shop and café. Maurice, however, had inherited his enthusiasm and all day on the Monday at technical college Jacques was fascinated as Maurice recounted his adventures in the bicycle race he had ridden on the Sunday. He was amazed to see his friend's name in local newspaper reports and began to realise that this minor fame could lead to success with the girls. He started to accompany Maurice – who was six months older then him – to events, and was very taken with the atmosphere and excitement of it all. He gave the matter an enormous amount of thought and decided that he would like to try it, but, like the hard-headed Norman peasant that he was, he reached the conclusion that the sacrifices and the training would only be worthwhile if he could win, get a kiss from the local beauty queen, and take a prize home.

Dieulois and other friends had real racing bikes, but even so Jacques was much stronger, and could always drop them on the hills. Maurice managed to persuade Jacques to visit André Boucher, the President of the A C Sottevillais, the best cycling club in Rouen. André was a quiet, modest man who ran a bike shop no more than 500 metres from the college. Boucher's passion was cycle-racing and training young riders. Before the war he had been a member of the VCL (Velo Club Levallois) in Paris, the most famous amateur club of all time.

In front of the shop window, Jacques gazed in wonder at the beautiful Automoto bicycles on display. He had been told that Boucher sometimes lent them to promising young riders, but he remained somewhat sceptical about such a tale. Boucher had already heard a lot about Jacques from Maurice Dieulois, so he was not too surprised when he turned up at his shop. What did astonish him was Anquetil's physical make-up – the slow heart beat, the lung capacity, the single-mindedness, the ease with which he turned the pedals, especially when climbing the hills: here was somebody very special indeed. After a few of the regular training rides together with other members of the club, Boucher was totally convinced and gave him two bicycles, one for training and one for racing. Indeed, he had such confidence in Jacques that he also gave him an unlimited supply of tubular tyres and promised him a bonus of 30 francs a kilometre for any race that he might win.

The 1950 season was over, but there was winter training in the gym. André Boucher's orders were clear: at least nine hours sleep, no eggs, no chocolate and no fried food. Anquetil was an enthusiastic pupil and always on time at the gymnasium. André said he was an example for all the others.

At the end of the year Jacques gained his engineering diploma and found a job with a small metal factory in Rouen. He started working there in January at a wage of 68 francs an hour, but by now racing was the thing that interested him most and he had acquired a habit of training on Thursday afternoons. Obviously, the director of the factory was not prepared to make any concessions for time off for a seventeen-year-old who had just started with him. So, after four weeks, Jacques asked his father whether he could work for him instead. Ernest had just bought another five acres of land so he readily agreed and Jacques handed in his notice.

Monsieur Anquetil senior was secretly delighted that his son was to ride races, but at the same time was determined to make a man of him. He said, 'OK, Jacques, you can work for me, you can train on Thursday afternoons, but only after you've done your quota of work in the morning. As far as bike-racing is concerned, there's only one thing that I know, and that is the winner's bouquet.' These latter sentiments were entirely Jacques' as well and he made a promise to himself that if he had not won anything after three races, then he would give up.

Boucher loved the bicycle before anything and insisted on the same hard training methods which he had learned from the legendary Paul Ruinart at the Velo Club Levallois. André was methodical and scrupulous, and passed this on to Jacques. However, his young pupil had a terrible weakness for things like chips and chocolate. In this respect, André was quite tolerant towards his young protégé, but was angry when Jacques went to Belgium for a wedding in the April of 1951.

Eventually, the great day came and he rode his first race for his club in Le Havre, finishing in the bunch. By the end of April he had finished third at Guillon and, finally, on 3rd May, he won the Grand Prix Maurice Latour, held over 110 kilometres at Rouen, when he managed to get away alone on the final hill. This was his first bouquet, but instead of being embraced by some ravishing beauty queen, the flowers were presented by a grandmother. Jacques was later to say that winning this first junior race was the most fantastic tonic.

From now on there was no going back. He was to ride his first season as a junior, accruing eight wins and finishing sixteen times in the first seven. A good start certainly, but one which gave no idea of his future rapid rise to fame. It was to be, perhaps, the fastest ascension in the history of the sport.

Chapter Two

In 1952, at the age of eighteen, Jacques became a senior and by now he was quite determined to make the sport his career. The previous summer he had followed the Tour de France with the greatest of interest. Few French households possessed a radio let alone a TV set, but Jacques had seen the race come through his area on the stage from Paris to Caen, and then followed it closely through the newspapers and the special editions of the sports magazines. He was fascinated by Hugo Koblet, the charismatic rider from Switzerland who won the event. His style, his elegance, his nonchalance, his originality were all qualities that Jacques deeply admired and he resolved to model himself on the incredibly popular Swiss.

In the AC Sottevillais Boucher continued to train and advise his precious discovery. Another club official, by the name of Sadi Duponchel, started to take an interest in Jacques. He drove him to races, followed him in a car or on a motorbike, and generally looked after the rider and his equipment. He rapidly acquired the nickname of 'guard dog' due to the fact that he would let nobody near Jacques before or after a race. He understood the young Anquetil very well, and although he understood his joy at winning and the accolades which this brought him, he also appreciated his shyness, his fear of strangers, and his horror of being surrounded too closely by a crowd. Duponchel would stay close to him for many years to come, acting as manager, chauffeur, mechanic and even masseur.

One of Boucher's main problems with Jacques was his lack of combativity. He tended to let things happen without reacting and could allow the race to slip through his fingers. In one race

Duponchel was following the event on his motorbike, watching as two riders had managed to get clear. Jacques had let them go and was at the back of the bunch almost going to sleep. Duponchel drew alongside his man and said, 'Bravo, Jacques. You're riding towards a magnificent third place.' Anquetil's sensitive nature was stung by such heavy sarcasm so he attacked immediately, quickly caught and dropped the leaders, and went on to win by himself.

It was not as if he lacked ability. His friend, Michel Billaux, later spoke of an event near Dieppe which he rode with Jacques: 'He punctured twice. I was dropped, but he came back to help me. He punctured a third time, but he still won.'

Jacques' reputation was beginning to spread throughout Normandy and he was to finish the season with a total of eleven wins, three second places, two third places and four fourth places, and all of them in top-class events. So in the regional championships he was a marked man. He was up against no less than fifteen riders from the big, powerful club from Caen which was run by the former Tour de France star Yvan Marie, who in his time had won Paris–Vimoutiers, the National Criterium and had finished second in the Grand Prix des Nations. After 100 kilometres had been covered, Anquetil was still in the bunch while the leading break, including three riders from Caen, had a lead of five minutes. Jacques was surrounded by several of their team mates who were doing their best to impede him; he had had enough of it, and said to Boucher, 'they're all against me. I can't do anything. I'm going to retire.' Boucher replied, 'You've got no right to do that, it's out of the question. There are still another 75 kilometres to go and that is where the race will be decided.'

Jacques loosened his toe-straps and dropped to the back. The Caen riders congratulated themselves for having eliminated him from the race, but Anquetil retightened them again, took a flyer and went past the whole bunch. He closed the five-minute gap on the leaders, raced straight past them and went on to win by three minutes. It was an incredible performance for an eighteen-year-old. Boucher had never heard of, let alone seen such an exploit before. It was now clear that he really did have a phenomenon on his hands. For Jacques it meant automatic selection to ride the national championships at Carcassonne in July.

Before then he won another big race, the significance of which was not fully appreciated at the time. It was a time trial at Caen and, in winning it, he gained the right to compete later in the season in the most important amateur time trial in France, the Grand Prix de France at St Etienne. It was, in fact, organised by the weekly cycling newspaper *Route et Piste*, printed on green paper and run by Jean Leulliot. Jacques made the long trip down south to the bicycle capital of France. The majority of the French bicycle and component manufacturers were to be found in this large, industrial city not far from Lyons. He had never been so far from home before and started to realise how much he liked travelling.

He duly won the Grand Prix de France by no less than twelve minutes and in doing so established himself as one of the top amateurs in the country. The following month he went south again to Carcassonne. André Boucher was proud of his protégé and believed in his chances, although he remained worried about his poor sense of tactics. Jacques himself was nervous and, the night before the event, he slept in Boucher's room with his bike. Permission for Boucher to follow the race was firmly denied so André placed himself at the top of a strategic hill. As the race was reaching its closing stages, and Jacques was climbing the hill in the middle of the bunch, Boucher jumped up and shouted, 'Now, Jacques, now! Give it everything you've got!' Anquetil attacked, went clear and won by himself.

In true French tradition, Quincampoix threw a party to celebrate the success of its champion when he got back home. The housewives produced the cakes and the flowers, the mayor produced the wine for the *vin d'honneur,* and a small band was hired to produce the music for the dancing. Jacques had not yet learned how to dance, but he felt at home amongst the villagers he knew so well and was touched by their tribute.

Jacques was now hot property even though he was still only in his first season as a senior. It was 1952, an Olympic year, so he was almost an automatic selection for the Games in Helsinki. Things were beginning to move fast. He had never flown before and André Boucher was at the airport to give him a medallion as a good-luck charm, which he proudly kept for the rest of his life. In the race itself Jacques rubbed shoulders with a young fresh-faced Belgian. He was to see much more of Henrik Van Looy in the years to come. Anquetil was not too worried about finishing twelfth, as he knew he had been up against some very experienced amateurs, and had the consolation of being awarded a bronze medal in the team competition.

A few weeks later it was off to Luxembourg for the World Championships. There he raced against another pale-looking youth who hardly looked old enough to compete against the seniors, but in fact Charly Gaul was two years older than Jacques. The race itself was 'of no sporting interest' since, as it was run on a totally flat course, it was decided by a big bunch sprint. On the line the first two could not be separated, but the officials were loath to declare the race a dead heat. The problem was solved when it was discovered that the Dutchman, de Brekel, had changed bicycles in an illegal zone, so Ciancola of Italy was declared the winner, with the Olympic champion, Noyelle of Belgium, in second place. Only the first seven were placed, and after that it was equal eighth for most of the field including Anquetil; the Englishman, King; and the Irishman, Edwards.

Jacques' mother had Belgian blood in her veins and, as was common in those days, the young Jacques had spent many holidays with relatives. He had stayed with an aunt in Amiens and, when he was fourteen, with an uncle in the Belgian Ardennes. So, a trip to Luxembourg may not have meant too much to him, but Finland, for the Olympic Games, was something else – a very exotic place that none of his friends had been anywhere near. In 1952 it was quite something for a young Frenchman to have travelled on an aeroplane at a time when a large number of French youths in the country had never even been on a train. He spoke enthusiastically of his trip to his father, but Ernest was not only a dour French peasant but a Norman as well, so he gave every impression of being neither impressed nor interested.

As the busy season came to a close it was time to take stock and look back. Boucher was very pleased with his pupil who had listened so carefully to his advice and had acted on it. He was clearly very strong for his age and now well known throughout France. One of his weaknesses was his lack of tactical sense and he always needed someone to inspire and motivate him. The couple of time trials that he had ridden were to his liking and they certainly seemed to suit him. He was later to say that he felt that the solitary effort suited him better as he disliked riding in a bunch. When he had few distractions around him his powers of concentration were considerable, and he always used his intelligence to study the course and paid careful attention as to the best line to follow through a bend or a corner. His memory never let him down and he gradually turned time-trialling into an art. Although he was so strong he was incapable of making the brutal accelerations which were necessary in a road race to open a gap. His long, hard turns at the front had the effect of asphyxiating his rivals so it was a little like a boxer who could punish his opponent to win on points, but was unable to produce the knock-out blow. Apart from his trips abroad and to the south, he had also been to Paris a couple of times, once for the classic amateur race Paris–Evreux in which he had finished tenth, and once to the Vincennes Woods on the east side of the capital for a race behind scooters in which he finished third. He felt quite at home in paced events, having trained behind Boucher's Derny. It was an incredibly hard discipline, but excellent preparation.

Racing was time consuming and he had seen less of his friends from his college days. On the other hand, he enjoyed the glory of winning, and was quite happy to be interviewed and photographed. To him, being questioned by the press was part of the pleasure of winning, so his inherent shyness was not a problem. Indeed, he expressed himself so well that only those very close to him had the faintest idea of his timidity. When total strangers tried to approach him they were suprised at how cold he could be, and assumed that he was being haughty and indifferent. He was accused of these faults for the rest of his career and few really comprehended the feeling of terror which overcame him at such unexpected encounters.

The balance sheet for the season was most promising: he had earned good prize money; and he had attained national recognition. With the progress that he had made he was virtually certain that he could make a living from the sport, but, still being only eighteen, what was the next step?

Chapter Three

For the 1953 season, Jacques took the step of obtaining an Independent's licence. It was half-way between being an amateur and being a professional. The actual term has no great significance and the category was abolished in 1966, but prior to that the number of Independents was greater than that of professionals. They normally rode for trade teams rather than a club and, although they had their own National Championship, there was no World Championship for this group of riders. In Britain at this time these semi-professional riders were virtually the only group of competitors who received any sort of financial recompense. Officially, the amateur cyclists on the Continent were not paid in cash, but in practice this was not the case. Being an Independent meant less national recognition for Jacques as he would be racing mainly in his own region with no expenses-paid trips abroad. But this hardly mattered as it would help him climb the ladder to a professional career. The main advantage for him was that he was able to race in professional as well as amateur races, plus, of course, those events reserved for Independents only. Financially he may have been a little better off, but only a little. Jacques was an intelligent young man who knew himself very well, and he also knew how to train hard for the big event. However, he still needed someone to push him into action and to motivate him, but by now his class was really beginning to emerge.

He began to win wherever he went and became the Independent Champion of Normandy. The really big test came at the beginning of August when he started the three-day Tour de la Manche against the professionals. Some of the field may well have been young and inexperienced pros, and many of them were in their first year in the paid ranks, but one thing they did not like was being beaten by an Independent. On the first leg Jean Stablinski went clear to win the stage by himself, but he was chased home by Anquetil in second place at 24 seconds. Most of the professional riders were enraged at this affront by a young unknown Independent and joined forces to pull Anquetil back, but, to their surprise, he managed to stay clear to put himself in a good position before the time trial on stage two.

Jacques loved the solitary effort and completed the 36 kilometres to St Hilaire in 59 min. 49 sec. This was 1 min. 57sec. faster than his nearest challenger and 2 min. 50 sec. quicker than the race leader. A time gap such as this was nothing compared to those that he had achieved in amateur races, but this was a different world with the professionals. Riding against them, such a gap, over such a distance, was quite considerable. Indeed, very few of these pros had ever been beaten in a time trial by an Independent. It was common practice amongst journalists to describe these races-against-the-watch by using a phrase which was normally reserved for bullfighting: 'the moment of truth'. Anquetil, an unknown, pale-faced youth, had outclassed many of the established 'names' and no amount of excuses could explain away the fact that this inexperienced, young rider from Rouen, or wherever it was, was clearly something special.

With just one stage to go Jacques was leading the race by a considerable margin. However, his small team of Independents was a comparatively weak one and had been brought together at the last moment for just this one race, and he was soon to discover what it was like to be really up against it. During the course of the 180 kilometres to Cherbourg he was attacked incessantly by the riders from the Stella and the Gitane teams. Anquetil was obliged to neutralise all these offensives single-handedly and had to avoid all the traps, but the riders in front kept 'closing the door'. Eventually, they had him off into a ditch. There was no damage done and, as he got back on his bike, he saw Pele, an unknown Independent from Nantes, waiting for him. 'That was diabolical,' he said. 'I'll help you get back on.'

Wounded pride amongst the pros in the main bunch meant that they pulled out all the stops to prevent the race leader from rejoining, but Jacques had the bit between his teeth and, after a long hard chase, he succeeded in latching on to the back of the bunch. It was enough to secure victory.

At the finish, as the prizes were being presented, Antonin Magne, the manager of the Mercier team was speaking to his man Redolfi who had just finished second overall. 'So you're letting yourself be beaten by a debutant now.' Redolfi pulled a face and said, 'Believe me, Monsieur Magne, what that young Anquetil did was really something. When he went clear on the first day, we were flat out trying to pull him back, but we just could not.'

Another very famous *directeur sportif* was present, Raymond Louviot, of the Gitane team. He was equally impressed, but he had never heard of Anquetil before, so he made a note of his name. However, the manager of the La Perle team had been aware of Jacques' potential for some time. Guillaume Mercader was responsible for the La Perle riders only when they raced in Normandy and had been looking forward to Anquetil's first big test against the professionals. After his win in the time trial Mercader had quietly taken Jacques to one side and surreptitiously promised that a couple of his riders would help him if he was in difficulties. The teenager was very surprised as this was clearly against the race rules, but he gratefully accepted the offer.

As the riders dispersed after the race the reason for the help became clearer when Mercader drove Jacques back to the hotel and turned on the charm. The main *directeur sportif* of La Perle cycles, a certain Francis Pélissier, was looking for a possible winner of the Grand Prix des Nations time trial in Paris in September. Mercader offered Jacques an exceptionally generous contract, but there were two conditions: first he must take out a professional licence; and second he must not speak to André Boucher about the offer. As he was still a minor, Jacques would need the consent of his parents, so a meeting was arranged at Quincampoix for the following day.

When Anquetil and Mercader went to Paris to sign the contract, Jacques took Sadi Duponchel with him. Maurice Guyot, the head of the La Perle company, was enchanted with the young Anquetil and offered him a two-month contract running from 1st September to 31st October at 30,000 f. a month, stipulating that if he won 'the Nations' then he would automatically ride the Grand Prix of Lugano. This was exactly the same contract that had previously been signed by Hugo Koblet, the winner of the 1951 Tour de France. Jacques was immediately fitted out with two special bikes for the forthcoming race in Paris.

André Boucher was furious when he heard the news and came close to breaking all ties with Jacques. He and Guillaume Mercader had been rivals for almost twenty years. When they were both riders, Mercader had stolen several victories from under the nose of Boucher and the rivalry continued after they both became team managers. They treated each other correctly, but no more. Boucher had plans for Jacques to become a professional a little later with Antonin Magne, who he believed would handle Anquetil in a sensitive way. However, faced with a *fait accompli*, he did consent to follow Jacques for one last time in his final race as an Independent.

Anquetil had been leading the season-long competition for the Maillot des As, run by the newspaper *Paris-Normandie*. The final event in the series was held on 23rd August and was run as a time trial over 122 kilometres. It came as no surprise when Jacques won the event, but the way in which he won it was hardly believable. He beat his club-mate, Claude Le Ber, by nine minutes and averaged an incredible 42.05 k.p.h. Jacques always maintained that it was the best ride of his life and the one of which he was the most proud. The news spread like wildfire, but few would believe that such a thing was possible and many thought that there had been some mistake in measuring the course. Alex Virot, the well-known reporter for Radio Luxembourg, gave a wry smile when he heard the news and said, 'In Normandy there can only be 900 metres in a kilometre!'

In the meantime Francis Pélissier had made the acquaintance of the young Jacques and, going on what Mercader had told him, announced to all and sundry that he had the future winner of the Grand Prix des Nations under contract. Francis was a huge man with a reputation for discovering new talent. Witty and urbane, he was very popular with journalists for his insight into the sport and his sharp repartee, although he could be vulgar and was not very well liked by other team managers. His elder brother, Henri, had had an even better career as a rider and they had both been sworn enemies of Henri Desgrange, the organiser of the pre-war Tours de France. But Henri Pélissier had died in 1935 and the third brother, Charles, had been left to carry on the family tradition. The youngest of the Pélissiers had been wildly popular with everyone, including Desgrange. Francis had won the Bordeaux–Paris a couple of times and after his retirement as a rider had turned his hand to producing unknown riders to win this prestigious event. It was not long before he was known as 'The Sorcerer of Bordeaux–Paris'.

In 1953 he had engaged the Swiss rider, Ferdi Kubler, to ride the Bordeaux–Paris for the La Perle team, but there had been a big dispute between the two men. Francis knew especially well how to prepare for the very special race from the Atlantic coast to the French capital and had given Ferdi a training schedule. But the Swiss thought better: He was a very experienced rider and a former winner of the Tour de France as well as the World Championship. Things came to a head, and in a grand gesture Pélissier sacked Kubler. Smarting from the insult, the man from Zurich finally won the event with ease, wearing a Swiss 'Tebag' jersey, thus making Francis look rather silly.

While Pélissier started to boast about his new discovery, Anquetil went to Brittany to ride the Circuit de l'Aulne. It was known as the 'Queen of the Criteriums' and always attracted some very big names. In 1953 Van Steenbergen was there along with one Louison Bobet, resplendent in the yellow jersey that he had recently won in the Tour de France.

Jacques was really on form and at the end of the race was part of the leading group sprinting for the finishing line. Suddenly, somebody pulled him back by his jersey, and he finished third with Bobet being declared the winner. He never discovered who had impeded him, but, one thing was for sure, nobody was at all interested in his protests. As a newcomer, he had no right to beat the first Frenchman to win the Tour de France in six years.

André Boucher had recovered from his anger and helped Jacques prepare in Rouen for the Grand Prix des Nations. It was easily the biggest event of his life so far, and he went to Paris to go over the course in detail. The route of 140 kilometres was not easy to memorise, so every so often Jacques would stop at a café, write down the precise details of a section of the course on a postcard and post it to himself in Rouen. In this way he was able to build up a complete picture. His preparation was completed by hard training behind Boucher's Derny, and finally he was ready for the big day.

At the start in Versailles Jacques looked confident and showed no sign of nerves – after all, Sadi Duponchel would be following him on his big motorbike. The press was talking about him a lot but, as a new professional, he was still rather an unknown quantity. A time trial of 140 kilometres was quite something for a nineteen-year-old and observers looked a little dubious when they saw him pushing such big gears. Nevertheless, he was a model of consistency and regularity, and he led from start to finish. He finally won the race by nearly seven minutes from the Frenchman Creton, at an average speed of 39.63 k.p.h., which was not very far off the race record held by Hugo Koblet. Most experts believed that the record would have been broken if the conditions had been better. The two English men in the race, Maitland and Joy, both finished nearly twenty minutes down.

Although Jacques was painfully shy, he usually felt at ease with journalists, but as he politely answered their questions he could not take his eyes off the Simca Chatelaine estate car which he had just won: 'Yes, everything went to plan'; 'No, I never really felt in trouble or went through a bad patch'; 'I was pleased to win, of course, who would not be? But, nevertheless, I was not going as well as I did during the final of the Maillot des As. That day I really could not feel the pedals.'

It was a day out for the family as his father, mother and brother were at the Parc des Princes track to share his triumph. They returned to Normandy, but Jacques stayed on in Paris for a celebration dinner in a restaurant on the Champs-Élysées with Pélissier and André Gusset, the journalist from *Paris-Normandie* who had always believed in Jacques' potential, from the very beginning.

A new star had burst on to the scene. Clearly, once again, Pélissier had brought off a miracle. However, he had done it before in 1948 with René Berton in this very same race and then the man had disappeared into obscurity. This end-of-season Parisian time trial was certainly a prestigious event and had in the past been won by Coppi, Koblet, and Bobet, but none of them had been riding. If the competition had been fiercer, some wondered how Jacques would have fared.

It was, nevertheless, a sensational win and filled several columns in the newspapers. Some of the more experienced and shrewder journalists remarked that he had the pale skin of the hyper-nervous. He gave the impression of being an anaemic and sickly teenager, rather frail, with only his legs showing any sign of strength. He really was a bit of a mystery.

In order to investigate the enigma and enlighten their readers, the Parisian journalists drove north to Rouen to search out the family farm at Quincampoix. The villagers got used to directing strangers to *chez Anquetil* and, on one day alone, Jacques was interviewed no less than eleven times. Francis Pélissier was there to grab some of the glory and get himself photographed. He adopted his normal pose of hooking his thumbs into the arms of his waistcoat, with a cigarette dangling from his lips.

With Anquetil himself the photographers really went to town: Jacques in his crumpled clothes, wearing clogs and pushing a wooden wheelbarrow; Jacques in front of a huge tub of apples; Jacques riding his old bike, complete with mudguards and dynamo; on the rollers, with the barn containing his new car in the background; Jacques admiring the roses round the door; Jacques leaving for a training ride; his mother holding his bike, pegging his La Perle jersey on the line, posing with Ernest, posing with Jacques and Ernest. As well as taking shots of the interior of the house, they also photographed the well-trimmed hedge in front of the house. Everything had been done to emphasise the fact that the family were nothing but poor peasants – 'slaves to the land', as one journalist wrote.

To the scribes from the newspapers the story was a godsend. Rags to riches, from the poor peasant to the national hero in just one afternoon. They stopped short of saying that now he would be able to wear leather shoes instead of wooden clogs, but the inference was clearly made. And poor Ernest, whose mother would never allow him to race, was fulfilling his dreams through his son.

Jacques played along with it all and even found it rather amusing. He had always enjoyed any game of bluff and would always do so in the future. No mention was made of the fact that his father employed several people or that he took his strawberries to market in his truck. They said nothing about the fact that they had been able to send their son to technical college for three years. Instead, the myth of the son of the desperately poor peasant was born, and endures until this day.

When Pélissier said: 'You've seen nothing yet', some people were a little dubious, but the fans were very excited at the news that Jacques was going to ride the Grand Prix Lugano, three weeks later. This was going to be a real test because Kübler, Bartali and Coppi had all been engaged to ride.

There were many well-wishers at the Gare du Lyon station in Paris when Anquetil caught the train to Switzerland. His old farm clothes had been swapped for an expensive-looking, open-necked jumper, an impeccable shirt and a silk cravat. The event was run on 19th October so it came as no surprise that the day was a bit chilly with some light rain. Unfortunately, Coppi had been banned from competing for having retired without reason from a race at Varese. To add to the disappointment Bartali had not put in an appearance, and it was only later in the day that the news came through that he had been seriously injured in a car crash.

Although the rain was not to his taste, Jacques performed very well. The gaps between the leading riders were minimal and Anquetil only moved into the leading spot on the last lap. After learning that he was two minutes down, he produced a storming finish to run out the winner by 1 min. 29 sec. from Fornara of Italy, with Kubler in third place.

The Italian press were as enthusiastic about his performance as their counterparts in France. Claims of the appearance of a 'new Coppi' were not so wild after all. This was clear evidence of the class of the young Norman. From now on the French would think of him as the young prince of cycling, who one day would be king. He was hot property and everyone wanted to photograph him.

It was not long before Italy was to see him as well. A rendezvous had been arranged for him to meet his hero, the great Fausto Coppi, at his villa on the Italian Riviera. The young Jacques was very touched when he was so warmly greeted by the great man, the most popular champion of all time. Jacques was certainly impressed by the expensive house, but even more so by Fausto's gentle simplicity. He assured the young Frenchman that he would go far, but warned him of the danger of accepting too many unsuitable contracts: 'You must get an adviser, Jacques, someone to help you through the jungle of professional cycling.'

The photographers recorded the event by taking pictures of the two champions in front of the luxurious and exotic villa. Coppi had not bothered to change out his track-suit bottoms and Jacques had reverted back to his crumpled farm clothes. They really did look an insignificant pair.

Jacques stayed on in Italy to ride the Baracchi Trophy. It was a two-up time trial based on the northern city of Bergamo, and Anquetil's partner was the experienced Frenchman Antonin Rolland. The winners were the elegant and popular pair Coppi and Filippi, both resplendent in their rainbow jerseys – while Coppi had won the pro World Championship a couple of months previously, his young team mate had carried off the amateur title. The French pair had finished in second place, and when Rolland was interviewed he said: 'I was well prepared and in very good form. Nevertheless, Jacques assassinated me and for the last 30 kilometres I could not go through; I was clinging on by the skin of my teeth.'

For his part, the young Jacques demonstrated his flair for saying the right thing, in front of the Italian journalists. It was surprising to find such a skill in a rider of such tender years, but one which ensured that the press would always give him generous coverage for the rest of his career. He said: 'Antonin Rolland was very courageous. I have had a much easier season than he has. I was doing turns at the front of five or six hundred metres while Coppi was doing only two hundred metres. Nevertheless, this would not explain away the fact that the two World Champions beat us by nearly six minutes. I have really enjoyed my trip to Italy. Coppi was wonderful with me at his home and told me how hard his career had been at the start.'

At the end of November Jacques kept a promise that he had made to his mother when he drove her, his aunt and his uncle to Lourdes. Although he was never to talk very much about his mother, he felt the greatest affection towards her until his dying day. The whole family was deeply religious and Marie Anquetil had a particular desire to visit the famous religious shrine. She had certainly never travelled so far in her life before. However, the press and the photographers could not be avoided. They followed them all the way to the south, duly recording the accident Jacques was involved in just outside Le Mans. All four of them were photographed at the famous church, in the grotto, in the souvenir shops and in the bar of the famous rugby player, Jean Prat. Although Jacques managed to give the press the slip at a reception laid on by the mayor, they stuck to him like a leech when he drove to the top of the Col du Tourmalet.

It had been an incredible year for Jacques, but things had not gone to his head. He had become distrustful and suspicious, especially after more than 50 people had tried to tell him how to ride the Grand Prix des Nations. His team manager, Pélissier, loved to give orders. Jacques refused to take them and, politely but firmly, insisted on following his own training programme. The orders for his diet were not only rejected, but Jacques demonstrated his determination to eat everything that he should not, especially in front of the journalists.

As well as being undisciplined and contradictory, he was also beginning to give evidence of his delight in being provocative. As Pélissier commented: 'I sometimes felt like slapping him, but, nevertheless, he's an incredible rider.' If he had started the year as an unknown regional Independent, he finished it as a household name. From now on, most people he would rub shoulders with were older than him and a good number of them in awe of him, as well. As he was accelerated into manhood he was virtually robbed of his youth. The consequences of this would only become apparent much later.

Chapter Four

By the start of the 1954 season, Jacques had grown tired of his Simca estate car – it was too slow and he had had a couple of accidents in it. He bought a larger and more powerful Renault Frégate, a red one, or 'crushed strawberry' as one wag called it.

He had signed a new two-year contract immediately after his first one had expired, so, with the La Perle team he went to the South of France for early season training. He knew few people and had no close friends in this new professional world. Being comparatively silent and uncommunicative, not many people fully appreciated just how mature he was for his twenty years. He remained very newsworthy as so much was expected of him, and came to the conclusion that all the attention he received could possibly be turned to his advantage.

During the winter he had appeared as a guest of honour at a whole number of local functions because he was too polite to turn them down. Pélissier had suffered from a minor heart complaint, but when he learned, through the press, of Anquetil's many engagements, he was furious. Jacques was forced to defend himself via the newspapers. He claimed that if he had not accepted these invitations then people would have said that success had gone to his head and that he was being pretentious. He said that he would have preferred to spend more time with his friends, rather than staying up late listening to compliments and answering questions, but he felt that it was his duty to do so.

He was always willing to pose for photos and was snapped with Bobet and Géminiani, and also Apo Lazarides, at whose hotel he was staying. He was photographed when training and when playing mini-golf. After making sure that a reporter was present, he sat down to a large plate of shellfish and a bottle of dry white wine. It was the sort of meal that most riders could never contemplate – it would have upset their stomachs too much; but Jacques' careful calculations proved to be right. His actions were widely reported and had a devastating effect on other riders, especially Louison Bobet, who dared not even consider such luxuries. It was an early example of his passion for bluff and provocation. Whilst it was true that he did have a very strong stomach, he usually limited his culinary excesses to moments when the press were present. His friend Jean Stablinski put it in a nutshell when he said: 'It's true. Jacques did eat a lobster in front of the journalists, but it was only half a portion.' He was to continue this war of nerves for the rest of his career.

So successful was Jacques' big con trick about his excessive consumption of alcohol and rich food that the media blew the whole thing up out of all proportion. To this day many people still believe that he lived on champagne and whisky. The fact was that Anquetil was an individualist with his own special philosophy on life. He reasoned that his career would buy him some of the better things of life. The profession entailed a lot of discipline and sacrifice, but he believed that these should be kept to a minimum so that life could be enjoyed to the full. He was particularly scornful of Bobet for whom no sacrifice was too big – he lived only for the glory of winning. Géminiani once said: 'Louison would think for a whole week about drinking a beer. His resolve would finally snap, but, after he had drunk it, he would chastise himself for two weeks for having done so!'

Jacques knew that he had talent and that it would develop more as he grew older, but also that his was a dangerous profession which could be brought to an end at any time by a bad accident, so, he took out an insurance policy to cover any such eventuality. He was also haunted by the fear that he would die young; life was precarious so it should be lived to the full. The sensitive Anquetil kept these thoughts to himself for the fear of being laughed at, and would only reveal them much later to his wife.

For the 1954 season Francis Pélissier had decided that Anquetil would not ride many classics, but of course there were lots of other races. Jacques made a couple of trips to Paris in February to ride the boards of the Velodrome d'Hiver, then a quick trip to Algeria at the beginning of March before the first real test of the season in the Paris–Nice.

When he was interviewed before the race he said: 'I have been designated team leader for this event, but I have never raced over more than 200 kilometres. What are my team mates going to say? People like Maurice Diot and André Darrigade who are both very experienced and successful riders? I am a little afraid of this event, especially if the weather is bad. But, above all, I want to finish as I never like retiring from an event.' When Jacques expressed himself so lucidly in front of the media, nobody would have guessed that this ease was, in reality, a cloak to hide his excessively shy nature.

This was the second time that Anquetil had come up against Coppi on the road and after Fausto won the third stage, everyone was looking forward to seeing how the two men would compare with each other in the time trial. It all ended in anticlimax when the World Champion retired from the race. Jacques duly won the test against the watch, beating the race leader and final overall winner, Raymond Impanis, by 29 seconds. Jacques finished seventh overall, a result which was more than promising.

After the finish Anquetil stayed on at the Côte d'Azur to ride another time trial. This time it was held on the Mont Faron and he was only able to finish eighth, 2 min. 9 sec. behind the specialist climber, Jean Dotto. The race was a comparatively minor event, but the lesson was clear: Jacques could go very fast indeed on the flat, but uphill was a different matter.

For the next couple of months he achieved a whole series of places in the top ten, such as ninth in the National Criterium and seventh in the Grand Prix Pneumatique at Montlucon. The Tour de France was approaching and although there was no question of him taking part, he was at the curtain-raiser, the Criterium des As, run behind Dernys at Longchamps, the site of the famous horse-racing track. It was a magnificent and exciting spectacle as both Jacques and his team mate, Hugo Koblet, incessantly attacked Louison Bobet, who was equally determined not to relinquish his lead. It was 1954, Bobet's best year, and in this event he overcame the intense pressure, finally to run out winner by three seconds from Anquetil. The Breton confirmed his good form by magnificently winning his second Tour de France and then the World Championship in Germany. For the moment, Louison was the uncontested number one in France, if not in the world.

For Jacques the really important part of the season was now approaching. First there were the post-Tour criteriums which paid so well; then the World Championships which were always to be of particular interest to him and finally the end-of-season time trials. However, criteriums alone were insufficient preparation for the title race at Solingen, on the other side of the Rhine, so he rode the Tour of the West, a prestigious and hard-fought stage-race in Brittany, and covered himself in glory with his magnificent display of aggressive riding. As one of the competitors said: 'Jacques was quite wonderful and made the race a very hard one. When he did one of his hard turns at the front, the bunch stretched into one long line.' Such youthful exuberance was to result in little material gain as he only finished tenth in the race, and as his career progressed there were to be far fewer examples of such aggressiveness in stage races. Nevertheless, he had certainly achieved his immediate objective of coming into top form at the right moment.

The summer of 1954 was one of the worst on record, and it was raining very hard as the riders started the World Championship race near Wuppertal in the industrial heart of Germany. As Jacques grew older he came to hate the rain, but it seemed to worry him less when he was young. The hard conditions whittled down the field to just a handful of the very strongest and, as the race was reaching its climax, the only survivors were Anquetil and Bobet of France, Gismondi and Coppi of Italy, Schaer of Switzerland, and Gaul of Luxembourg. On the final lap Bobet punctured, but still managed to catch and drop Schaer for a superb victory. They were followed home by the fresh-faced Charly Gaul who was totally at ease in the rain; then Gismondi, outsprinting Anquetil for fourth place, and finally Coppi, who had cracked on the final lap.

So Anquetil's first attempt at the world title had been most promising; with such class, and at his age, few doubted that he would put on the rainbow jersey one day. For the immediate future he had a couple of very important races against the watch before starting his military service in October. At the Grand Prix Martini in Geneva he was beaten into third place by Koblet and Fornara – but for his puncture, Fornara would have given Hugo a very close run indeed, but Jacques, at 2 min. 17 sec., was well beaten. Francis

Pélissier said that Anquetil did not have the right gears on his bike, but the young Jacques made no such excuses.

Jacques Anquetil and Hugo Koblet met again in the Grand Prix des Nations, and here there was a problem of a different sort. When Koblet rode in Italy he was a member of the Guerra team, but when he competed in France he was part of Pélissier's La Perle organisation. So, when the Swiss decided to ride the Grand Prix des Nations, it meant that Francis Pélissier had two top men in the event. Which one was he to follow? He opted for Hugo, and Jacques was greatly upset by this lack of confidence shown by his *directeur sportif*, even if Koblet had won in Geneva.

On the day of the event Anquetil was very well prepared and rode a perfect race while Koblet retired. However, few had taken into account the Belgian, Jean Brankart. Riding the race of his life, he was still in the lead with just twenty kilometres to go, but Jacques was kept well informed and pulled out all the stops in a desperate finish. He finally took the victory by 22 seconds, breaking Koblet's 1951 race record into the bargain. Then, in a gesture that many described as 'totally Pélissier', Jacques Anquetil drove to Francis Pélissier's café outside Paris and presented his winner's bouquet to Mrs Pélissier. 'He's a funny boy,' she said. 'You can never be sure whether he's pleased or not.'

An eleventh place in Paris–Tours and then it was off to the barracks at Rouen to enrol in the army. He was quickly transferred to the sportsmen's battalion at Joinville where he was to rub shoulders with several members of the national football team. There were one or two officers who were sticklers for discipline, but they were quickly overruled from above – there was capital to be made from Jacques' successes.

Morale in the army was at a low ebb. There had been the humiliating defeat of 1940, then the government had involved the country in a useless and unpopular war in Indo-China, without giving the army sufficient support. The whole thing had ended five months previously in another catastrophe at Dien Bien Phu. To make matters even worse, there were the first signs of an uprising in Algeria. Any prestige the army could obtain through the sporting achievements of its soldiers was, therefore, most welcome. It was hardly surprising, then, that Anquetil was informed that he would be free to race where and when he wanted.

The date of the Grand Prix of Lugano was fast approaching, but only at the last moment did he manage to get leave to compete. Despite the short notice, it was quite an easy victory for Jacques. Wearing uniform had clearly not affected his form.

He was to cross the Alps a second time in order to ride the Baracchi Trophy with the World Champion Louison Bobet as his partner. Once again, his leave did not come through until very late, but this time it had more unfortunate results. The long drive to Italy was made worse by thick fog, and by the time Jacques arrived in Bergamo, having had only three hours sleep, Bobet had been in the town for four days and was fretting as Jacques calmly sat down for something to eat. He was not one to make excuses, so Bobet put his late arrival down to carelessness.

The French pair finished second, 1 min. 26 sec. behind Coppi–Filippi, and Bobet was furious at being robbed of victory. Not a word passed between them at the finish and Louison complained bitterly to the newspapers. He was the World Champion and, as such, he believed victory was his right. Jacques was not serious – even the papers said so – whereas he, Bobet, always wanted to win so much it was said that he would give up five years of his life for a major victory. Above all, Bobet was really irritated by Jacques' 'cast-iron' stomach, annoyed that things seemed to come so easily to him, and worried that one day Jacques would take away from him the number one spot in the affections of the French public. In short, Bobet never really liked Anquetil.

Coppi saw things quite differently, and in his calm, polite and gentle way explained to the newsmen that if Jacques had been able to obtain his leave earlier, then the French pair would undoubtedly have won. On the other hand, if he, Fausto, had been paired with Koblet then he would have gone even faster.

Back in France most people took Bobet's part mainly because, by now, most fans had formed a certain idea of Jacques Anquetil. A report in a journal summed it up: 'He does not attack, he does not seem serious and he always looks bored. He pushes gears that are far too big and seems only interested in money. He is cold, indifferent and unapproachable. His successes do not seem to make him happy and he never seems to try.' He was seen as the young prince of cycling and many considered that he was taking the title too literally.

Jacques defended himself with mature words of wisdom. He assured people that he was very serious indeed and trained very hard. He pushed big gears because he found it easy to do so. He did not attack because the other riders would never allow him any freedom. As for his nature, well that was the way he was: he had a horror of pulling faces in public and was incapable of making excessive gestures. He was a racing cyclist, not an actor. But the real problem was that when anybody thought of Jacques, the first thing that sprung to mind was his cold blue eyes.

The fact was that he was a highly intelligent young man who simply did not conform to the normal rules. He had got used to going to bed late and getting up late. Perhaps it was a reaction against the early rising on his father's farm, but he was far from being unique in this respect: it was well-known that during stage-races Coppi himself was a very poor riser and always stayed in bed until the last possible moment. Jacques accepted that the profession demanded sacrifices, but thought that these should be kept to a minimum as there were other things in life apart from the bicycle. He had an enormous appetite and just loved to eat chips. What was the point of being well paid if you could not enjoy the fruits of your labour? The majority of riders could only dream of the big win and were willing to try just about anything in order to pull one off. In short, Jacques was a painfully shy twenty year old who hid behind a mask which gave every appearance of indifference.

The year ended with more contracts at the Velodrome d'Hiver in Paris. These meetings attracted large crowds and acted like magnets for stage and screen stars – it was said that you could see more film stars at the Paris Six-day race than anywhere outside a film festival – and Jacques was later to form a number of close and enduring friendships with show business personalities through these meetings at the famous Velodrome. His appearance fee remained at 30,000 f. and he was always newsworthy. Often when his name cropped up the Press asked: 'If Jacques Anquetil has won virtually all the time trials he has ridden, then surely he should be able to break the hour record?' The journalists went to the shop of Maurice Archambaud, the last French holder of the record back in 1937, for advice. Maurice was quite adamant: 'Anquetil will be the first one to beat 46 kilometres.'

Chapter Five

From the beginning of the season it started to become clear that it was going to be the last year that La Perle would be running a pro team. Sales of bicycles were falling as mopeds, motorbikes and cars were becoming so popular. Francis Pélissier had a series of minor illnesses and thought that it would be an appropriate time to retire as well. With his energy and drive considerably diminished, he was no longer the man he used to be. There was some hope that companies from outside the cycle trade could be induced to sponsor some teams, but the governing bodies in France thought that this could be very dangerous and would do everything they could to oppose it.

At 21, Jacques was still considered to be too young for the Tour de France, but perhaps he could be risked in a few minor stage races, especially those which took in some mountains. More appearances on the summer tracks might give some extra experience for the hour-record attempt he was expected to make. However, records were normally attempted in the autumn so it was assumed that Anquetil would compete in the traditional time trials first.

His early season form seemed reasonable and he made a good start by finishing fourth at Oran in Algeria. A crash put him out of the National Criterium but he seemed to be riding very strongly in his first real classic, the Paris–Roubaix, before he was eliminated with a broken chain. The following month saw his biggest test up to that point when he started the Tour of the South-East

Provinces which spent a couple of days in the Alps. All of the La Perle team were somewhat disgruntled with Francis Pélissier: he only told them that they were riding at the last moment and he was not much use to them during the race itself. The riders were left to fend for themselves.

An early leader in the race was the English man Brian Robinson, but Anquetil went away with Charly Gaul on the sixth stage from Annecy to Gap and the Frenchman won the sprint at the finish to notch up his first ever victory in the mountains. Yet Gaul was in superb form when the race went over Mont Ventoux and the stage win enabled him to take the final victory overall by seven minutes with Anquetil in ninth place at 15 min. 9 sec.

A few days later Jacques started an even harder event, the Criterium du Dauphiné Libéré. It lasted for nine stages and was virtually a dress rehearsal for the Tour de France. In racing circles it is said that nobody who does badly in the Dauphiné has much chance in the Tour.

At the start in Valence, Jacques was worried that the team did not seem to have a masseur. When he expressed his anxiety to Pélissier he got the sharp reply, 'Listen kid, don't make a fuss about it. For a race over only one week you don't need a masseur, you can get all the massage you need on the bike. Now go away!' The stars of the race were Bobet and Walkowiak. Even in the time trial Jacques could only finish third behind Bobet and Privat. Unsurprisingly, Anquetil finished the race in fifteenth position, nearly an hour down.

A few weeks later the National Championship was held at Chateaulin in Brittany. It had always previously been held on the motor-racing circuit at Montlhéry to the south of Paris. So, in place of the wide open spaces the course now comprised of twisty country roads with no straight longer than 300 metres. This encouraged breakaways and there were certainly to be no shortage of them during this hard, fast and exciting race. Bobet was clearly on form and, as wearer of the rainbow jersey, desperately wanted to win in his own backyard. Most people regarded him as race favourite and he had the backing of the powerful Mercier team.

Anquetil was clearly very strong but the sprinter of the team, André Darrigade from Dax, had had a lot of bad luck up to that point in 1955. Still, things had to change for the better sometime.

In the end, just about the whole field took part in one or another of the many short-lived escapes. One of the longest was by Schodeller and the Mercier rider René Privat, but their lead never went much above 30 seconds. They were caught with twenty kilometres to go as the field broke up and reformed with dizzying speed. Twelve men were left at the front as Bobet was doing long, hard turns to ensure the success of the break and especially to distance André Darrigade who was not up with them.

André went hard up the final hill in a desperate attempt to close the gap, but with the inevitable Mercier rider sitting on his wheel. Bobet urged Anquetil to greater efforts to prevent the danger man from rejoining, but Jacques shook his head: André was a friend as well as a team mate and as he latched on to the back of the leading group, despair could be seen in Bobet's eyes. The front group now contained twelve riders and half of them were wearing the Mercier jersey, as opposed to three from La Perle.

Incredibly, René Privat went clear again with Schodeller, but their lead was never more than 30 metres. As they all came together again the finish was getting very close. With just over one kilometre to go Pierre Molineris escaped, but this time it was Anquetil who was solely responsible for bringing him back. Darrigade claimed that Jacques was very strong on the day, but after he started his long sprint he saw Jacques sit up. André was sprinting in the middle of the road when he saw Bobet move up to his shoulder on the right. Darrigade went again, but in doing so moved slightly to the right and on the finishing line won the race by a mere three inches, with Jacques in fifth spot.

Bobet simply could not accept the result. His will to win had taken possession of him. He was beside himself with rage at being beaten and wanted to lodge a protest that he had been impeded in the sprint. His brother, Jean, put a hand on his shoulder to calm him down: 'Louison,' he said, 'now is the time for you to act like a World Champion.' The volatile and excitable Darrigade was mad with delight as he put on the tricolour jersey and embraced Jacques passionately. Their friendship was well and truly sealed. A rather drawn looking Pélissier made sure that he was photographed alongside the newly attired Darrigade. At last the team manager had something to celebrate. The La Perle company were on the edge of bankruptcy and the riders had not been paid since April.

Bobet explained to the journalists that if he had officially protested, the judges would undoubtedly have given the race to him as it was unjust that he should lose in this fashion. An impartial observer, André Leducq, writing in the magazine *But et Club*, said that although Darrigade had moved off his line a little, it certainly did not stop Bobet from coming through. Jacques' right-hand man, Sadi Duponchel, said to his young protégé: 'There, Jacques. There's your partner for the Baracchi.'

André was nearly five years older than Jacques and a few days later won a stage in the Tour de France for the second time in his career. Anquetil, meanwhile, rode mostly criteriums, but his thoughts were on the World Championship in Rome. He was certainly well prepared for the event and the hot weather was to his liking, if not to that of Coppi and Bobet, who both retired. Jacques and André Darrigade spent most of the race in front of the main bunch either in the leading group or in the chasing group until Darrigade was eliminated with a puncture. British hopes were raised when Mitchell, Pusey and Ilsley were seen at the front, but the weather and the distance were too much for them, and none of them finished.

With twenty kilometres to go Jacques was in the leading break with the Italians Nencini, Fornara and Coletto; the Frenchmen Géminiani and Rolland; and the Luxembourger Schmitz. The Belgian Stan Ockers had also finally got up to them after closing a nine-minute gap in 40 kilometres.

'What are we going to do?' said Jacques to Géminiani.

'It's every man for himself,' said the experienced rider from Clermont-Ferrand.

Jacques attacked and went clear, but was caught by Géminiani and Ockers. Whether or not the Frenchman had cooperated with the Belgian to get up to Anquetil was something that Jacques was never able to establish. The whole thing was rather academic as Ockers was so much stronger than either of them. When the Belgian attacked Géminiani cracked immediately and then Jacques, too, was obliged to sit up as Ockers went on to win in great style. Schmitz came past both Frenchmen to take the silver medal. Anquetil finally finished sixth at 1 min. 55 sec. with Géminiani eighth at 2 min. 45 sec. Just as in 1954 Anquetil's performance was quite outstanding, but, nevertheless, insufficient.

It was an amazing win for the little smiling Belgian who was in his thirteenth year as a professional. At 36 years of age he had twice finished second in the Tour de France without once wearing the yellow jersey. Nor had he ever put on a National Champion's jersey, so this was a completely new experience for him. He laughingly said that he felt he had to finally bring off a big win, otherwise all the customers in his café in Antwerp would go somewhere else. More seriously he added that he had always been accused of being insensitive, but when they played the Belgian National Anthem in his honour he could not hold back the tears.

Three weeks later Jacques took his revenge, winning his first Grand Prix Martini at Geneva in front of Ockers, Brankart and Fornara. A week later he started the Grand Prix des Nations as undisputed favourite. In spite of the adverse weather conditions he beat the race record and, according to one distinguished journalist, won the event with 'miraculous ease'. Not since the 1930s had anyone won the race three times and Jacques was still only 21!

More rumours began to circulate about an attempt on the hour record. Jacques was on form so why wait? The army was all for it and had even persuaded Jacques to give all his profits from the attempt to army charities. For Anquetil himself, the position was a little delicate. His contract with La Perle did not finish until the end of October and the company had made it plain that it was not willing to pay his expenses for the record attempt. However, his contract with his new sponsors started at the beginning of November and they were quite prepared to pay for the whole thing.

His new team was Helyett Cycles, supported by a new *extra-sportif* sponsor, Felix Potin, who owned a chain of grocery shops. Jacques was happy to see the last of Francis Pélissier and found his new team manager, Paul Wiegant, much more *sympa*. When the Vel d'Hiv (as most fans called the Velodrome d'Hiver) opened its doors for the start of the winter season in the second week of October, Jacques finally broke the news to the journalists – a week later he would be in Milan for an attempt on the hour record. Out of respect for his current sponsor he was to ride a La Perle bicycle. His jersey was to carry no name at all, but instead of being the red and white of La Perle, it was to be the green and white of Helyett.

The previous record had been established by Fausto Coppi in November 1942. When the last French holder, Maurice Archambaud, saw his five-year-old record broken he complained that there were irregularities in the way that the mandatory sandbags had been positioned. Fewer of them had been placed on the bends than during his successful attempt. Jacques was surprised to see so many of them at the bottom of the bankings again, rather too close to the track. Jacques' schedule was based on Coppi's previous one and the aim was just a modest improvement on the distance.

He was joined by 10,000 people in the stands, including many French roadmen who were in Italy for the forthcoming Tour of Lombardy and who had come to witness the attempt. Daniel Dousset was also there. He had been Anquetil's 'manager' since the start of his professional career, in other words he was the link between the rider and the race promoters, the man who arranged the contracts. However, he had quickly become a personal friend, too, and so he was also at the trackside.

Jacques started his attack on the record very fast and was soon up on his schedule. Dousset was worried and implored him to slow down. It had always been Anquetil's policy in a time trial to start fast, ease up a little, and then finish fast, but this time it just did not pay off. His blistering pace had taken too much out of him and when he eased he had nothing left for the finish. The result was a disaster and almost a humiliation: he was more than 600 metres short of the old record. The Italian crowd were happy enough and started to chant 'Coppi, Coppi, Coppi!' Jacques had been the usual marvellous pedalling machine, but he had not gone fast enough.

Jacques said that he was disappointed, of course, but he had never thought that the sandbags would have bothered him so much. On the straights they were no problem, but on the bends too many of them meant that he had to ride further up the banking and thus increase the distance covered. To ride at the very bottom would have meant risking touching one of them with a pedal. None the less, it had been a useful experience and he was sure that one day he would be able to break the record. The experts agreed with him, but the Italian spectators went home happy that day.

For what it's worth, Francis Pélissier later said that he had refused to go with Jacques to Milan as he was expecting him to fail. He said that he was bound to make a mistake, and if he didn't he would invent some excuse – and that he was badly advised and even when he was given good advice he wouldn't listen. A previous record holder, Maurice Richard, said Anquetil was embarking on an attempt without serious preparation. Perhaps the last word, though, should go to the journalist Pierre Chany, the man who was to become a close personal friend of Jacques. He wrote: 'He made so many mistakes that it would have been a miracle if he had taken the record. Conditions were against him. He had ridden very little after his arrival in Milan and was bored with all the sterile discussions of his advisers.' Chany then went on to say that Jacques' bike weighed six kilos against the seven and a half of Coppi's machine, and the nine kilos of Archambaud's mount.

The road season finished with the Baracchi Trophy and this time Anquetil was paired with Darrigade. For the third year running Jacques finished second behind Coppi and Filippi.

The year came to an end with a few more contracts on the track in Paris, but what Jacques was really looking forward to was riding in a new team alongside his friend Darrigade. His new *directeur sportif*, Paul Wiegant, was an entirely different kettle of fish to Francis Pélissier.

Chapter Six

At the start of the new season there was much talk about another attempt on the hour record. Maurice Archambaud had died, but not before giving his analysis of Anquetil's mistakes to the journalist René de Latour, who had witnessed Jacques' unsuccessful attempt.

According to Maurice, Jacques had chosen a hotel too near the centre of the town making it impossible for him to get the required peace and quiet so necessary for concentration. His stay in Milan had also been far too short, not allowing him enough time to wait for ideal weather conditions: on the day of the attempt there was a light wind blowing, it was a little cold and the air was too damp. His physical preparation had been hampered by the rain. The bicycle itself, he thought, was too light and therefore not rigid enough, and he had made no attempt to find the most aerodynamic position. Maurice himself had spent some time in the wind tunnel at the Eiffel laboratories in Paris. Furthermore, he claimed, Anquetil had not respected his schedule and had started far too fast. Finally, he thought his gear of 52x15 had been a little too high, especially in the last fifteen minutes. Archambaud probably knew what he was talking about: he had only broken the record after several unsuccessful attempts.

Back in Rouen Jacques discussed his plans for the season with Sadi Duponchel. After his first win in the Grand Prix des Nations, he had found it increasingly difficult to meet up with his old friends, and Sadi was the one person with whom he had stayed in close contact. Together they bought a ten-roomed flat in the centre of town. Jacques was not a man to make friends easily, and many people found him somewhat argumentative and distrustful. He was certainly not one to listen to people's advice. As Jean Bobet was later to say: 'Anquetil only obeys Jacques and Jacques only listens to Anquetil.' And, yet, he could not stand being alone for very long, and he really needed someone to divert him from his secretive and reflective nature. Apart from Duponchel, his only really close friend was André Darrigade, and he was a godsend – warm, volatile and enthusiastic, he was just what the young Anquetil needed.

Jacques was going to be posted to Algeria before the end of the year so, in his discussions with Sadi, he concluded that any record attempt would have to be made in the summer. All Frenchmen conscripted into the army were obliged to spend some time in North Africa, and the army could not make any exceptions for their sportsmen; the senior officers, however, were clearly anxious for him to make an attempt on the record, and would do everything to help and encourage him. Thus, the main objective for the season was set.

The year started with the customary trip to North Africa, then it was back to France where Jacques beat Andrieux at the Vel d'Hiv for the national indoor pursuit title. Just after that came the Paris–Nice. It was a new-look peloton which lined up for the start of this important stage-race: this was the first year of the *extra-sportif* teams. Amongst the new products being advertised on the team jerseys were petrol, coffee, beauty cream, grocery shops and coffee machines.

Jacques crashed on stage three and, although Darrigade and two other team mates dropped back to help him, they were not able to rejoin the bunch. He retired that day, before the time trial, totally demoralised. Anquetil did have the small recompense of seeing Shay Elliott, his new team mate from Ireland, finish third in the race against the watch, but a disappointed press criticised him for having a fragile morale – as usual the media were expecting too much of him. Although his contract required him to ride most of the major races, he was using them mainly as preparation for his principal objective of the season – the hour

44

record in the summer. If he was successful it would mean much more than a couple of major wins on the road.

The National Criterium was a very fast, hard race, and Jacques and André rode extremely aggressively. However, the race came together again before the finish and was won in magnificent style by the flamboyant Roger Hassenforder in a big bunch sprint at the Parc des Princes. Darrigade was a disappointing fifth and Jacques was given equal eighth place. André later explained that towards the end of the race he was obliged to do an enormous amount of work and no arrangements had been made to lead him out in the sprint. He was, by nature, somewhat loath to ask any of his team mates to help him. All the same, he was later to make a comparison between this race and the Tour of Lombardy which he won a few months later as a member of an Italian team. In the race around the Italian lakes all plans had been finalised before race day in order for him to receive the maximum amount of support.

Next came Paris–Roubaix, which turned out to be a wonderful race for the French, if not for Anquetil, as Bobet outsprinted six other breakaway companions, including three previous winners of the event. The decisive move came when a group of twenty of the strongest men went clear to be whittled down to seven by the finish. At the decisive moment, Jacques was off the back with a puncture and finally finished in 31st place, nearly four minutes down. Nobody knew at the time, of course, but it would be 25 years before another Frenchman won this 'Queen of the Classics'.

Then it was back to Paris once more for the start of the Paris–Brussels, one of the longest single-day races on the calendar. As the race was approaching the Belgian capital André Darrigade was in the leading break with a real chance of winning. But his hopes disappeared with a puncture and the race was finally won in great style by the new young star of Belgian cycling, Rik Van Looy. He had played a prominent role in Paris–Nice a few weeks previously, but many had considered that his lack of experience had caused him to make too many useless efforts. Anquetil was credited with equal eighth place at the finish in Brussels, after nine hours in the saddle.

In the Three Days of Antwerp Jacques won a stage, then finished ninth in the hilly, single-day Midi Libre, six and a half minutes behind the winner, Antonin Rolland. By now his string of top-ten places was of less interest to the press than the form he was showing for the forthcoming hour-record attempt.

At the beginning of June he won the National Pursuit title at the Parc des Princes by a margin of eight seconds. He claimed, however, that it had not been as easy as it might have looked because, having warmed up on his road bike in the woods near the stadium on a very big gear, he had felt awkward and uncomfortable when he rode the pursuit on a much smaller one. He reported that his team manager wanted him to do two more weeks of specialised and intensive training before going to Italy.

In the end Jacques flew to Milan on Friday 22nd June with Daniel Dousset, Sadi Duponchel, André Boucher and Captain Guéguen, and that same evening did twenty laps of the Vigorelli track and said that he felt in very good condition. In Milan, they were surrounded by journalists determined to find out where they were staying. Following Archambaud's advice, they tried, without much success, to keep this a secret. The problem of the sandbags had, however, been resolved: they were thinner, there were fewer of them and, being filled with foam rubber instead of sand, they were less dangerous. Dousset suggested that the attempt should be made on the Sunday, but Jacques preferred the Monday.

Over the previous couple of months Daniel Dousset had been on the phone to Anquetil quite regularly and had been puzzled at the number of times that Jacques had said that he'd not bothered to go out training, but the truth was somewhat different. Anquetil had been training very hard indeed, with long, high-speed sessions behind Boucher's Derny. At the age of 22 he was the master of such preparation and the lies he told Dousset were just another example of his taste for provocation.

His military superiors were most anxious that Private Anquetil should break the record, especially after the previous year's failure. Once again Jacques had agreed, amid much publicity, to give all his gains to an army charity.

On Monday 25th June everything was ready. Anquetil wanted to attempt the record in private, but the owner of the track would not hear of it and tickets at 150 lire a time were soon sold out. Throughout the day the wind made an attempt inadvisable. By seven in the evening, however, it had dropped considerably and the Italian spectators were getting impatient. Although conditions were not ideal, it was decided that the attempt to improve on Coppi's distance of 45.798 kilometres should go ahead.

Once again, Jacques started too fast, but this time it looked as if he might be able to maintain the pace, covering just over 23 kilometres in 30 minutes. He had followed his usual practice of starting fast, easing a little, and then finishing fast, but he had started too fast, and not eased enough. He was still going well at 40 minutes, but then he rapidly began falling behind schedule. With ten minutes still to go he sat up.

Captain Guéguen immediately contacted his battalion headquarters at Joinville and received a prompt telegram in reply which congratulated Jacques on his efforts, expressed confidence in his next attempt, and told him to take all the time he needed. Then came the post-mortem: Duponchel impressed on Jacques the importance of keeping to his schedule, and local experts were called in to examine his bicycle closely. For the whole of his career Jacques was notorious for being indifferent to the technicalities of his machines. The bike in question was the chromium-plated one on which he had recently won his pursuit title. The wheelbase was judged to be rather short – ideal for pursuiting but not entirely suitable for an effort lasting for 60 minutes. This would probably have accounted for the extreme pain which he had felt at the top and back of his legs. His road saddle was more comfortable and would be used in any future attempt. Coppi's personal mechanic, Pinella di Grande, agreed to supervise the building of a new frame in three days.

In the meantime, Anquetil needed to get away from the intense atmosphere which had been disrupting his sleep, so he went north to Lake Como with Sadi Duponchel and spent an evening in a night-club. They danced until very late in the morning before eventually returning to the hotel, where Jacques finally got what he had been missing for several days – a long, deep sleep. Nevertheless, the journalists were scandalised and wondered just what sort of a Frenchman this was.

Captain Guéguen claimed that conditions would be ideal for another attempt on Friday evening. So, after carefully warming up behind a scooter, Jacques announced: 'It's now or never. If I fail, I'm going home.'

Interestingly, the new schedule was slightly slower than that of Coppi back in 1942. In this way he hoped to save himself for the final fifteen minutes when Fausto had suffered so much and only just survived. Coppi, in fact, had not prepared all that carefully and was rather lucky to have broken the record at all. They knew that it would not be easy to put a break on Anquetil's enthusiasm to go too fast, so three men were placed strategically around the track. 'The record is yours for the taking,' said Sadi Duponchel. 'If you blow it this time I'm going to break your face.'

This time everything was perfect. He followed his schedule scrupulously and seemed to be turning the pedals as if in time to a metronome. So perfect was his style and position that he made it look so easy. With six minutes to go he had already ridden 100 metres further than planned, and then released his powerful final burst. At the end of 60 minutes he had ridden 46.159 kilometres, bettering the old record by 311 metres. Just as Archambaud had predicted, he was the first man to break the 46-kilometre barrier.

The Italian press went into raptures over the performance, as did the French army: when Jacques eventually returned to barracks he was greeted by a guard of honour and a couple of months later he was promoted to corporal.

An interesting sidelight on Jacques' attempts on the hour record was later provided by his wife, Janine, although at this stage she did not really know him. She claims that his heart was not really in his first attempt in 1955: he liked and respected Coppi too much to really want to rob him of his precious record. In 1956 he was certainly more motivated and perhaps felt that taking the record only after a couple of attempts was, in itself, a compliment to Fausto.

No Tour de France again, but Anquetil took pleasure from Darrigade's performance in the *Grand Boucle*. The event was finally won by a little-known regional rider, but André was convinced he could have won the race himself. He complained that he had been let down by the team in general, and Marcel Bidot in particular. However, given that he finished 40 minutes down in Paris, most people did not take the claim too seriously.

For Anquetil the next big test was the World Championships in Denmark. This time he gave the road race a miss and set his sights on the pursuit title, but he was beaten in the final by the

Italian expert, Messina. After a lot of thought he came to the conclusion that too many pursuit races could shorten his career, just as Coppi himself had claimed. Anquetil's main objective was to race for as long as possible in order to derive the maximum advantage from his talents. He was always worried that one day an accident would bring his career to an end. A further factor in his decision to restrict his pursuiting might have been the appearance on the scene of another young Frenchman who gave every indication that one day he would be virtually unbeatable in pursuit races – a certain Roger Rivière.

For the second year in a row Anquetil did not ride the Grand Prix of Lugano but was successful at the Grand Prix Martini at Geneva, once again beating the Belgian star, Stan Ockers, this time with an increased margin of 3 mins. 35 secs. The distance of the Grand Prix des Nations had been reduced to 100 kilometres, but Jacques, as always, was the favourite. After 50 kilometres he caught Albert Bouvet, another expert against the watch, for four minutes. Anquetil went past him like an express train, without even a glance, but Albert held on, and on, and on. He even overtook Jacques and opened up a lead of 100 metres. Jacques had never experienced anything like this before and, disconcerted and disorientated, he was on the point of retiring from the race. Of course, those in his following car would have none of it and he duly went on to win the event at record speed.

Towards the end of the season Jacques and André made the trip to Italy where they had been taken on by the Bianchi team to ride the Tour of Lombardy. The whole thing had been arranged some time previously by Fausto Coppi himself. In the meantime, however, Coppi had had a disagreement with Bianchi and was wearing the colours of his own team, named Coppi–Carpano. It was an exceptionally hard day and, as the race approached the finish at Milan, Coppi and Ronchini – a team mate of Anquetil and Darrigade – were clear of the rest of the field. Then, acting on the orders of their team manager, Ronchini stopped working and the pair were caught with five kilometres to go.

Darrigade had been riding particularly strongly in the chasing group; so too had Fiorenzo Magni, angered at having been insulted by Coppi's wife who was following the race in her own car. The group which rode on to the Vigorelli track for the finish also contained the young Belgian, Rik Van Looy, who had, as he was given to do, been making too much unnecessary effort at the front of the group. The partisan Italian crowd went wild with delight as Coppi went to the front and stayed there. Magni was clearly beaten, as was Van Looy, De Bruyne, Forestier, and Fornara, but not the sprinter Darrigade who caught and went past the *Campionissimo* just before the line. The crowd groaned in despair and the organisers were so upset that Darrigade had to ride his lap of honour without a bouquet.

Jacques congratulated André warmly on this prestigious victory, and the Bianchi team were obviously very pleased as well. As for André, himself, his joy was somewhat tinged with regret at having robbed his friend Coppi of a win that he knew would have meant so much to him; he was amazed, too, at the support he'd been given by his Italian team mates. Although France was his home and he didn't really want to make the move, he did wonder if it would not be an idea to look for a permanent position on an Italian squad.

Now obviously very hot property in Italy, Darrigade stayed on to ride the Baracchi Trophy, but without Anquetil. Jacques had been posted to North Africa and had to leave immediately, so a partner had to be found for André. It was suggested that he form a team with Bobet. Darrigade categorically refused this, but he readily accepted the Swiss specialist, Rolf Graf. It turned out to be a happy choice as the pair ran out clear winners. It was rather ironic that, partnered by Jacques, he was to manage two second places, a third and a fourth place, but never a win. During the winter season, however, André refused to ride with any partner at all on the track. Jacques was away for the whole of the winter so André rode the boards as an individual.

Anquetil was to spend six months in Algeria. The army could not afford to show him too much favouritism, but they did keep a close eye on his safety. A racing trip to North Africa was one thing, but, as a soldier, he was a target for terrorists. He had to obtain permission to go training and, when he did, he was given an armoured escort.

During his time in the French colony it was rumoured that he had a passionate affair with a ballet dancer, the wife of one of his friends. He quickly realised there was no future in such a liaison and that it would be much wiser to concentrate on his career. He had proved himself on the track, and against the watch, but much more was expected of him. To fulfil his potential, and become a top-money earner, he would have to win some classics or major stage-races Everyone believed that he had the class to do so, and he couldn't use his age as an excuse for much longer.

PART TWO – THE YOUNG KING

Chapter Seven

On 1st March 1957 Jacques was finally discharged from the army. For the first time in his career he had had a complete break from racing for almost six months, so he quickly had to buckle down to training and lose some weight. This proved to be no great problem and in his first race, from Genoa to Nice, he finished second behind Louison Bobet. In the restaurant of the hotel where he was staying he recognised a familiar face. It was Madame Boeda, the wife of his doctor, who was taking a short holiday with her children.

Frankly, Janine Boeda did not have a very high regard for this young hypochondriac who was five years her junior. He sometimes came twice a week to her husband's surgery with worries about his constipation. She had trained as a nurse and had seen some really sick people in her time, so she could not understand why her husband spent so much time with this fit, youthful athlete with the cold, blue eyes. Nevertheless, when Jacques invited her and her children to dinner she accepted. In the evening, she saw a different side to Jacques: he could be so charming and he was really wonderful with the children. One thing was for sure: he led a full, exciting and glamorous life – a far cry from her mundane existence, working in her husband's surgery at Rouen.

This was the start of Anquetil's fourth season as a professional and, so far, it had been rather a bizarre career. He had delivered much less than was expected of him. He had won most of the late-season time trials, of course. Indeed, by now, it was surprising if he did not. No other rider had ever dominated these specialist races like he had, and he continued to beat most event records. He had also taken the hour record, albeit after three attempts. He had won a handful of criteriums, too, but nothing of any great importance. It appeared that he was not a brilliant climber as, in 1957, he could only finish seventh in the time trial up Mont Faron. So it looked as though he couldn't expect to do well in the Tour de France, the most important event on the cycling calendar, but André Darrigade was continually pressing him to make a decision about riding it. 'It's marvellous, Jacques,' he said. 'An experience you will never forget. You should waste no more time.'

The first big test of the season was Paris–Nice. It was a very controlled race with nobody being able to open any big gaps. Jacques started the race three kilos overweight and suffered for the first two stages, but in the time trial on stage five, pushing a gear of 53x14, he averaged 45.535 k.p.h. to beat Brankart by nearly a minute. This enabled him to put on the leader's jersey and, with the help of his strong Helyett–Potin team, which included Darrigade and Elliott, and able to call on the help of a 'sister team' Essor–Leroux (also managed by Paul Wiegant) which contained Forestier, Hassenforder, and Stablinski, he kept it until the finish. According to the journalist Roger Bastide, Anquetil rode 'with authority and maturity' to make sure that none of the danger-men went clear. This was a sensational victory. 'Jacques Comes Of Age', screamed the headlines as he won his first big stage-race. So, what next?

Unfortunately, he proceeded very much as he had done in previous years when he was seventh in the National Criterium. Then, in a slow and uneventful Paris–Roubaix, he arrived with the main bunch just over a minute down on the Belgian winner, Fred Debruyne. He was classified equal sixteenth in the massive sprint for second place. A couple of weeks later he flew to Ravenna in Italy with Forestier and Darrigade. They were riding a rather bizarre three-up time trial over a distance of 100 kilometres on a small, five-kilometre circuit. They beat the Italians, the Spanish and the Dutch, running out winners by just under a minute.

Here, Darrigade and Anquetil both confirmed that they would not ride the Tour without each other. André stated that he was disappointed with the support he had received from the rest of the French team when wearing the yellow jersey in the 1956 Tour. Jacques, on the other hand, proclaimed that he was not looking forward to three weeks in hotels, and would take a suit to wear in the evenings to get away from the atmosphere of the race.

Despite having previously announced that he had no intention of defending his pursuit title, Jacques relented at the last moment. The press speculated that Paul Wiegant wanted him to ride the Tour of Romandie in Switzerland and his insistence on contesting the track title again was his way of avoiding the stage-race in the Alps. Such a refusal would not have been possible with Pélissier, but Anquetil had learnt by now that he could dominate Wiegant. In the pursuit final Jacques was well beaten by Roger Rivière, but many people still saw him as good potential Tour material, and Darrigade had sworn to ride only for him.

The manager of the national team, Marcel Bidot, was certainly interested, but had his own difficulties. In 1954 and 1955 he had allowed Bobet to pick the team, and, since he had been a previous winner as well as a world champion, nobody had objected. But the previous year, 1956, had been a catastrophe for Bidot: it was generally considered that his man, Bauvin, had let victory slip through his fingers, permitting a little-known regional rider, Roger Walkowiak, to win the race. Marcel Bidot had been booed by the public at the Parc des Princes.

In 1957, Bobet, a three-times winner of the Tour, still remained an obvious choice, and with Bobet automatically came Géminiani. The previous year's winner, Roger Walkowiak, was also an automatic selection, even if Géminiani was opposed to him. Anquetil's class should also have seen him selected, but Bobet made it plain that he did not want him on the team. Darrigade suggested that the pair of them should ride for a regional squad and this looked like being the best solution. Marcel Bidot, meanwhile, was being plagued by journalists as to his plans and intentions, but, well-used to such pressure, he remained politely evasive. Towards the end of May, at the start of the Tour of Italy, there were still no solutions in sight.

Bobet was riding the Giro accompanied by Géminiani – a most useful colleague since he had once finished fourth in the race and, having an Italian father, spoke the language fluently. No Frenchman had previously won the event and this was Bobet's first major stage-race since the Tour de France in 1955, almost two years previously. By the time the race reached Loretto, Louison was wearing the leader's pink jersey. He and his faithful ally, Géminiani, discussed their tactics and decided that they would concentrate on what they were doing here and now, trying to win in Italy, and miss the French Tour. Louison Bobet would fight with all his strength to defend the pink jersey. Approached by a French radio reporter and questioned about his plans for riding *Le Tour*, he casually said he would not be at the start. This was sensational news and the reporter could not wait to broadcast it.

The next day, Marcel Bidot, following a stage-race as an observer to check the form of some of the potential members of his team, was having lunch with the journalist Pierre Chany. Chany asked if he had heard the news on the radio, but Bidot had no idea what he was talking about. When he was enlightened, he could scarcely believe it: Bobet should have informed him first, before releasing anything to the press. To learn of his decision via the radio was simply an insult.

Then, as Marcel recovered from the shock, he realised that this could spell the end to his problems. Now he could go ahead and select Walkowiak, Anquetil and Darrigade without any worry. The remainder of the team was rapidly picked from good, solid, experienced and, above all, disciplined French riders. Why, there were even some potential winners amongst them, such as Gilbert Bauvin, runner-up the previous year; Jean Forestier who had won Paris–Roubaix in 1955 and the Tour of Flanders the following year; and René Privat who had been promising so much for so long.

Jacques was delighted with his selection and went out of his way to prove that he was able to climb the mountains in the Midi Libre, even though he did not finish the race with the leaders. Marcel Bidot followed the Boucles de la Seine – a major race in those days – to check the form of his team in the forthcoming Tour. He was gratified to see Jacques riding so strongly that he managed to take fourth place in the big sprint which decided the race. Darrigade had been dropped on one of the hills and, although Anquetil helped him to regain the bunch, he was still paying for his efforts in the Bordeaux–Paris, and was unable to finish.

In Nantes, at the start of the Tour de France, Jacques was the only débutante in the team. Bidot told them what was expected of them: nobody at this stage was designated as the team leader and they would all support each other until one of them proved that he was stronger than the rest. Whoever that might be would then have the unqualified support of the whole team. Strict discipline was required of everyone, and anyone not complying with this would be fined.

The race began in intense heat as they headed north-east to the Channel coast. Anquetil always liked the heat: 'He was a camel, a dromedary. He could ride 200 kilometres without drinking,' Géminiani was later to say. However, one of his worst attributes was his lack of attention: he would sit at the back of the bunch and his mind would wander. On the first stage he touched a wheel and came down, fortunately with only minor cuts and grazes. As he was chasing hard to get back to the bunch, Marcel Bidot drew alongside and said, 'Mr Darrigade would like to know if you'd like to see a representative of the health service?' Jacques gave a wry grin and was impressed to see three team mates waiting to help him regain the shelter of the peloton.

On the second stage the tar was melting on the roads as the day got hotter and hotter. The riders became more interested in filling their bottles from the roadside fountains and raiding cafés for bottled drinks. Charly Gaul, the race favourite, was feeling particularly bad, and any water that he consumed he vomited up again. His terrible suffering continued for 72 kilometres before he put his brakes on and, in a state of semi-consciousness, wearily climbed into the broom wagon along with another nine riders who were also weakened by these record temperatures. Charly Gaul just could not take the extreme heat.

This was a disastrous season for Charly: a few weeks earlier he had been robbed of victory in the Tour of Italy when Bobet and Géminiani broke the unwritten law that says you don't attack a rival when he is answering a call of nature. The two Frenchmen did, and got clear away. As the Luxembourg climber fell further and further behind, Coppi, who was following the race in a car, wondered why he did not buy himself some help from some of the Italian riders. No doubt Charly believed he could close the gap alone, but he totally misjudged the pace and, by the finish, he'd lost eleven minutes, and all hope of winning the Giro.

He was furious and promised he would turn Bobet into a string of sausages (Gaul was an ex-butcher!), and he got his revenge, ensuring that Bobet did not win, and helping Nencini, the new race leader, to keep his pink jersey. Charly waited for the Italian when he punctured, made sure that he never went short of anything to eat or drink, and personally neutralised any attacks by Louison. Gastone Nencini had never had such a de luxe team mate in his life, and it was especially frustrating for Bobet when Nencini beat him into second place by seventeen seconds.

Gaul's retirement from the 1957 Tour was a big boost for the French team, none of whom had any hope of staying with him in the mountains. It seemed as if Bidot could do no wrong. The first stage was won by Darrigade, who obviously put on the yellow jersey. René Privat went away on the second leg, opening up a three-minute gap in twenty kilometres to take the stage victory and the overall lead. Then Darrigade helped Anquetil to win the third stage into his home town of Rouen. Besieged by reporters, Jacques told them that, but for his friend Maurice Dieulois, he would never have raced at all and then, after receiving his bouquet, he rode slowly past the crowd and made a point of giving his flowers to Janine Boeda. By this time they had seen each other on several occasions.

Although it was proving to be a very 'fluid' Tour, with the race lead frequently changing as breaks arrived at the finish with considerable time gaps, the French national team had the race in a grip of iron, and relinquished the yellow jersey for just one single day. Anquetil went away with Bauvin on the road to Charleroi, with Bauvin taking the stage and Jacques the yellow jersey, but he only kept it for two days. Jacques had, by now, virtually established himself as team leader, but the big test in the Alps still awaited them. Then, the day before the major climbs, Jacques went away in a long break, won the stage into Thonon-les-Bains, and put on the yellow jersey which he was not to relinquish again before the remnants of the race reached Paris.

There had been no let up to the incredible heat: spectators, and even the fire brigade, had been out with their hose-pipes trying to cool the riders down. By the rest day, at the foot of the Alps, no less than 45 riders had retired from the race due mainly to the heat. Even the Spanish climber, Bahamontes, had had enough, and no amount of supplication could make him continue. He was urged to think of his career, of his team, of Spain and even of Franco, but it was all to no avail. Only the French national team seemed to be unaffected: they were the one squad left with a complete team. However, appearances were deceptive and

Darrigade, in particular, was suffering badly. He later confirmed that he had come very close to retiring on the stage to Thonon-les-Bains.

Jacques' sponsor, Felix Potin, had a house at this beautiful lakeside town, so he invited Anquetil and Darrigade for lunch. In later years there were wild reports that Jacques drunk champagne throughout this Tour, but his team mates insisted that he celebrated with a glass of 'bubbly' on only one occasion, and it may well have been Monsieur Potin who persuaded him to do so.

The next day was the one that everybody had been waiting for – the first day in the mountains. Finally the question that was in everyone's mind would be answered: could Jacques really climb mountains effectively, and not lose time on his main rivals? And would the Belgians and the Italians, who up to now had had a comparatively quiet race, find the will to attack? On the road to Briançon, the highest town in Europe, the race crossed over the Télégraphe and the Galibier. Anquetil was in third place on each summit and in fourth place at the finish, less than two minutes down on the Italian, Nencini, and the Belgian, Janssens. The rest of the French team lost some time, so only Forestier was left in contention for a high overall placing, but this certainly established Jacques as uncontested leader of the team. From now on they would work only for him, and he seemed to be in a very comfortable position indeed, with Janssens eleven minutes down and Nencini twenty minutes adrift.

The second full day in the Alps finished on the shores of the Mediterranean at Cannes and, despite all that had been anticipated, nothing changed at the top of the general classification. This was followed by the flat stages linking the race to the Pyrenees and, as the heat continued, some of the riders could not resist the temptation of a quick dip in the sea to cool off. Again, Jacques found himself riding at the back of the peloton with his mind on other things, and more than once his team mates had to drop back to get him to the front when the action started. On the stage to Perpignan, a group of seven danger-men (they were all in the top ten on general classification) took advantage of Anquetil's lack of attention: they escaped from the bunch and rapidly opened a serious gap. Darrigade immediately dropped back to warn Jacques. After he had finally convinced him of the peril, the two men embarked on a long chase at 60 k.p.h. and finally caught the leaders. Darrigade maintained this was the greatest exploit of his career. However, generally speaking, these flat stages were not very animated, and a couple of times lowly placed riders were allowed to escape and win by enormous margins.

The race followed the shores of the Mediterranean all the way into Spain, finally to stop at Barcelona for a short time trial. As expected, Jacques won this chrono to add a few more seconds to his overall lead. There now remained the Pyrenees to cross, and then the final, longer time trial which they all said Anquetil was bound to win. This 23 year old was beginning to look unbeatable: somebody would have to do something very spectacular to knock him off his perch.

In the Pyrenees Jacques did look vulnerable a couple of times and suffered a lot on the final mountain stage to Pau, but he lost very little time and, with a comfortable lead and the time trial to come, the race was virtually over. As expected, he won the time trial from Bordeaux to Libourne, thus putting the issue beyond any possible doubt, and the race ended in anti-climax in Paris where the Belgian, Marcel Janssens, was in second spot at nearly fifteen minutes. For Marcel Bidot it was a total triumph – 21 days in yellow, first overall, the team prize and twelve stage wins. In the words of one journalist, 'It was a hold-up'. No one realised at the time, but this was to be the pinnacle of Jacques' popularity. He had been dubbed 'Jacquot', but, in effect, 'The Prince of French Cycling' had become the young king.

How different this Tour had been compared with the previous year, when the issue was in doubt right up until the last moment. The yellow jersey had kept changing hands as long breakaways had finished with enormous leads. The winner, Roger Walkowiak, was the shy and modest son of a Polish immigrant and, to many experts, his win was one of the best and most exciting in the history of the Tour. Unfortunately, his form deserted him and he slowly slipped back into obscurity; it even seemed as if there was a conspiracy to assassinate his character. Poor Roger's life was made a misery and he rued the day he ever won the Tour.

Jacques' win was competent rather than sensational, but, most importantly, he had proved that he was much more than just an excellent time trialist: it seemed he could win anything on the cycling calendar. The most significant headline was: 'Jacques Wins His First Tour'.

The World Championship was held at Waregem in Belgium and, as expected, it was a hard, exciting race. As the finish approached there were three Frenchmen and three Belgians left to sprint for the title: Bobet, Darrigade and Anquetil were faced by Van Steenbergen, Van Looy, and De Bruyne – which is to say five wonderful sprinters plus Anquetil. What was Jacques to do? He did not want Bobet, his main rival, to win, but if he helped Darrigade he was worried that he would be criticised for acting against Louison. It was an insoluble dilemma since he was going to be criticised for whatever he did. In the event, he did nothing and finished in sixth place. The Belgians were much more organised and De Bruyne led Van Steenbergen out to win his third rainbow jersey. Bobet got on 'Steen's' wheel to take second place, with Darrigade third and Van Looy fourth. Quite frankly, Jacques need not have worried quite so much as even the most ardent French fan would have been forced to admit that Van Steenbergen was virtually unbeatable in a sprint, especially on home ground. He was, perhaps, the best sprinter of all time.

In the end-of-season time trials a new force emerged: although in only his first year as a professional, an Italian, Ercole Baldini, had beaten Anquetil's record for the hour and was now gaining a reputation of being one of the best time trialists in the world. Jacques was able to beat him, both in the Grand Prix Martini in Geneva and again at the Grand Prix des Nations in Paris, but at last he faced a serious rival in these races against the watch. And in the background stood Roger Rivière from St Etienne: in September he had improved upon Baldini's hour record and many experts prophesied that he was going to be an even more dangerous rival to Anquetil than the Italian.

The last French classic of the season was Paris–Tours and, as usual, the race which linked the French capital to the elegant city on the river Loire was fast and furious, and ended in a bunch sprint. Anquetil offered to lead out Darrigade, but André was 'cooked' and Jacques could only manage tenth place. The spectators were wild with delight as an on-form Bobet was sprinting clear of all the others, but, in a last desperate surge, the Belgian De Bruyne pipped him on the line. 'Shit!' said Bobet, and he was still repeating the word an hour later in the dressing room. It summed up his feelings – he had always wanted to win this prestigious race, and this was the third time he had come close only to fail at the last moment. It also summed up a season which had seen him second in the Tour of Italy and second in the World Championship. Winning was the only thing that counted for him; places of honour meant nothing. But if Louison was unhappy, then Fred De Bruyne was delighted. He had won the Tour of Flanders, the Paris–Roubaix and now this. Three major classics in one season is something that has only ever been achieved by a small handful of riders.

Back over the border in Italy, Jacques could only manage 23rd in the Tour of Lombardy and, partnered by Darrigade, fourth place in the Baracchi trophy – a quiet end to a great road season.

Then Anquetil and Darrigade teamed up again, and were joined by the Italian track specialist, Teruzzi, for the Paris Six-Day. For many years this had been the top event of the winter season and, for 1957, it was run on the basis of teams of three. They won, and it proved to be one of the most popular victories ever in that famous 'Temple of Cycling'. For some years Anquetil's mother had been living in a modest flat in Paris and never failed to buy a ticket to see her son race. The following day she always sent her son a note telling him of any mistakes he had made. Although Jacques was always annoyed by her criticism, he did have to admit that she was often right.

The year 1957 really had been Anquetil's: Paris–Nice, Tour de France and now the Paris Six. Nobody had ever won the latter two races in the same year, and he was still only 23. What would be next – a big classic win, perhaps?

Chapter Eight

Professional road-racing cyclists work hard during the season and take their holidays in the winter. They might possibly end or start the season with indoor track appearances or, as Rik Van Steenbergen did until the age of 42, ride throughout the summer and winter. Nowadays many will fly to the other side of the world to get some sunshine but, in the 1950s, such holidays were very expensive. The two most traditionally popular winter-time activities for road riders were hunting and skiing. Jacques did a little hunting but was too fond of animals to be much of an enthusiast. On the other hand, he loved winter sports, and cyclists usually make good skiers because of their in-built sense of balance.

At the start of 1958, Jacques went skiing to his favourite resort of St Gervais, accompanied by Dr Boeda, his children and his wife. The relationship between Janine and Jacques had started to become serious, but they had managed up to that point to keep it secret. At the end of the holiday, the two lovers' parting was very difficult because Anquetil had asked Mrs Boeda to come to live with him.

A few days later Jacques was in Cannes and could bear their separation no longer. He jumped on a plane and flew back to Rouen with the romantic notion of carrying her off, and Janine followed him blindly. According to legend, she put a fur coat over her nightdress and just left; according to Janine herself, this was not true – she put a raincoat over her pyjamas. Either way, the couple drove straight to Paris in a borrowed newspaper van and, in the Rue St Honoré, one of the smartest shopping streets in the capital, she bought daytime clothes. Very quickly, she obtained an official separation from her husband and applied for a divorce.

The affair did not cause anything like the same scandal in France as had been the case in Italy, some five years earlier, when Fausto Coppi had taken a married woman to live with him. Of course, Jacques had no wife and child, and for the romantic French it was the *coup de foudre* – they were head over heels in love and that was all that mattered. Jacques' father, however, disapproved strongly: 'If he stays with this woman,' he said, 'then he is done for.' Whilst it is unlikely that his religious mother approved of the liaison, she was no doubt pleased at her son's obvious new-found happiness, and there was little she could do about it, anyway. Janine was to make enormous efforts to allay the fears of Anquetil's parents and was later to prove a model daughter-in-law.

As for the cycling, the season started in much the same way as previous seasons had done, but Jacques was now a fully mature rider and much was expected of him. He won the time trial in the Paris–Nice, but could only finish tenth overall. He was also tenth at San Remo before finishing twelfth in the National Criterium. Prior to 1957 Anquetil's main objectives had been the autumn time trials, but from 1957 onwards the Tour de France usually became his main objective for the season. It has always been recognised that it is difficult to maintain top form throughout the entire season, so his lack of success in the spring classics was perhaps largely due to lack of ambition as much as preparation. As Jacques was later to say: 'I sacrificed everything for the Tour de France, even the classics.'

The terms of his contract would certainly have stipulated that he rode most of the top single-day classic races, and whether this pleased him or not is not clear, but he usually managed to finish them because he hated retiring. However, he had big plans for the Paris–Roubaix. He really wanted a big win to please Janine and thought the race suited him: it was an event for the strongest riders as the weak were always eliminated by the strength-sapping cobblestones. What's more, he had plans for making the event even tougher than normal.

It was a hard day with a strong head wind, and was to prove to be the slowest edition of the race for thirteen years. Early on, still with 200 kilometres to go to the finish, Jacques attacked and took a big group with him – no less than seventeen riders, from seven different teams. His long, hard turns at the front ensured not only that the break stayed clear, but also caused many of the weaker riders to drop off the back. Others were eliminated with punctures so that, finally, there were just four left – Jacques, another Frenchman and two Belgians. With thirteen kilometres to go Anquetil punctured, but rejoined after a stupefying three-kilometre chase. Then, four kilometres short of the line, they were reeled in by the main bunch. 'Poor Jacques,' said the newspapers. 'Robbed of certain victory by a puncture. What rotten luck after such a magnificent ride.' This is one version of events, and, unfortunately, the version that Jacques believed –unfortunately, because the conclusions he drew from the race were to affect, and spoil, the rest of his career.

There is a more realistic interpretation of the events of that day: when Anquetil escaped the break was taken very seriously, and the top Belgians, who were the real experts of Paris–Roubaix, sent their team mates to the front of the peloton to make sure that the gap never grew too wide. Anquetil's leading group was never allowed to gain more than four minutes, and, more to the point, when the hard, cobbled section was reached the lead was down to a minute and a half. From that point on, the break was doomed. The pace in the bunch was such that in the final kilometres all the *domestiques* had been dropped and the twenty men left contained most of the stars. Amongst them were five previous and three future Paris–Roubaix winners, and the speed with which they then caught the break was nothing short of phenomenal. And even if the break had stayed clear, Anquetil could certainly not have been sure of winning since both the Belgians, Truye and Verplaeste, were excellent sprinters. To say that you were robbed of winning Paris–Roubaix by a puncture is also rather contentious: dozens of riders could make the same claim. In fact, there are several Belgians who have punctured no less than three times and still gone on to win.

But Jacques didn't see that; he made it clear to all and sundry that, from now on, one-day races no longer interested him – the element of chance was too great. It was only in time trials and stage-races, he said, that the strongest rider usually won. Perhaps this was a mixture of sour grapes, provocation and establishing future alibis. In reality, Anquetil was probably no different from any other rider – they all want to win Paris-Roubaix. Nevertheless, many took his remarks to represent an attack on the very essence of bike racing, with its implication that a large part of the sport was inherently unsatisfactory. Others saw it as arrogance, as if these wonderful races were in some way beneath him.

Another point of view was that, because the Belgians had dominated this type of racing for so long, the French had acquired an inferiority complex which had affected even the one Frenchman who had the class to redress the balance. From now on Jacques' poor results in one-day races made people feel frustrated and fuelled the belief that they were due more to his unwillingness to take them seriously, rather than an inability to succeed. In short, it laid the foundations of his unpopularity.

After his failure at Roubaix, Anquetil gained some recompense by winning the Dunkerque Four-Day and then a three-day event in Belgium. His victory at Dunkerque was due solely to winning the time trial, in which he beat Brankart and Darrigade. His team mate, Elliott, won two stages, so it was a very successful, long weekend for the Helyett–Leroux team. Jacques finished his Tour preparation with an eighth place in the Paris–Vimoutiers, third in the Boucles de la Seine and eighth in the National Championship. It looked as if he was coming to form in time for his main objective of the season. However, all was not well in the French camp for the Tour which, this year, began in Brussels.

Jacques was obviously the number-one choice for the national team, but Marcel Bidot could hardly leave out Bobet. Jacques said, 'OK, but I'm not putting up with a coalition against me in my own team. So, it's Bobet or Géminiani, but not both.' 'Gem' had always been unwavering in his support for Louison, and now he expected Bobet to stand by him; but the solidarity was not forthcoming and it was the end of their friendship. Above all, Géminiani blamed Marcel Bidot; he was furious with the French team manager and spent the whole Tour, riding as captain of the Centre–Midi team, trying to get even.

Always a favourite with the journalists, Géminiani paraded a donkey around at the start for all to see . 'I'm calling him Marcel,' he announced loudly, 'because he is just like Bidot – stubborn and stupid.' When, during the race, the French team attacked, he shouted, 'Look everyone, the French team is attacking. They're attacking. Give them a big round of applause!' He continued in this vein for nearly three weeks.

The first big surprise of the race was in the first time trial – 46 kilometres on an easy course at Châteaulin in Brittany – when the Luxembourg climber, Charly Gaul, beat Anquetil. It was a hard psychological blow for the young Norman, but he managed to hide his anxiety. It was going to be a very different Tour from the previous year when he had played such a prominent role in the first half of the race. He gave the expected, routine interviews to the press: early days – not as strong as in 1957 – time will prove him right, etc. The truth was that the result of the time trial had sown doubts in his mind about his form.

He took some pleasure from Darrigade's stage wins, but was unhappy with the cold, rainy weather and so thought it unwise to make too many attacks. He would save his strength and take a back seat; so much depended on what happened on the Mont Ventoux. For the first time in the Tour a mountain time trial would be held on the Ventoux and Anquetil, like everyone else, was worried about how much time Gaul would take out of him. Then, as the Tour progressed down the west of France, he started to express his unhappiness at having Bobet on the team, and even believed that Bobet and Géminiani, although in different teams, were 'up to something'.

Géminiani was delighted to put on the yellow jersey for one day in the Pyrenees: it was one in the eye for Bidot. Jacques' worst fears were then realised on the 'Giant of Provence'. On the climb he lost five minutes to Gaul, while Géminiani lost six. For once, things were going well for Charly as he moved into third spot overall. Géminiani was again in the yellow jersey with Jacques sixth overall, seven minutes down.

The following day, on the road to Gap, high drama developed when Charly Gaul stopped to repair his bike. Géminiani attacked immediately and a break quickly formed. As was his habit, Jacques was at the back of the bunch taking little interest in events. Darrigade dropped back, screamed at him and catapulted him to the front. At the finish the break was down to four men as Nencini sprinted to victory from Géminiani, Anquetil, and the consistent Belgium, Adriaenssens.

Gaul had finished the day eleven minutes down; he was now fifteen minutes behind race-leader Géminiani, and apparently out of the picture. The 'mechanical problems' which had caused his downfall had, in fact, been the result of sabotage – his chainset had been loosened and his tyres cut. Whilst the culprit was never caught the finger of suspicion pointed at those who benefitted from his misfortune, one of the winning break most probably, but certainly not Anquetil: his sense of fair play was considered beyond question. Jacques might have been a hard-nosed Norman, but he hated injustice and was highly regarded by all the riders.

The following day Bahamontes won the big stage in the mountains, and, with just one final day in the foothills of the Alps and then the time trial, Géminiani looked a likely winner. But Jacques had other plans. He was not going to pull back seven minutes in the chrono so he would have to put some time into Raphaël on the climbs.

Janine had come to visit Jacques at the hotel. Women were normally barred from the Tour but, right from the very start, she had been accepted by everyone. She was so strong a character that many found her overwhelming – she hardly qualified as a 'woman's woman'. However, she was always newsworthy and photogenic, and certainly received far more publicity than any other rider's wife before or since. As Raymond Poulidor later remarked: 'She could walk through the riders' changing room without raising the slightest comment.' Marcel Bidot said to her, 'Madam, rest assured that Jacques will win this Tour. Nothing could be more certain.'

Anquetil, similarly, sought to reassure her: he told her to drive back to Normandy and do all the washing for the dizzy round of post-Tour criteriums. At the same time he asked Sadi Duponchel to prepare all his criterium bikes, as well.

The next day dawned bright and sunny so the team managers sent all the luggage on ahead, including the extra jerseys and rain capes. When Charly Gaul went away alone, early on the stage, nobody took too much notice: he was no longer a danger overall and was clearly going for the stage win to salvage some honour from the Tour. Then Anquetil attacked and dropped Géminiani. Things were going well. Then the sun went in, the skies clouded over, a light rain turned into heavy rain which very quickly became icy. Gaul was in his element, now – he loved these conditions, whereas Anquetil hated them. Jacques' legs went heavy. His breathing became difficult. All his strength drained from his body. First, Adriaenssens caught him and went straight past. Then Géminiani, Bobet and Favero, and Anquetil was powerless to react. Meanwhile, Charly Gaul was going faster and faster, and the gap was beginning to reach alarming proportions. Walkowiak caught Jacques and loyally stayed with him to the finish, but in just 60 kilometres Gaul had put 22 minutes into Anquetil. Not only was the Frenchman exhausted, he was sick as well.

At the end of that day – after one of the most dramatic stages in the history of the Tour – Gaul was back up to third place, and expected to win the final time trial and the race overall, while Géminiani was in tears at the loss of his yellow jersey. In a theatrical style, of which only he was capable, he screamed that the French team were 'Judas. All Judas', but nobody was quite sure why.

Jacques began the next day surrounded by his team mates, but when he started spitting blood he stopped, dismounted and was taken to hospital in Besançon. Janine heard the bad news on the radio, and, after just a few hours sleep, jumped back into the car and drove to the hospital. A pulmonary congestion was diagnosed and the doctors ordered a complete rest from the bicycle. If not, his future would be in jeopardy.

During the night Jacques had a very strange nightmare. He was riding through the mountains chasing a 'rain man' a few hundred metres ahead. After a prolonged effort he saw that it was Charly Gaul, made up from thousands of tiny droplets of rain. When he drew alongside him the apparition vanished and then reformed a few hundred metres in front. Then the process started all over again.

After a couple of days in the hospital, Janine drove Jacques back to Normandy, but it seemed France had forgotten about Anquetil. He had been humiliated and nobody expressed any concern about his health. They were all enthralled with Gaul's triumphant arrival in Paris and Darrigade's terrible crash on the track at the finish. It was the very lowest point of Jacques' career. He was not offered a single contract, either in a criterium or on the track. It was as if the whole world had turned its back on him.

He was so demoralised he discussed with Janine the idea of giving up the sport altogether.

Luckily, Janine was a nurse – *his* nurse – and well-experienced at restoring the morale of the sick. She was also older than him and, to some extent, played the role of his mother as well. Even so, she had her work cut out repairing his confidence. They decided he should make his come-back in a small race in Belgium, away from the limelight, and Jacques insisted that if he failed to finish it would be his last race. He did finish – last but one – but, most importantly, he regained something of his morale.

One of Anquetil's most amazing qualities was his rapid rate of recovery and this, perhaps, was the first evidence of it. Few people had been aware just how seriously ill Jacques had been and, when he won the criterium at Château-Chinon, they assumed him to be back to full strength, and he was nominated as the favourite to win the World Championships at Rheims. However, he retired from the race while, once again, Bobet, his arch rival, distinguished himself with a fine performance. It was not good enough, however, as the new Italian star, Baldini, the man who had beaten Anquetil in a time trial in Italy earlier in the season, won by two minutes from Louison, with André Darrigade third again.

In the late-season time trials Anquetil finally completed the salvaging of his reputation when he managed his first 'triple' by winning the Grand Prix at Geneva and at Lugano, and the Grand Prix des Nations. He was twelfth in both the Paris–Tours and the Tour of Lombardy, before finishing the road season with yet another second place in the Baracchi Trophy.

However, the racing season was not entirely over as, partnered once again by Darrigade and Teruzzi, he won his second Paris Six-Day. This was a very special race – the last Six-Day event on the hallowed boards of the Velodrome d'Hiver, the most famous cycling arena of all time. Despite the howls of protest, property speculators had bought the valuable site and were going to demolish the stadium in order to build a block of flats. It was a blow from which track cycle-racing has never fully recovered.

At least Jacques' winters would be much freer now because he had little enthusiasm for riding the winter boards in Belgium or Holland. His two wins in the Paris Six-Days had brought in large sums of money – along with Coppi and Bobet he had been able to command appearance money of 350,000 f.

When Janine moved in with Jacques he bought a large house at St Adrien, a somewhat rambling and pretentious place, but beautifully located at the bottom of a hill alongside the river, some five miles south of Rouen. This, together with a motor boat he acquired for pottering about on the Seine, was the achievement of a boyhood dream.

Anquetil's house at St Adrien, beside the River Seine

In other respects, Jacques' life took a different direction because he really did have a need for someone in whom he could confide. A close friend like Darrigade was all very well, but he could not share his most intimate fears and worries with him. With Janine he could. She quickly learned that he was haunted by the spectre of death and, above all, by the incredible fear that one day he would not wake up. It was for this reason that he was so determined to live life to the full and refused to make too many sacrifices. She came also to appreciate his sensitivity, and horror of being approached by strangers in public. He even refused to go into a restaurant if there were too many people there. Slow to make friends, he only made very genuine ones, stuck by them and was very generous with them. Liked and admired by all riders, and at ease with journalists, he was not very well understood, still less popular, with the public.

Jacques and Janine purchased a flat in Cannes and, before the year was out, a skiing chalet at St Gervais. It was there, in December 1958, that Jacques and Janine were married. It was a very big affair, with virtually the whole family present at the Alpine ski resort. The mayor of the town, a personal friend of Jacques, made sure that there were no press photographers present during the civil ceremony in the town hall to spoil the occasion. It was only after they all went outside to the snow that any pictures were allowed and, with their blond hair and blue eyes, they did make a very attractive couple.

Chapter Nine

The big question at the start of the 1959 season was how well Roger Rivière would do against Anquetil. Perhaps to whet everyone's appetite, the two men disputed an omnium at the Velodrome d'Hiver, before it closed forever a few weeks later. Rivière won the series by three matches to two.

With the majority of the French professionals, Anquetil installed himself in the South of France for some early season training in the warm weather, on the shores of the Mediterranean. In the evenings he spent some time with Louison Bobet and his brother Jean, where the conversation inevitably turned towards racing. Anquetil insisted that Rivière was purely a trackman and would never be any good on the road. The Bobet brothers strongly disagreed with this theory and it would not be very long before they were proved right.

Louison was also right in another prediction – that the national team formula would not be retained for much longer in the Tour de France: there was too much commercial interest at stake, he maintained. The Italian team sponsors were certainly beginning to put pressure on the Tour organisers to revert to the formula of trade teams. If not, they might not be contesting the race much longer, which was especially worrying because most of the top Belgians and many of the top Spaniards were members of Italian squads. By way of some sort of concession, a new rule was brought in which stipulated that all the top French riders must be in the French national team, or not ride at all. This may well have seemed a reasonable rule, especially to the foreigners, but for Marcel Bidot it was going to prove a nightmare.

The Anquetil/Rivière question was taken up once more in the Paris–Nice race, which had been increased to eleven days and now finished in Rome. This was to be Rivière's first full season on the road as a professional and this race between the two capital cities was going to be a big test. The event was very tight, with most stages being decided by bunch sprints. Neither Anquetil nor Rivière were allowed much freedom, but it was clear that the man from St Etienne was in better form, and even dropped Jacques on one or two of the climbs. Nevertheless, when it came to the short time trial, Anquetil was the better man, even if only by one second. Roger's team mate, the very tall, young Gérard Saint from Normandy, finished third in this race against the clock, confirming the promise he had previously shown by his second placings in the Grand Prix de Lugano and the Grand Prix des Nations at the end of 1958.

By the time the event finally finished in the Eternal City, Rivière was seventh overall and Anquetil eleventh. They had both spent a large part of the race helping their team mates and finally it was Jacques' team mate, Jean Graczyk, the son of Polish immigrants who scratched a precarious living from a small farm in the centre of France, who beat Gérard Saint by a handful of seconds.

'Popof' Graczyk* was finally blossoming out into a fully fledged professional and one of Jacques' best *domestiques* on the Helyett–Leroux team. Although he was now in his third season as a team mate, Jacques said that he really did not know him that well as they had never seemed to have ridden the same stage-races, and he had always thought of him as a rather shy and timid man until he got on his bike, when he was transformed. The silver cup that Graczyk received in Rome he promptly gave to Anquetil, saying that he deserved it as much as he did. Jacques was very touched.

---

*Why 'Popof'? Because on the way back from the Melbourne Olympics in 1956, Graczyk was with the French team that stopped off in Fiji for a couple of days. There were rumours that there was a Russian spy in the area and Jean was arrested by the local police who thought his surname somewhat suspect. He was immediately released, of course, but his delighted team mates promptly christened him 'Popof', and the name was to stick for the rest of his career.

At the beginning of April Anquetil went to Belgium for the Trophy of Flanders run by the newspaper *Het Volk*. He attacked hard on the first stage, but Van Daele and Hoevenaers outsprinted him at the finish. Perhaps of more significance was an event that took place that same day in the Alpes Maritimes – the hill climb up the Mont Faron. Here, Rivière won convincingly, beating the established climbers Bahamontes and Dotto.

The Anquetil/Rivière rivalry looked as if it would be maintained at Paris–Roubaix, and the 1959 edition proved to be an exceptionally hard race, with non-stop rain from start to finish. In the end the Belgians proved that they were the masters of this 'Hell of the North' by providing eleven of the first twelve finishers. It seemed as if Rivière was going to be in at the kill, but he blew up; meanwhile, Jacques crashed and could only finish 24th.

Marcel Bidot's task of putting together a team for the Tour de France was becoming ever more difficult: Roger Rivière had, by now, fully established himself and was an automatic choice; so were Bobet and Anquetil; Géminiani, who had finished third in 1958 after his quarrel with Bobet, was also a certainty, and he had since taken Rivière under his wing and refused to be separated from him; and Roger was also using Bobet's former *soigneur*, Raymond Le Bert, with whom Louison (who was famous for his grudges) had fallen out so spectacularly that he would not even tolerate him in the same hotel. There was little or no hope of any sort of reconciliation.

Jacques now embarked on a new adventure when he started the Tour of Italy. He certainly had a very strong Helyett team to back him up, but foreigners usually had a hard time in the Giro. The sponsors always need an Italian win, so the organisers turned a blind eye to certain 'irregularities'. Riders from the home country could normally expect to be pushed up the hills by the fans, whereas foreigners were as likely to be impeded, or even punched in the back. It was all quite scandalous, but it was Italy.

Everyone was looking forward to an exceptional race and there was enormous speculation in the peninsula as to the outcome. Fausto Coppi tipped Anquetil, Gaul, Nencini and Favero, in that order. Ercole Baldini was wearing the world champion's jersey, however, and his fans refused to believe that he would not be playing a major role. Although the best-paid rider in Italy, he was criticised for being timid and lacking self-confidence. He said that he'd been suffering from appendicitis and bronchial pneumonia, but few believed his form had been that badly affected.

Anquetil, too, came in for his share of criticism. It was claimed that he was more interested in the joys of life than in making sacrifices. They said that too much cinema, too many restaurants and pretty girls had been the real cause of his retirement from the 1958 Tour de France. In short, he still had to establish himself as a serious contender, but people close to him, such as his masseur, Robert Pons, dismissed all such claims. Marriage and his big new house had changed him, he said, and Jacques had come to Italy to win. His own fans went even further. They expected the calm, confident Anquetil to win the first time trial and then to control the rest of the race, especially with such a strong team: André and Roger Darrigade; Delberghe; Elliott; Graczyk; Pavard; Stablinski; and Vermeulin. Then again it might rain, and if it rained in the mountains Gaul would be hard to beat.

There was also the Belgian, Rik Van Looy, who could not be ignored as a possible winner and everyone remembered Van Steenbergen's second place in 1951. There were commercial links between Van Looy's Faema team and Charly Gaul's EMI squad so the question of a possible collusion between the two teams arose in some people's minds – in Anquetil's, for one, apparently, when he remarked in an interview: 'Gaul is very strong and this mountainous Giro seems to be made for him – and he has eighteen team mates.' Gaul, himself, when questioned about this, laughed ironically: 'You must be joking,' he said. 'Van Looy is riding to win,' and he went on to add that Anquetil was, indeed, a great champion, but that he, Gaul, was in very good form too.

As expected, Jacques put on the leader's pink jersey after he won the time trial on the second day, but he was not particularly unhappy to lose it to Charly Gaul the following day. It was going to be a most memorable Giro, and the race really came alive when it moved south from Naples. There was a short, eight-kilometre climb up Mount Vesuvius. The press, of course, had a field-day with their speculation of an eruption of the famous volcano inspite of the fact that it had lain dormant since 1944. Gaul supplied the evidence of his good form when he won the climb, putting 52 seconds into Anquetil in the process.

An opportunity for Jacques to get his revenge occured on the next stage when the race moved west into the little peninsula which looked down on the Bay of Naples, Capri, and Ischia – all blue sea and sunshine. This leg consisted of a 31-kilometre time trial over very twisty roads. To make matters worse, the roads had a lot of loose gravel on them – indeed, some of Jacques' team mates had fallen off when inspecting the course. Nobody took any risks, but the final result was interesting: Jacques was beaten into second place by the little-known Italian Catalano, with Van Looy third. Gaul was sixth, but, more importantly, Anquetil had taken back 30 seconds from him and left himself in third spot overall, 1 min. 57 secs behind Charly.

As the race moved north to the Dolomites there was high drama on the road to Bolzano. Anquetil dropped Gaul on the descent and regained the pink jersey from him. Charly, who had been leading the race for some thirteen days, claimed that his bike had been 'got at' and was very dangerous on the descents. It had certainly happened before, in the 1958 Tour de France, but on neither occasion did Charly blame Jacques. Indeed, when Anquetil later punctured Gaul told Darrigade not to worry as he was not the type of rider to attack when an adversary was in trouble.

As the race moved west towards the Alps all the fans were wondering whether Jacques could gain enough time in the 51-kilometre time-trial stage, between Turin and Susa, to ensure his final overall victory. It was an intensely dramatic moment when Jacques caught Charly after only 21 kilometres in the race against the watch. The drama continued for another 21 kilometres with the Frenchman unable to drop the Luxembourger. Only with nine kilometres still to go was the pink jersey able to rid himself of his main rival. At the finish Jacques had gained another 2 mins 4 secs on Charly. Normally, this would have been a comfortable enough lead, but the race was set to pass through the Alps before the finish in Milan.

The final show-down of this amazing race came two days later, on the stage to Courmayeur. At the start, Anquetil was leading Gaul by four minutes and nobody was really sure if this was going to be enough. On the first climb of the day, Gaul was first over the summit, but Jacques rejoined on the descent. On the climb up the little St Bernard, Gaul was quite superb and was climbing at a speed of 36 k.p.h. Nobody had ever seen anything like it and Charly, himself, said that he had never felt so strong in all his life. Three kilometres from the summit Jacques suddenly cracked. He was seven minutes down by the time he reached the top, and by the finish had lost ten minutes after puncturing three times. On the day, Nencini lost three minutes, and Van Looy lost five. It was a sensational climax to a wonderful race. At the finish, in Milan, Anquetil was second at six minutes. He had found Italy, in general, and the Giro, in particular, to his taste. Second place at his first attempt was not bad, and he vowed that he would return and do better.

In fact, he was soon back in Italy when he and Rivière flew out to ride the big time trial in Baldini's home town of Forli. The Italian World Champion was desperate to re-establish himself in the eyes of his fans after his poor showing in the Giro. In a magnificent display he beat the previous record, with Jacques one minute down in second place and Rivière fourth at 2 mins 45 secs. By now, however, all three of them were thinking only of the most important race of the year.

The highlight of the season – the Tour de France – was fast approaching, and now that Roger and Jacques were back in France something had to be thrashed out with regard to the composition of the French team. The principal parties would have to be brought together and some decision reached. Daniel Dousset, the manager of all the riders concerned, offered the use of his restaurant in the forest of Rambouillet, to the west of Paris. Bidot, Bobet, Anquetil, Rivière and Géminiani had lunch together, which put them in a better frame of mind, but Marcel Bidot was still going to have to use his gift for diplomacy to the full.

'Look Marcel,' began Jacques. 'Roger and I have always got on well together, but for most of the season we are rivals. We ride against each other. To be team mates for three weeks won't really work out as I'm not going to sacrifice my chances for him.'

Géminiani said that his main objective was to help Rivière, implying, but not saying, that he was uninterested in whatever Bobet did. It was understood that Louison was getting a bit long in the tooth, but nobody could suggest such a thing to him. He was a proud man with his reputation still intact, especially after winning the Bordeaux–Paris a few weeks previously.

Bidot patiently explained that each one of them would have a couple of team riders at their disposal, and that an accident or poor form could put any of them out of the picture. As far as Anquetil and Rivière were concerned, there was plenty of time for both of them to win several Tours. Bobet was only the second man in history to win three Tours and the French public expected to see him in a French jersey. The same applied to Géminiani, last year's hero. They were the best four riders France had had in a long time and France would expect all of them to cooperate for a French victory. If they did not, the fans would never forgive them.

The meeting broke up after an agreement, of sorts, had been reached. As they dispersed, Marcel Bidot said, in private, that the whole thing had been exhausting and, although peace had been reached, there was no hope at all of any of his men winning, as none of them were really prepared to work for each other.

As was traditional, the French championship was run off seven days before the start of the Tour, and the revelation was Henry Anglade, the elegant rider from Lyon. He had dominated the championship race, and won stylishly and convincingly. 'Napoleon' – as he was called, due to his authoritarian manner – started the Tour in the Centre-Midi team and would prove to be one of the strongest of them all.

The Tour, for Bidot's men, started as badly as expected. Jean Stablinski put it best when he said: 'You just did not know where you were or what to do. Anquetil attacked, Bobet went after him and Géminiani screamed at Rivière to get up to them both.' Yet, the outward signs were that things were going reasonably well. The first big test came on the time trial on stage six. Rivière won this race against the watch from Baldini and Anquetil, with Gérard Saint fifth, Gaul sixth, Anglade eighth and Bobet twentieth. Added to that were two stage wins by Darrigade, one by Cazala, Graczyk, Hassenforder and Rivière, and all before the Pyrenees. It was looking promising. Furthermore, both Bobet and Géminiani had lost quite a bit of time overall which put them out of the picture and forced them to take a back seat – this, at least, was a load off Marcel Bidot's mind, especially as the other two principals, Anquetil and Rivière, seemed to be cooperating well with each other.

Then came the sensational stage from Albi to Aurillac on which the whole outcome of the Tour was to hinge. It was a boiling-hot day and, although the route went over no real mountains, there was no let-up from the incessant hills: the whole day was spent either climbing or descending. In short, it was a stage for the strong. The weaker men were slowly eliminated from the break until, at the finish, there were only four left. The stage win went to Henry Anglade in front of Anquetil, the Spanish climber, Bahamontes, and the Englishman, Brian Robinson.

Rivière had spent the day protecting Anquetil by preventing anyone from getting up to the break, but he put in a storming finish to reduce the gap to less than four minutes. However, after the first dozen finishers, the time gaps were quite alarming. Charly Gaul had suffered enormously in the heat and, although he finished in sixteenth place, he lost more than twenty minutes, and all hope of winning the Tour. When the rest of the exhausted field struggled in it was realised that no fewer than fifteen men had retired or been eliminated.

Anglade was now in second place on general classification with Bahamontes and Anquetil at seven minutes, and Rivière at nine. Then came the dramatic time trial up the very hard climb of the Puy de Dôme just outside Clermont-Ferrand. As expected, Bahamontes won the stage, three minutes faster than Anglade, Rivière and Anquetil. This meant that the Spaniard was now second on general classification, 39 seconds in front of Anglade, 5 mins 4 secs in hand on Anquetil, with Rivière at 7 mins 24 secs. The race was now finally taking shape and it was obvious that the eventual winner would be one of these four because the current wearer of the yellow jersey, the Belgian Hoevenaers, would undoubtedly crack in the Alps.

When this second mountain range was reached Bahamontes stretched his legs again and went away with Gaul on the road to Grenoble. This not only eliminated Hoevenaers from the picture but also placed him firmly in the lead. Anglade was at 4 mins 51 secs, Anquetil at 9 mins 16 secs and Rivière at 11 mins 36 secs. It was clear to everyone that all of the three Frenchmen would beat the Spanish climber in the final time trial at Dijon, but this would leave Anglade as the one most likely to take the race lead and the final victory. The prospect pleased neither Roger nor Jacques – two major stars in France were quite enough. Their appearance money was bigger than that of any other rider, but a Tour de France win by the charismatic Anglade would no doubt make him the top earner.

There was another reason for their opposition to the man from Lyon: in France there were two managers – Daniel Dousset, who had the majority of the stars, and Roger Piel who, for the most part, had less important riders. Both Anquetil and Rivière were contracted to Dousset, while Anglade was tied to Piel. Jacques and Roger were unwilling to risk Piel's group rivalling Dousset's as this, too, might lead to them losing money. So, whatever happened, Anglade must not win. Yet they were both too far behind to beat him.

Roger and Jacques talked the matter over. It was said that they were visited by somebody – perhaps an intermediary from the Spanish team, perhaps a representative of the Coppi bicycle company whose machines the Spaniards were riding – suggesting that it would be in their interests to help Bahamontes win. So, the decision was made, but Bidot was unaware of what was happening.

On the big mountain stage to Aosta, Bidot could not understand why neither Rivière nor Anquetil would attack when the yellow jersey had been dropped on a long descent (Bahamontes had always been a poor descender) and was five minutes down. They both claimed that they were having a bad day, but he found this hard to believe. Bahamontes was allowed to rejoin, and it was the non-climber, Baldini, who won the stage.

In the time trial Bahamontes lost a full six minutes, but it hardly mattered. He ran out a comfortable winner in Paris, followed by Anglade, Anquetil and Rivière.

The public had not been too sure about what exactly had been happening, but were pretty sure that Anquetil and Rivière had stopped Anglade from winning. The day before, Roger and Jacques had finished first and second in the time trial, proving that they were two of the strongest men in the race, yet neither of them had made any attempt to attack Bahamontes. There was mild applause for the winner, a huge ovation for Anglade, and then the crowd vented their fury on Bidot, Rivière and Anquetil.

Marcel was used to these receptions whenever he failed to produce a winner. Rivière was totally shocked and upset by the boos and whistles, and he rode his lap of honour at sprinting speed. Jacques thought his reception totally unjust and could not understand it at all. He put on a bold front and slowly rode his lap of honour with a small smile on his lips.

Henry Anglade, a highly intelligent and articulate man, gave his views on this remarkable Tour later. In spite of appearances he had suffered a lot in the Alps and had never really believed that he was strong enough to beat Bahamontes. He was not in the same team as Rivière and Anquetil so, he said, they had a perfect right to ride against him – just because he was a Frenchman did not mean that they were obliged to collude with him. Indeed, it was against the rules of the race. There had, in the past, been cases where two Italian teams had cooperated with each other and, although it may have been a little difficult to prove, the organisers immediately limited the Italians to one team. French teams, national and regional, had never ridden for the benefit of each other.

Anglade was as aware as anyone that this was the hard world of professionalism, and one of the rules of this 'jungle' was that nobody gave any presents to a member of another team. The French national champion may well have been disappointed, but personally felt no rancour towards Jacques and Roger, the two 'Golden Boys' of French cycling.

The 1959 Tour was to be a turning point in Jacques' career. Always admired rather than loved, the boos that greeted him in Paris were the first signs of the hostility that would dog him until the end of his career. He had drawn the wrong conclusions from his magnificent ride in the previous year's Paris–Roubaix and this time seemed to be totally incapable of comprehending the rage of the public. He was to pay dearly for this lack of understanding.

The next big race was the world championship in Holland where Jacques won the sprint for ninth place after his friend, Darrigade, had won the sprint for first place. The two of them were beginning to drift apart now, as both were married and did not need each other so much. Nevertheless, André was full of praise for Jacques' strength, and for the warmth with which he had congratulated him at the finish. And the French riders in general, and Anquetil in particular, had redeemed themselves in the eyes of the public, at least temporarily. This time they had all been seen to be working for the common good. In a contrary, and rather bizarre episode, the Belgian federation wanted to suspend Van Looy and a couple of team mates for not winning, but were forced to change their minds. It was all too ridiculous.

For Darrigade himself it had been the most incredible week of his life. Eight days before the title race he had won a very hard criterium at Vayrac, so he was reassured that he was in excellent form. However, the following day he crashed heavily at Felletin and injured his knee badly. The French Cycling Federation was informed of his injury and immediately contacted Jean Stablinski, the first reserve. Darrigade promised them that he would give them his final decision on the Thursday before the race. On the way back to Paris he happened to meet Louison Bobet who offered to lend him his Derny, and his pacer, to test his form. André gratefully accepted the offer, but, for the first twenty kilometres, he was in agony and crying with pain. As he gritted his teeth, the suffering slowly disappeared and, after 150 kilometres, he was really 'flying' and realised that he had regained his very top form.

On Thursday evening André arrived at the hotel in Holland ready for the race but was suffering from the most awful toothache and was quite unable to sleep for the whole night. On his return to the hotel the next day, after a short training ride, he met Antonin Magne who took a close look at his lean face. He said, 'You're either ill or very, very fit.' This boosted his morale in a way that nothing else could have done. On the Saturday morning his heart went down to his boots when the doctor told him that he had a tapeworm. Nevertheless, he was told not to worry too much as it had been there some time and by now he was used to it.

On the day of the race Darrigade went with an early break that never gained more than one and a half minutes on the bunch. It meant that although many riders were dropped a lot of others managed to get up to them. With five laps to go Darrigade thought that his hopes had disappeared when Gérard Saint, riding strongly at the front of the main bunch, looked like closing the gap on the leaders. Henry Anglade rode alongside Darrigade and said that he was 'cooked' and could not last much longer. André pleaded with him to make one last big effort before he went off the back. Henry stayed at the front for almost a lap before he retired, but the gap opened sufficiently to ensure that the break stayed clear.

André was particularly worried by the presence of the Belgian, Noël Foré, who, in the interests of Van Looy, had done no work at all in the break. He was even more worried about the new, young English professional, Tom Simpson, who had ridden so strongly in the recent Tour of the West in Brittany. In the final kilometre he looked over his shoulder to check on the Briton and unwittingly touched the derailleur of the Dutchman, Geldermans, with his front wheel, and it was a miracle that both men could stay upright. As the line was approaching the Italian, Ronchini, shoved his team mate Gismondi twenty metres into the lead. For Darrigade it was a gift as there was a strong adverse wind blowing in the finishing straight. André came flying past him in the final 100 metres as Simpson finished in fourth place.

At the very beginning of September Jacques won the prestigious Criterium des As run behind Dernys at Longchamp in Paris. He attacked very early in the race and that was the last the others saw of him until the finish. It was a wonderful demonstration of style and strength, and only the Belgian, Noël Foré, who had won the Paris–Roubaix in April, and Louison Bobet, offered any sort of resistance. Among those who were so decisively beaten were: Anglade, Darrigade, Rivière, Bahamontes and Saint. As a headline in the weekly *Miroir-Sprint* said: 'Anquetil Is Reconciled With Paris'.

Then the annual round of important time trials came round again, and Jacques duly won in Geneva from Gérard Saint and the Italian Aldo Moser, whose younger brother, Francesco, was to become even more famous in years to come.

Jacques refused to ride in the Grand Prix des Nations, airily telling the journalists that he had won the event six times and had nothing left to prove. He went on to add that his reason for riding the two Swiss time trials was to keep an agreement that he had made earlier in the season. Daniel Dousset had told him that there was no way out of it – promises had to be kept. Of course, it was a disappointment for the fans who were looking forward to a confrontation with Rivière, and Jacques naturally came in for considerable criticism. Some said that he had too much to lose while others remarked that, unlike the Swiss race, the Grand Prix des Nations did not pay start money. Rivière's supporters said that it did not matter too much as Roger would undoubtedly beat

Jacques' race record, but few expected it was going to be such a memorable event.

The Italian, Aldo Moser, was given the honour of starting last, with Rivière just before him. Also on the start card were Gérard Saint; Henry Anglade; the Swiss, Vaucher; Vermeulin, a team mate of Anquetil and the young Englishman who had made such an impression at the World Championship, Tom Simpson.

Rivière started very fast indeed and covered the first part of the course at more than 50 k.p.h., and quickly relegated the Italian to more than two minutes. As the wind strengthened the experts started to criticise Roger for continuing to use his big 54x14 gear. Nevertheless, he caught Vermeulin who had started four minutes in front, but Roger could not drop him and Vermeulin even went past him on some of the hills. This disconcerted Rivière as much as Bouvet's resistance in 1956 had upset Anquetil. Poor judgement caused Roger to dig too deep into his reserves as he slowly lost ground and, at the entrance to the Parc des Princes track, he was exactly level on time with the revelation of the race, Aldo Moser. Over the required two laps of the velodrome the Italian was four seconds faster, thereby winning the race. Rivière's defeat was not the only disappointment for the French, as Gérard Saint could only manage fifth and Anglade finished seventh. For Simpson it was a disastrous day as he finished next to last in 24th place. The Swiss, Vaucher was third.

While Anquetil had beaten Aldo Moser by three and a half minutes at Geneva, he put nearly five minutes into him at Lugano where even an ageing Fausto Coppi beat him. But, although Jacques won the event as expected, he did not have things all his own way because, by then, Baldini had fully recovered his form and was only 28 seconds behind the Frenchman at the finish.

Both the Paris–Tours and the Tour of Lombardy were decided by bunch sprints and both were won by the impressive-looking Rik Van Looy. Jacques finished both events in the same time as the winner, but many places behind. He completed the European road season by finishing third in the Baracchi Trophy, partnered by Darrigade. The pair had lost just over a minute when they arrived late for the start, but they were clearly off-form and had no hope against the winners Baldin–Moser, who had been carefully preparing for the event over a considerable period.

No more Velodrome d'Hiver, so Jacques was happy to spend some time at *Les Elfes*, his house by the river. In a gesture which perhaps summed up his character, he named his boat *Whistles of '59*. Being rather proud of his speedboat, he gave a high-speed demonstration to the journalist Robert Chapatte. Over-ambition, combined with inexperience, caused him to overturn the boat and dump himself in the river. There were fears that his thick clothing would drag him down, but he managed to reach the shore and was to roar with laughter at the anxiety of his spectators. After he had changed, he proudly showed his visitor the new gun that he had bought for his forthcoming trip to Africa

It was Géminiani who arranged a racing trip to Upper Volta – more of a holiday than serious competition, and there would be an opportunity to get in some big game hunting for those who were interested. The party was made up of Coppi, Géminiani, Hassenforder, Anglade, Rivière and Anquetil. Wives could accompany their husbands if they wanted and, of course, Janine went with Jacques. Giulia Locatelli, the 'white lady', did not go with Coppi. Rumours were beginning to circulate that Fausto was growing tired of her and was thinking of terminating their relationship; she was certainly not very popular with many riders.

Géminiani shared a room with Coppi and, one night, they were kept awake by the mosquitoes. After returning to Europe they were both struck down with what appeared to be a very heavy form of 'flu. Eventually, Géminiani's doctor diagnosed this as malaria and he was treated accordingly. In Italy, Coppi's doctors refused to listen to such a diagnosis and continued to treat him for 'flu. He died on 2nd January 1960. Anquetil was shocked, and he became even more aware of the fragility of life.

Chapter Ten

When the news of Coppi's death came through, Jacques was staying at his skiing chalet. Along with the majority of the stars of cycling, and another 30,000 mourners, he made the trip to the little village of Castellania in Piedmont which had been Fausto's birthplace, and was to be his final resting place. After a simple but moving ceremony, Coppi was finally laid to rest alongside his brother, Serse, who had died in a racing accident some nine years previously. Jacques was particularly moved at the death of the man who had shown him such kindness while he was still a teenager and against whom he had competed for some six years.

After people slowly recovered from their shock and disbelief that the Italian *Campionissimo* was no longer with them they vented their fury, and anger on the doctors whose careless diagnosis cost the life of the man who was, perhaps, the most popular champion in the history of the sport. Maybe in an attempt to vindicate themselves, these medical men, from the hospital in Tortona, pointed out that during the last few years of his career Coppi was no longer able to really compete at top level, and had taken an excess of stimulants just to keep going. This had weakened his resistance, they maintained, making it even more difficult to fight his fatal disease. There were also other suggestions that Fausto had already suffered from a bout of malaria in 1943 in North Africa, when he was a prisoner of the British army.

The latter hypothesis was not taken very seriously, but rumours of drug-taking were beginning to emerge in some of the sporting press. In France, at the end of the previous season, it had been hinted that Rivière had taken 'something'. He strongly denied the claim and said that what he had consumed amounted to nothing more than 'performance-enhancing vitamins'. Then, the weekly sports magazine, *But et Club*, interviewed four riders –

Magne, Leducq, Speicher, and Bobet – who had won eight Tours de France and three World Championships between them. The three older men tended to play the issue down, while Bobet at least made some attempt to be honest. The consensus of opinion among the four was that drugs had always existed, but now they were becoming stronger; there were too many races on the calendar; drugs might be taken but you must not generalise; it was all really the fault of the *soigneurs,* and drug tests were a bad idea. In short, it was hypocrisy on a grand scale because the truth was very different. Only riders who had retired and cut all ties with the sport gave any sort of accurate picture, but even then, not until years later. The *Omerta* – the law of silence – was strictly enforced and nobody dared to break it.

For Anquetil it was a different matter: being such an honest man, he was totally sickened by all the lies, but he obviously would not point the finger at anyone. He used small quantities of stimulants, himself, on a regular basis, but it was more in the nature of helping him through a difficult and exhausting season rather than trying to cheat in any way. He was later to say that you could certainly race without the help of drugs, but you could not race so often. Rivière, long after his retirement, admitted that he had broken the hour record with the help of drugs, which only confirmed many people's thoughts at the time, but to this day it does not seem to have detracted from his exploit.

Jacques' plans for the season were that he might give the Tour de France a miss after the hostility of the crowd in 1959. He blamed the organising newspaper, *L'Equipe,* for his bad reception and, as they were also the organisers of the Grand Prix des Nations, he had demonstrated his displeasure by not riding it. But he desperately wanted a big win to re-establish himself and what better way to do it than by winning the Tour of Italy? He had come close in 1959, so it was well within his capabilities, and no Frenchman had ever won it before. In this way he could afford to leave the Tour de France to Rivière – after all, Roger had proved Anquetil's match in the time trial, was, possibly, a better climber. He certainly had no intention of playing second fiddle in a French team to help his principle rival win.

In a way, Jacques was at the crossroads of his career. He had broken the hour record which had stood for fourteen years, but this had largely been forgotten as Baldini (riding as an amateur) had improved on his figures and Rivière had gone even further on two separate occasions. He had won the Tour de France in grand style, but had then been well beaten by Charly Gaul in both the French and then the Italian tours. Bobet was no longer a force to be reckoned with, but now Jacques had to share 'The Top of the Bill' with Rivière. There was certainly no animosity between the two of them, but all friendship went out of the window once they were on their bikes.

As a teenager, Jacques had been hailed as 'the New Coppi', but very few people saw him in that light now – a top professional, certainly, but one who had yet to prove that he was in the same class as Bobet. In short, in the eyes of most people, he was a bit of a disappointment. Nevertheless, he had come a long way. He had a magnificent house on the river; a beautiful, intelligent and supportive wife with whom he was still madly in love; a skiing chalet in a fashionable area of the Alps; and a luxurious flat in an even more fashionable part of the South of France. He took enormous pride in his appearance and was often to be seen wearing very expensive suits. It was no exaggeration when the journalist Jean-Paul Olivier called him 'The Prince of Elegance' and 'The Epitome of French Good Taste'.

He indulged himself with expensive cars and loved to drive fast. He enjoyed skiing in the winter but, in future, he would also seek the winter sun in the West Indies. In his private life he had realised all his boyhood ambitions, but it was not enough. There was still something missing. For a man who adored children it was a bitter blow that Janine could have no more. With regard to his work, his team manager, Paul ('Mickey') Wiegant, had been competent, helpful and supportive, but had never pushed his man to achieve a really great exploit, and Anquetil certainly needed something to keep himself at the top.

The season began with three races in Algeria. In the Criterium of Oran Jacques' team mate, Shay Elliott, escaped to win the race by himself but, behind him, the event was enlivened by the personal battle between Anglade and Anquetil, and it was finally Jacques who beat Henry in the sprint for sixth place. It may have all seemed somewhat strange to the casual spectator, but it was really all a question of prestige. Next came a trip to Italy for the

Genoa–Rome, and then it was back to France again for the Paris–Nice.

Paris–Nice proved to be a rather curious race. In the team time trial on the second stage, Anquetil was dropped by his team mates after suffering mechanical problems. He went through a very bad patch, and finally lost four and a half minutes on the stage. A couple of days later, on the leg to St Etienne, an important break went clear. Roger Rivière clearly wanted to finish well in his home town and was all for bringing the escapees back. His team mates dissuaded him as their man, François Mahé, was part of this leading group. It was clearly up to Anquetil and his Helyett team to do the chasing, but none of them budged, and the break continued to increase its lead. Van Looy found the whole thing very amusing as his team mate, Impanis, was the best-placed man in the leading group and looked like taking over the race lead while the rest of the stars sat in the bunch simply looking at each other.

At the finish, the leaders crossed the line a massive twenty-three and a half minutes up on the bunch. The race was virtually over, and Paul Wiegant was furious with Anquetil for his lack of effort; but Jacques was not interested in his complaints: all was not well – he seemed to have no strength in his legs and he could only finish fourth in the time trial. He retired, disillusioned, the following day, leaving people to guess as to the cause of his problems. Whatever it was, he got over it quickly enough to ride Milan–San Remo and finish in his usual lowly place. It was rather curious that while Jacques normally finished this Italian classic, he was never able to shine in it.

On 16th March the racing world was shocked when Gérard Saint was killed in a road accident. The tall, elegant 24 year old left a wife and three children. Although he normally rode in Rivière's team, Jacques was very fond of this fellow Norman and remained in close contact with Gérard Saint's family for the rest of his life. The association of French professionals organised a collection for his widow and, then, two days before the Paris–Roubaix, a track meeting at the Parc des Princes, the benefits of which also went to Madame Saint. A large number of the stars of cycling – Anquetil, Bobet, Van Steenbergen, Darrigade, Altig, De Bruyne, Anglade, Simpson, Graczyk, Bouvet and Van Looy – took part. The stadium in his home town of Argentan was later named in Gérard Saint's memory.

Most of the French professionals crossed the Mediterranean again to Oran where, for the first and only time, the National Criterium was being run. It was disputed over just one single race and it was won by Jacques' team mate, Jean Graczyk, while Anquetil himself finished third at 2 mins 4 secs. Then, back in northern Europe, Jacques finished in fourteenth place in the Tour of Flanders as preparation for the Paris–Roubaix.

The 'Queen of the Classics' was animated by an escape of Bobet and Rivière: they were away together for more than 90 miles before they were caught. Then Tom Simpson escaped by himself, and was riding with such strength and ease that most expected him to stay clear to the finish. However, he was chased by the Belgian, Pino Cerami, and the Frenchman, Sabbadini, who caught and went straight past the English man when he blew up. The 38-year-old Cerami, who had ridden most of his career as an Italian before finally managing to obtain Belgian nationality, then dropped his companion to win alone at Roubaix – it was the biggest win of his life. Anquetil launched a powerful counter-attack, but it was far too late and he finally finished in eighth place.

This was to be Jacques' highest placing ever and, for most experts, this 'Hell of the North' should have been well within his capabilities. He certainly wanted to win it, no matter what he might have claimed. It will always be a mystery as to why he never did; perhaps the reason is that he never really made up his mind to do so. But, for the moment, his thoughts were on the Giro.

At the beginning of May, before going to Italy, Jacques rode a five kilometre pursuit race against Rivière at the Parc des Princes track. Since this was Roger's speciality, many were surprised when Jacques ran out winner by 35 metres, although most Anquetil fans believed that he could have been one of the best pursuiters of all time if he had concentrated on the discipline.

The start of the Giro brought another surprise: Anquetil was beaten in the first, short time trial by the Italian rider, Venturelli, who showed the most enormous potential, but, although his star shone so brightly, it was extinguished a couple of days later when he retired from the race.

At the end of the third day it was Jacques who put on the pink jersey, although only for three brief days. Once again, Charly Gaul was the joint favourite, along with Anquetil: the little climber planned to win the race on the very hard climb of the Monte Gavia, while Jacques was pinning his hopes on riding a good time trial at Lecco.

When Anquetil rode the 68 kilometres against the watch at an average speed of 45.356 k.p.h., he put more than six minutes into Gaul. Everyone was stupefied. The journalists said they thought they had seen the best of him before, but nobody had seen anything like this. Jacques said that he had not felt the pedals, had thought of nothing but the race, and had just concentrated on going faster and faster. It was to remain one of the most impressive performances of his long career. Jacques' morale was high throughout the whole of the race as Janine was waiting for him in the hotels in the evening and knew exactly how to boost her husband's confidence. She drove their big Simca before the start of a stage while Jacques warmed up behind it and, such was their popularity in Italy, they were followed by crowds of fans wherever they went.

The show-down on the Monte Gavia was not entirely as had been anticipated. It was the first time the race had used the climb which was, in effect, an enlarged goat track. It had a steep wall of mountain on one side and an even steeper unprotected drop on the other. This stony road contained several sections at 22 per cent. However, when Gaul accelerated away, twirling his tiny gear, it was obvious that he was not going to make up seven and a half minutes, especially as he was believed to be suffering from bronchitis. More of a danger was Gastone Nencini who received so many pushes from the Italian crowd that he was able to freewheel uphill. It was claimed that a French motorbike was attempting to stop the Italian fans from cheating in this way, but other fans were throwing stones at it. In spite of this, Jacques dropped him before the summit, but punctured, so it was the Italian who was first into the descent. Nencini was one of the best descenders of all time and, to make matters worse, Anquetil crashed. Picking himself up, Jacques chased as hard as only he knew how. The gap slowly came down and at the finish the Frenchman had saved his jersey.

The next day the Italian *commissaires* apologised to Anquetil for the monstrous behaviour of the Italian crowd and assured him that if Nencini had taken over the race lead as a result of their actions then he would have been disqualified. Jacques went on to win the race in Milan by a mere 28 seconds. Nencini was something of a specialist at close finishes – in the 1957 Giro he had beaten Louison Bobet by just nineteen seconds. On that occasion, too, Charly Gaul had been a major player and this time the Luxembourger finished third.

The Anquetils took a short holiday in Venice, hoping for a little peace and quiet, but they were mobbed wherever they went. So Jacques played bridge for three days before returning to France in triumph; the country had been waiting nearly 60 years to see a compatriot beat the Italians on their home ground.

Jacques returned to Italy, with Roger Rivière, to ride their most important time trial at Forli, on Baldini's own territory. This time Anquetil got the better of his Italian rival, while Rivière finished a long way down. A picture was beginning to emerge of the man from St Etienne: although he could be quite brilliant against the watch, he could also be very erratic – a claim that nobody could ever make about Jacques.

After finishing eighth in the national championships at Rheims behind his team mate, Stablinski, he continued to maintain that he would not be at the start of the Tour de France. Many people still refused to believe him – after all, he had bluffed so much in the past. However, those who were aware of his racing programme in the week before the start of the Tour should have been convinced: he raced at Milan; then rode the Antwerp Three–Day; a pursuit match against Venturelli in Italy; a *nocturne* at Caen; then Paris; Toulouse two days later; and then back again to Paris the following day!

It was Rivière who was made favourite to win the Tour and, for once, Marcel Bidot had no trouble in picking a team. To be out of the public eye for the entire month of July was not, however, to Anquetil's taste. So, during the race itself, he wrote a column for a sports paper. As expected, he made some very interesting and relevant points on the racing and the riders.

The whole of France was expecting Rivière to win even though Nencini was proving to be the stronger in the mountains. Then, when laying in second place overall, a couple of minutes behind the Italian, Roger lost control of his bike on a small mountain descent. He finished up at the bottom of a ravine, still conscious, but fully aware that he was paralysed. It was to prove to be the end of his career.

When the Tour finally arrived in Paris, on this very sad note, Anquetil had been riding the accompanying track meeting. He wanted to console Darrigade, who had lost any chance of a stage win when he punctured at the entrance to the velodrome, and he also wanted to congratulate Nencini on winning the Tour, which was quite an achievement after the efforts that he had made in the Giro, but he kept out of the way. He was worried that he might be seen as seeking publicity, trying to grab some of the limelight which was not really his.

Jacques started the round of criteriums early. The racing might not have been as tiring as in the Tour, but the travelling between events certainly was. Fortunately Janine was an excellent driver and, while Jacques slept during the journey, Janine slept during the racing.

The world championship took place at the end of the month in East Germany. Jacques had embarked on some special training behind André Boucher's Derny over a circuit that was very similar to the Sachsensring, but Boucher observed that he was not on form. In the race itself he made few efforts, but did manage to finish ninth. The French were encouraged that they had finished three men in the first ten, with Darrigade second and Poulidor fifth, and, on top of that, the Frenchmen Rohrbach and Graczyk had animated the race. But the true fact was that the French had ridden as a bunch of individuals, making very little attempt to organise themselves. In total contrast was the Belgium team which ensured that their man, Van Looy, won. Rik's sponsors, Faema, had put up half a million Belgian francs, to which Van Looy added an equal amount out of his own pocket, to be shared amongst the Belgian riders if, and when, Rik Van Looy won.

After the Worlds, Jacques arrived at the Criterium des As with no hope of doing well, not having been able to sleep for a couple of nights. His friend, Noyés, a healer, spent ten minutes with him before the start, putting his hands on Jacques' throat. He felt no immediate difference and was sure he would have difficulty just finishing the race, but he rode like a man transformed, winning in a record time, and completely outclassing the field. From then on Jacques had total confidence in Noyés' therapy.

Now, at the end of the season, Jacques said he was tired, and promised Janine that he would not ride many of the late-season time trials, except for the Grand Prix of Lugano. When, in this Swiss event, he found that he had not been placed last man to ride he was furious, and threatened not to ride at all. In fact, he did ride, and won, and the organisers promised him that he would be assured of starting last the following year. Jacques, however, insisted that he would never come back again.

He also teamed up with the Swiss time-trial specialist, Rolf Graf, for the Bracchi Trophy, and they were leading up to the point where Graf crashed. Jacques finished alone, well down on the winners, Ronchini and Venturelli, but even they had red faces when it was announced that a pair of unknown Italian amateurs had gone even faster over the same distance.

So, 1960 came to a close. Many people may have considered this to have been Anquetil's third successive disappointing year. Sure, he had won the Tour of Italy in fine style and the prestigious Criterium des As in Paris, as well as some of the top criteriums, but very little else – there was no pleasing some. But, perhaps things would change now that Bobet and Géminiani had retired, and Rivière had been eliminated. In fact, the following season was to see the emergence of a new Anquetil – stronger, more mature, more successful, yet less popular. The young king was about to become the old king.

It had been a very black year for cycling, with the deaths of Coppi and Saint, and the crippling injury to Rivière. No one in France seemed to be in the same class as Anquetil, and his total domination would lead to boring racing and falling sales of newspapers. The journalists needed to find a new rival for Jacques.

Tour de France 1959 (with Ercole Baldini)

PART THREE – THE OLD KING

Chapter Eleven

As the fans looked forward to a new season it was evident that some things were going to be different. The Helyett team was now co-sponsored by the Italian drinks company Fynsec, but André Darrigade would not be riding for them: he had put on the light-blue Alcyon-Leroux jersey. His friendship with Jacques had cooled considerably since the two men got married and Anquetil's new 'right-hand man' was Jean Stablinski. Jean was, by now, recognised as one of the most astute riders in the game and fully understood Jacques' need to be motivated. Indeed, he was to some extent his adviser and, in the years to come, many people came to regard them as more like brothers.

Antonin Magne was making a lot of noise about his new team leader, a certain Raymond Poulidor. The journalists were a little sceptical as Raymond was, by now, in his twenty-fifth year, and had yet to win anything of any great importance. However, the reason for his comparatively late start with the pros was that his military service had been delayed, so 1961 was only his second season in the paid ranks.

Jacques was now 27, the age at which riders were normally expected to reach maturity, so perhaps it was for this reason that he planned to ride a long, hard season of races. He was determined to establish himself beyond all possible doubt as the number-one rider in France and, after studying the route of the forthcoming Tour de France, he decided that it would suit him; he was determined to bring off something spectacular.

The cycling world was somewhat scandalised when Van Looy admitted to the Belgian press that he had helped his Belgian rival, Emile Daems, to an overall win in the Tour of Sardinia in return for a couple of stage victories. He explained to the journalists in Brussels that, if he could not win himself, he preferred to see victory going to another Belgian. Anquetil responded to this by claiming that Van Looy had ridden specifically against him in the past two Tours of Italy, but that he had sought his help in the Tour of Lombardy against one of his (Jacques') own team mates, Graczyk. He had refused, of course, and went on to say that if Rik continued to act in this way then people would start talking about a 'blue train'* on the road. Certainly Van Looy's conduct in Sardinia brought no credit on him and upset many in the peloton.

Winning the Paris–Nice proved that Jacques had come to form early in 1961, but would he be able to hold it for the whole season? French hearts were filled with joy when Raymond Poulidor won the Milan–San Remo. Antonin Magne had not been joking when he said he had somebody special on his hands.

Then it was back to Paris, to the former motor-racing circuit of Montlhéry, where the National Criterium was being held. The course took in the banked track as well as the twisty, flat circuit alongside it. Just like the Brooklands circuit, south of London, Montlhéry had seen its heyday before the war. Unlike Brooklands, however, the Parisian track had been kept in good condition as it was used on a regular basis for record attempts. The race was fast and furious, and Anquetil, as one journalist remarked, rode 'a la Bobet'. In other words, he spent the whole race in the front quarter of the field.

With three laps to go a front group of fifteen had established itself and Jacques managed to join them after closing the gap by himself. Paul Wiegant, his *Directeur Sportif*, drew alongside in his car and urged Anquetil to attack. Jacques shook his head and said, 'You must be joking. Not in this wind.' Jean Graczyk also urged him to try to get clear. 'No, Jean,' he said. 'You go and if they bring you back, then I'll try it.'

The words were hardly out of his mouth when there was a loud 'pffit' as Graczyk's back tyre went down. Jean Stablinski then had a try at persuading him. 'Go to the front Jacques. Ride to win. If you decide to go clear, you can drop any peloton. Just try and you'll see that I'm right.'

---

*The so-called 'blue train' was reputed to be a system in the Six Day races on the track whereby the top riders shared the main spoils amongst themselves, thereby making it difficult for any new riders to establish themselves.

Jacques had total confidence in Stablinski's judgement. On the last lap he said to his team mate, 'Is this the time?' 'Yes,' said Jean. 'In the name of God, go now!' With just 1,500 metres to the finish Anquetil went clear for what virtually amounted to a long sprint. On the line he was two lengths clear of Darrigade.

This was really a red-letter day: after nearly eight years Anquetil had won his first single-day road race, excluding criteriums. Antonin Magne had announced at the very beginning of the season that 1961 was going to be Anquetil's year and to many it was beginning to look as if he was right.

The next day most of the French pros were riding a criterium at St Claud when a dispute arose between Anquetil and Hassenforder. The man from Alsasce had been excluded from the traditional share-out of the primes among the top riders, and he held Jacques responsible. Roger Hassenforder did everything he could to impede Anquetil while shouting abuse at him all the time. Finally, he put Jacques into a ditch, fortunately resulting in only very minor injuries. It was intolerable, and this was by no means the first time that he'd been in hot water. When called in front of the Committee of Professionals, he feared the worst, and was judged by, amongst others, Bobet, Anquetil, Wiegant, Bidot and Darrigade. Luckily for him, they took into account his excitable nature and his lack of recent form. Their verdict was suspension for one month, and a request to his sponsors that they should reinstate him.

The Paris–Roubaix saw Jacques finishing well down in 60th spot nearly six minutes behind the winner, Van Looy. It was total humiliation for the French as their best man was fourteenth. It was beginning to seem as if the Belgians were unbeatable in this northern classic.

Jacques returned to Forli for the Grand Prix, even though the race was not totally to his liking – he found the course too flat and designed to favour the local hero, Ercole Baldini. The Italian was now past his best, even though still extremely well paid by his sponsor. Jacques beat him into second place by 4 mins 24 secs to prove that there was nobody who could now really challenge him at this discipline.

Then it was north again to Switzerland for the Tour of Romandie – a short, mountainous stage-race usually used by the more important riders to bring them to top form in preparation for a bigger event – in Jacques' case, the Giro. Winning the time-trial stage was mainly a question of pride, but also a warning that he would be the one to watch in the forthcoming three-week race around the Italian Peninsula. He spent the rest of the time in the Swiss race simply watching his rivals and keeping himself out of trouble.

Anquetil's prospects started to look good in Italy when he put on the pink jersey after an excellent performance in the first time trial, but there was still a very long way to go and anything could happen in this stage-race, as he was to discover. A few days later Pambianco, one of the top Italians, went away early in the day in a break which finished with an enormous lead, while Jacques sat day-dreaming at the back of the bunch. This stage win put the young Italian into the overall lead by a huge margin. What's more, it meant he would be supported by all of the Italians in the field, thus giving Anquetil no chance of reducing the gap to any great extent. One of the unwritten laws of racing is that you can never expect to win a major tour if you have one really bad day. This had happened to Jacques in the Tour de France of 1958. However, the Tour of Italy was different: here the unwritten law was that if you were a foreigner you could not possibly let any of the top Italians gain a lot of time because he could count on the help of most of the field to protect him. The Giro was indeed a unique race. Jacques finally finished in second spot. In three years he had achieved two second places and one first place. The only *straniero* to do better than this was Charly Gaul.

Interviewed after the race, Jacques said that Pambianco had been pushed so many times on the climbs that several riders had told him that the race had been stolen from him. However, the event had finally taught him that he could climb well enough to fear nobody. He had always had difficulty in breathing at very high altitude, although this was getting better. He went on to say that, generally speaking, racing was becoming faster and harder, but that he was feeling stronger than ever and the proof was that he had been in second place at the top of the Stelvio behind Charly Gaul.

A very good ride in the National Championship resulted in a fourth place behind France's new hero, Raymond Poulidor.

Jacques would have dearly loved to have put on the red, white and blue jersey once in his career, but his friend and team mate, Jean Stablinski, had been away in the break with Poulidor, so he could hardly have made an attempt to bring them back.

It was beginning to look as if Raymond Poulidor was going to emerge as his main rival; he was a man with the huge hands of a peasant, a big smile and lots of promise. If Jacques was not quite the son of a lowly peasant that he always pretended to be, Raymond certainly was. In fact, as a farm labourer, his father came somewhere below a peasant in the social hierarchy. Poulidor did not go to a technical college for three years; he worked for his father without any pay at all. The first money he ever received in his life was in a bike race which, of course, made him all the more committed.

Raymond Poulidor achieved popularity almost immediately. He really was a man of the people, warm hearted, generous and modest. When he won the Milan–San Remo it seemed to herald a revival in the fortunes of French riders in foreign classics. René Privat had won this Primavera the previous year, and now Poulidor had copied him at the very beginning of his career.

Jacques had never won a foreign classic, apart from in time trials, and it seemed as if he never would. Everyone assumed that Poulidor must be much younger than Anquetil although, in fact, he had been born only two years after Jacques. He had not turned professional until his military service had been completed which was one of the reasons why he was to race at top level until after the age of 40. Fanned by the newspapers, the rivalry between the two men was quickly established. Although there was no personal animosity between them, Jacques was very jealous of Raymond's popularity.

In 1961 Poulidor was 25, and this was certainly old enough to ride the Tour de France. However, his team manager, Antonin Magne, would not hear of it: riding in the French team alongside Anquetil, and working for him, was totally out of the question. When the Tour de France started, it was without its French national champion.

The great event began in Anquetil's home town of Rouen and, even before that, Jacques had done something very rash: he had announced that he would wear the yellow jersey for the whole of the race, from the first to the last day. It had been done before the war by Bottecchia of Italy, Frantz of Luxembourg and Romain Maes of Belgium, but none of them had dared to predict it. If he did manage to bring it off, it would be magnificent, but if he did not then he would look very silly indeed. Jacques was pretty sure of himself and, of course, all his supporters in Rouen had no doubts at all. Jacques had always liked a challenge and, in a way, he was challenging himself. He also wanted everyone to know that his domination of the race had been planned in advance and therefore was no accident.

The general opinion in the racing world was that Jacques would be unable to hold onto the jersey for the whole race because if he did not crack, then his team would. The main danger-man was Charly Gaul, again: nobody was expected to stay with him in the mountains. But Charly's fears about his Swiss team mates proved to be completely right, and he later claimed that if he had had Anquetil's strong team then it would have been a very different race indeed.

The first stage was split in two – a road race to Versailles in the morning and a time trial after lunch – with the yellow jersey only being awarded at the end of the afternoon. On the morning stage Anquetil got in the winning break and Darrigade was first across the line at Versailles, with Gaul timed in four minutes down. Jacques and André were now in different trade teams, but Marcel Bidot had brought them together in the French national team. In the afternoon Jacques won the race against the watch by more than three minutes to put on the yellow jersey. His position was already looking impregnable – nobody had ever started a Tour as well as this.

On the orders of Marcel Bidot the French team then started to control the race, to 'close it down'. 'We're not here to make a film for the cinema,' he said, and went on to point out that the Italians had employed this tactic before. His words did not go down well with the press, or with anyone else for that matter. The Italians to whom he was referring were, of course, Fausto Coppi's team in 1952 – after just eleven stages the race was effectively decided – but not before Coppi had escaped by himself on the road to Namur, and won not only the time trial but also two marvellous stages in the Alps.

Anquetil and Bidot had planned things right down to the millimetre. Jacques would never make an effort that would not pay off 100 per cent. He would gain more time in the time trial, limit his losses on Gaul and go with any danger-men on the flat, or in the mountains. Any form of attacking was out of the question. He thought that, as the race leader, it was up to the others to attack and for him to defend. It was all totally logical, but, rather like the football team that scores two early goals and then put all eleven men in their own goal-mouth for the rest of the match, it robs the competition of any spectacle.

When Bidot said that they were not there to make a film, he could not have been more wrong. The story of any Tour de France is more dramatic than anything that has ever appeared on a cinema screen. Robbed of any real drama, the Tour is of only minor interest. The 1961 Tour de France was not completely like that, but it came close to it. It is the 'glorious incertitudes' that make sport what it is.

The stage to Châlons-sur-Saône saw a break gain seventeen minutes and threaten Jacques' yellow jersey. So, Anquetil went to the front of the bunch and it stretched into one long line, and stayed that way for 30 kilometres until the gap was reduced to a reasonable level. On another occasion, Charly Gaul launched a solo attack in the Alps, but Jacques fought very hard to limit the damage. After crashing before the finish, the Luxembourger had gained a mere 1 min. 40 secs.

Jacques Goddet, Director of the Tour de France and Editor of the organising newspaper, L'Equipe, dipped his pen in vitriol as he criticised the lack of action which was causing daily sales to plummet. When groups of twenty or more riders, containing Anquetil, arrived together at the finish of mountain stages Goddet called them the 'dwarfs of the road', and a storm in the Pyrenees was deemed to be the angry protestations of the gods.

Goddet unleashed his venom on page two of his paper, while on page three, Pierre Chany, was telling a different story. Chany had known Anquetil personally since 1953, and although the two men had fallen out over what Jacques had considered to be unfair criticism, they had reached a reconciliation. He, a cycling reporter who was considered to be one of the best of all time, emphasised how strong the French team was, with what mastery they had neutralised any dangerous attack, and how their complete domination was due to their superiority. He pointed out that Anquetil was obviously under an enormous strain, yet showed no sign of cracking.

This went on for a week before Goddet could no longer put up with being contradicted by one of his employees. He called Pierre to his hotel and ordered him to stop making them both look stupid by disagreeing with him in print. Chany was not inclined to abandon his principles, but, at the same time, did not want to risk losing his job. He went to see Felix Levitan who not only wrote for a Paris daily paper, but was, along with Goddet, joint head of the Tour de France. Goddet and Levitan never really liked each other. Coming from a wealthy, upper-class background, Goddet tended to patronise Levitan, whose parents were humble shopkeepers. When Chany sought out Levitan for his advice, the answer came immediately: 'Ask him to put it in writing, my boy.' Chany followed the advice and Goddet, aghast at the very idea, let the matter drop.

Anquetil and the French team were both grateful and amused. After French national team mates had won two consecutive stages, Jacques rode alongside Chany and, within earshot of Goddet, shouted, 'Hey, Pierre! That's one in the eye for that big, bad boss of yours.' Goddet did not move a muscle in his face.

The race continued on its uninspiring way. Stages were won by Belgians and Italians. Darrigade won a couple; Jacques won the time trial, of course, and Charly Gaul had overall second place snatched from him at the last moment by the Italian, Carlesi. Anquetil, in a very unconventional move, decided to animate the last day. He attacked on the road to Paris, was first on to the Parc des Princes track, and helped his team mate, Cazala, win the stage.

By taking nine stages, keeping the yellow jersey for the whole of the race, winning the team prize as well as the green points jersey, it could be considered a virtual clean sweep for the French team: total domination. As Jacques himself put it, 'What more could they ask?'

But the Parisian crowd did not see it that way. There were boos, whistles, howls of anger, clenched fists – everything. It was even worse than in 1959, as fans demonstrated their disapproval in the most violent possible way. If the wire fencing had not been in place to keep the crowd off the track, anything might have happened.

Anquetil was amazed, puzzled and mystified. He was suffering from mental and physical exhaustion from the efforts he had made; he had used his judgement to perfection; he had demonstrated complete mastery over his rivals; and he had never cracked. In spite of all this, although he may have suffered enormously, especially in the mountains, he had never given any indication of it; he was always stylish and relaxed, giving the impression of effortlessness. It was this stylishness that Géminiani later commented on: 'In the whole of my life I have never met such a courageous rider. His courage defies imagination, but nobody notices because his style is so perfect.'

At the finish Jacques showed no emotion, no pleasure and no sign of triumph. 'He was bad tempered and argumentative after being whistled at in Paris at the end of the Tour,' said Janine. 'The criteriums were morose.'

The truth was that Jacques loved people, but was terrified of crowds and could not bear to be surrounded too closely. Only those who knew him well could testify to the fact that he really was a painfully shy person. During interviews he always seemed so relaxed – perhaps it was his greatest bluff. The hostile reception at the Parc des Princes had a devastating effect on his sensitive nature.

Jacques had entered the third period of his career. He was now the dominator; the old king – the despot. There was a certain cruelty in the way he imposed his will on the other riders in this Tour. You could hardly love him, even if you had to admire him. As usual, Jacques gave all his prize money to his team and embarked on the exhausting, dizzying, but lucrative round of criteriums. He always fulfilled his obligations, rode at his best and gave the crowd their money's worth. He may well have been whistled at the start, but was often mobbed at the finish by delirious fans. What a tragedy that he was unable, or unwilling, to produce such a spectacle in the Tour de France.

The French team had a considerable sum in prize money to share out between themselves at the finish of the Tour, but few considered that they had covered themselves in glory, even if Darrigade had won four stage. They had done little to enhance their value to the organisers of the criteriums. Groussard, for example, had had an opportunity to take the yellow jersey, but had been forbidden to do so. Anglade, in particular, was annoyed at his own loss of prestige which resulted in him being offered a mere eight contracts in France. The blame for this must lay on the shoulders of Marcel Bidot, who had organised the whole thing and had not allowed even very minor riders to escape.

However, at the World Championships in Switzerland French morale was sky-high when their amateur compatriots took the first three places. The winner, Jean Jourden, came from Jacques' home town of Rouen, and had been trained by his former mentor, André Boucher. After the finish, André himself approached Jacques and said, 'It is up to you to make it a double for France tomorrow.' André was irritated when Anquetil replied, 'I don't see the point because it would not increase my contract money one iota.' The remark was typical Anquetil and, whilst it certainly increased his reputation for provocation and cynicism, he was also indulging in his usual habit of inventing an alibi for future failure.

The Championship race itself was fast and extremely hard. Only the very strong were included among the fifteen men who sprinted for the finish. Van Looy won his second title, and Poulidor raised hopes for the future by finishing third. Jacques finished in thirteenth spot and said to the journalists, 'Rik is just so strong that it is hopeless trying to beat him.' Others remarked that with Stablinski finishing in the leading group, as well, the three Frenchman should have combined better to attack the Belgian non-stop in the closing stages. Even if Rik was too strong for them, at least they would have brought more honour and glory to their country. A couple of weeks before the world-title race Anquetil announced that matters were now much better between him and Van Looy, which inevitably led to speculation later as to whether this had played a part in Van Looy's victory.

By now it was becoming clear that Anquetil did not have the mentality to win single-day races. He was too ready with alibis before the start, and excuses after the finish. If he remained 'the King' in France then Van Looy was 'the Emperor' in Belgium. Like Jacques, Rik Van Looy was a pleasant, polite and agreeable person, but once on a bike he was transformed into a tyrant. Whilst his aggressive determination, combined with his considerable strength, enabled him to win an enormous number of top-class events, he had no friends in the bunch, unlike Jacques. Between them, the two men dominated cycle-racing in 1961, but it was somewhat ironic that Van Looy was paid bigger contract fees than Anquetil in France, whereas Jacques received more remuneration than Rik in Belgium.

Jacques reached a new pinnacle when he won the Grand Prix des Nations by a record nine minutes from the Belgian, Gilbert Desmet. During the race he kept receiving time-checks from his manager, Paul Wiegant, and was puzzled at being told that he was down on schedule when things seemed to be going well. He redoubled his efforts and rode himself into the ground, finishing totally exhausted. Wiegant's policy of supplying him false information had paid off with Jacques pulverising all records, but when Anquetil learned that his manager had told him lies, he was beside himself with rage, and he never forgave him.

Victory in the Grand Prix of Lugano was followed by his customary low places in the Paris–Tours and the Tour of Lombardy. Partnered by Stolker, he was fifth in the Baracchi Trophy – his worst place ever. After nine years, Jacques was beginning to despair of ever winning this Italian event which most people thought was his by right. However, at the end of the season, he was rewarded with the Super Prestige Pernod, which was just starting to gain some real significance in the pro cycling world as the 'other' World Championship and, although it had a clear bias towards the classics, its winner was meant to represent the year's best all-rounder. Anquetil, it would seem, did place a great deal of importance on winning this award, and when he won again in 1963 the public's perception and the eyes of the cycling world became firmly fixed on the result of the year-long competition.

This year, 1961, marked a turning-point in the history of the Tour de France because Anquetil had proved that the race could be won purely in the individual time trials. When these had first been introduced, back in 1934, it was never envisaged that they would play a decisive role. The race had always been decided in the mountains and, largely as a protest by the riders against the inhumanely long distances, the flat stages were a slow crawl round France; because of the problem of maintaining public interest in the race between the end of the mountains and the finish in Paris, a time trial was introduced. It was intended to add a little extra excitement and colour. In the early post-war years, the Tour time trials were held over considerable distances and, while they affected the outcome of the minor places, nobody could ever claim that a race had been won on time trials alone.

Then came Anquetil. His victory in the 1957 Tour had been achieved in the traditional way, and his time trial success had only had the effect of underlining his superiority, which had been Henri Desgrange's real objective back in 1934. Then, in his cool, calculating way, he estimated that if he had won two Paris–Nice, two Dunkerque Four-Days and a Tour of Italy principally in the time trials, then he should be able to do the same in the Tour de France. Of course, in 1961, he succeeded brilliantly, but in doing so he virtually neutralised the mountain stages, giving the impression of a slow crawl through the Alps and the Pyrenees.

The following year, 1962, would see even greater changes in the race.

Tour de France 1961 (with Charly Gaul)

Chapter Twelve

The main talking point at the start of the year was the difference trade teams would make to the Tour de France. The formula of national teams had been introduced by the 'Father of the Tour', Henri Desgrange, back in 1930, as trade squads looked as if they were going to destroy the event. There had been widespread corruption and intimidation to an extent that there was a danger of the Tour losing all credibility as a sporting event. National teams not only saved the Tour, but also ushered in a golden age that was to see some of its riders elevated to the level of film stars. The reputation of the Tour is based on this period in which the most memorable races took place.

However, for many people, the writing was on the wall with the advent of the *extra-sportif* trade teams in 1956. Chairmen of large, powerful companies were less than lukewarm about the idea of paying their riders to help a man representing another company win the Tour de France and benefit from the ensuing publicity. The Italians, in particular, were unhappy about a race which would never take more than ten or twelve of their country-men while the French had, perhaps, 70 or 80 men in the field.

In France, the St Rapha drinks company wanted to win the Tour and they thought the best man to do it was Anquetil. Most of their top men were foreigners, but none of them were really potential Tour winners. To give Jacques more of a chance they wanted him to be supported by an experienced and powerful team. So, they made an approach to Felix Potin who had Anquetil under contract along with Helyett cycles. Officially, Potin had pulled out of sponsorship the previous season, and Helyett had then been supported by Fynsec. Unfortunately, the Italian drinks company found themselves unable to fulfil their financial responsibilities, so Potin had agreed to meet the expenses of the team for the rest of the season, even though he got no return in terms of publicity. It was Monsieur Potin, therefore, whom the directors of St Rapha approached when they proposed a merger between their men and the Helyett team. Their previous *Directeur Sportif*, Raymond Louviot, would transfer to the new Gitane–Leroux formation, and Raphaël Géminiani and Paul Wiegant would be joint *Directeur Sportifs* at Helyett–St Rapha. The deal was concluded in principle, and a phone call was made to Anquetil at his home at St Adrien.

When they broke the news to Jacques it was followed by a very long silence. Eventually, Anquetil explained that, although it may have sounded silly to them, he was a very superstitious man and thought it would be bad luck to join a team which had once included Géminiani, Rivière, and Gérard Saint. Look what had happened to them! After much thought, and a little persuasion, he finally agreed to be part of the new organisation and, with Stablinski, went to his flat in Cannes for early season training. However, who was going to be the team manager had yet to be fully resolved.

The very cold, early season weather was more than Anquetil could take: he retired from Nice–Genoa–Nice and was also unable to finish Paris–Nice. Something was clearly wrong because he had only been able to manage tenth place in the time trial. He did finish most of the other spring classics, but always some way behind the winner. However, Jacques had set his heart on a new adventure. He wanted to be the first to win all three major Tours, so he was at the start of the Tour of Spain

By now he was very close to Jean Stablinski, much closer than he had ever been to Darrigade. André remained a friend, but they did not see a lot of each other. Their wives did not get on well together and now André was in another team. The last time they really worked together was in the national team during the previous year's Tour de France and even this association was never to be renewed. However, Stablinski was, by now, like an elder brother to Jacques; he was a wise but cunning man, and the stories of his manipulation of other riders were legendary. They always shared the same hotel room and confidences. Jean was the son of a Polish immigrant who had moved to north-eastern France to work in the coal-mines. Jean never tired of telling Jacques that 'it's a hard profession alright, but it's even harder down the pits'.

This close association of the two Frenchmen was to last for another five years.

The merger of the new teams brought Jacques the immediate problem of having to ride alongside another team leader – Rudi Altig. This blond-headed German was the current World Pursuit Champion; he was very strong and an excellent time trialist. Due to his weight he was not a very good climber, but this was not considered, at that time, to be too important in the Tour of Spain. Anquetil did not trust him, and saw him as a potential rival – the last thing he wanted on his own team. Some time previously, Jacques had driven all the way to Berlin for a pursuit match against Altig. When he arrived he was exhausted, and asked Rudi to go easy on him, but the German took no notice and absolutely humiliated him. Anquetil thought such an act was totally unpardonable.

Raphaël Géminiani had been appointed their team manager for the Tour of Spain. Since his malaria in the early part of 1960 Raphaël had tried racing again, but had been unable to find any sort of form – perhaps he was too old. He had briefly tried to make a career in journalism, but then found that running a team suited him better. He was inexperienced at the job, but many regarded him as a natural *directeur sportif* because of his racing experience and his strong personality. When he told his team in Spain that as long as one of them won the race he did not mind who it was, Jacques started to bristle. He remained unhappy and suspicious when, throughout most of the race, Altig wore the leader's jersey. Jacques made it clear that he thought he was being betrayed.

The race would finally be decided in the time trial on the penultimate day. Jacques was not in good form at all, but had managed to hide the fact. In the race against the watch Altig beat Anquetil and, that same evening, Jacques left Spain for the long drive back to Normandy. Through not finishing the Tour he lost the other members of the Helyett–St Rapha team a lot of money, and thereby made himself most unpopular. On the other hand, Altig had made a considerable contribution to the team's coffers.

The fact was that Jacques was actually very ill, and should not have ridden the time-trial stage at all. In the car on the way home Janine said that he looked like a ghost, nothing interested him and he could hardly stand. Once home, he had no appetite and his wife had to nurse him like a sick child; the doctors even talked of the possibility of cancer. Eventually, after a trip to the Pasteur Institute in Paris, the real problem was diagnosed – viral hepatitis.

The rift that had opened between Anquetil and Altig had to be healed at all costs if both men were to ride the Tour together. Daniel Dousset, acting as manager for both Rudi and Jacques, knew he had quite a job on his hands. Anquetil was always loath to listen to any advice, and claimed that those who criticised him were either jealous or incompetent. His team mates obeyed his orders without criticism, but secretly complained that his habit of sitting at the back of the bunch made life very hard for them. If he rode at the head of the race then life would be much easier and they would obtain better results. Dousset told Jacques that he had not been betrayed by Altig in the Vuelta, but by his own health. Rudi would be no danger to him in the Tour because he was too heavy to climb the high mountains effectively. On the other hand, he was going to need someone as strong as the German to counter the expected attacks from Van Looy

It was quite a serious illness that Anquetil was suffering from and meant a complete break from the bicycle. Nevertheless, he had a great capacity for recovering quickly and it was not long before he could embark upon some light training. His next big objective was the Tour de France. To get into any sort of form for it, he just had to ride the Dauphiné Libéré stage-race in the Alps. The doctor was horrified at the very idea and forbade him to take part, but Jacques knew that there was no choice. At the start, his team mate, Pierre Everaert, said, 'What are you doing here in this state, Jacques? You'll ruin your health.' Géminiani described him as 'looking like a bird who had just fallen from its nest'.

For the first three days he was surrounded by five or six team mates. Slowly and gradually his strength returned. On the fourth day the sun came out which made him feel a little better, but then the cold and the mist returned the following day and caused Jacques to take a terrible hiding, and to lose seventeen minutes. At the start of the next day he was aching all over, and most people thought that he was on the point of retiring, but Anquetil summoned up his considerable courage. In the words of Géminiani: 'he was no ordinary human being, but few realised that because he made it look so easy'. He survived his week of perdition and had put himself in a position to start the Tour. But there were a couple of problems to be resolved first.

A meeting was called in Paris to resolve the problem of who was going to be the permanent *directeur sportif* of the team. Most of the team riders were present and Jacques made his position clear from the very start: 'Under no circumstances,' he said, 'will I accept anyone other than Paul Wiegant. Géminiani is very amusing and a good companion, but he treats me like a child. Why, he even called me a lackey. I have never spoken to anyone like that in my life.' But all the other riders – Stablinski, Graczyk, Rostollan, Anaert, Le Lan, Stolker, Altig and Geldermans were for Géminiani. Finally, it was put to the vote and Anquetil had to give way. A journalist made the comment that at last Jacques had someone close to him who could contradict him and get away with it.

At the start of the Tour 'Gem' made it clear that Jacques Anquetil was the leader, and all the riders would work for him. 'But I have my own chances,' protested Altig. 'I am a world champion and have just won the Tour of Spain. I haven't come all the way to France to be treated like a child.'

The *Directeur Sportif* explained that the Tour de France was different to that of Spain. He had no chance at all in the mountains but, if he wanted to go for the green jersey, then the team would back him up. If this was not acceptable then they would phone the Irishman, Shay Elliott, to replace him, and he could go back to Germany. Rudi gave in.

The new trade-team formula meant that Raymond Poulidor could start the Tour with the full support of his Mercier team. He was thought of as Jacques' number-one rival, but Jacques, already irritated by his popularity, was even more annoyed by this claim. Journalists who questioned him on the subject got short shrift. 'Poulidor, my main rival? You really think so? I certainly don't! For me the danger-man is Van Looy. He will really enliven the race with his constant attacking. All Poulidor does is to follow other people. He never takes the initiative.'

When Poulidor started the race with his forearm in plaster he received more sympathy and support than ever before. Jacques was never the victim. He rarely crashed and never once in his career did he crack a bone, let alone break one. You never even saw a plaster or bandage on one of his limbs. If Poulidor was famous for his bad luck, then Anquetil was notable for his good luck. Jacques always hid his feelings – in a way, he even thought it shameful to show them – so, when he won, it seemed always to be without effort. His serenity upset people and his victories were so overwhelming that they seemed easy.

Unfortunately, his taste for provocation seemed to run away with him and his attempts at cynicism were catastrophic – France is not a cynical country and cycling is not a cynical sport. His remarks about not liking the bicycle and racing only for the money stained his reputation. He cultivated paradox and anarchy, best summed up by the phrase: 'he was sawing through the branch on which he was sitting'.

At the start of the Tour the word was that Jacques was not fully on form, and Van Looy, riding his first Tour at the age of 29, was out to make an impression and to attack Anquetil. Many of his fans sincerely believed that Rik would win so many stages that the time bonuses that he would accumulate would help him challenge for the race leadership.

However, it was not to be. His aggressive riding made the Tour interesting and exciting, and forced Anquetil in person to neutralise his attacks. This gave the impression that Jacques was as strong as ever and, after his win in the time trial at La Rochelle, he established himself as the master of the race and beyond the reach of them all. When Van Looy crashed out of the race before the Pyrenees, without winning a single stage, most people thought that the race was virtually over.

In reality, Jacques Anquetil was having a very hard Tour indeed, even though he succeeded in convincing everyone that he was not. If anyone had the strength to challenge him, nobody had the confidence. When they reached Paris he had more than five minutes in hand over the Belgian, Jos Planckaert, with Poulidor third at ten minutes. There had been one considerable scare on the last stage when Jacques crashed quite heavily. He could have lost the race through the incident, but Planckaert, very sportingly, did not attack and all was well.

It had been a promising first Tour for Raymond, who had won the mountain stage to Aix-les-Bains, but for the public it had been another lack-lustre Tour: Jacques' victory had been based on his two time-trial wins. The main interest in the Tour de France has always been in the mountains; the rest of the race counts for far less. So, when Jacques arrived in Paris, it was no wonder that his reception was lukewarm. Yet again, he had robbed the race of its main spectacle. As somebody remarked at the time: 'When the Belgian sprinter, Emile Daems, can win the hardest stage in the mountains, then something must be wrong.'

There was something wrong, although nobody knew at the time. It was only discovered later that Anquetil had ridden the whole event with a tapeworm. It was amazing that, despite this handicap, he was still able to pull something special out of the bag for the two time trials. Jacques had won his third Tour de France by a mixture of bluff and supreme courage. Indeed, bluff and courage were what best summed up his whole career.

After the Tour many people were anxious to know what the relationship was between Anquetil and Altig, and journalists questioned the German at length. Rudi was a friendly and open person, very different to Jacques. He said that he had stayed at Jacques' house at St Adrien for a few days and they had got on marvellously well; in fact, they had been just like brothers. During the Tour of Spain he saw a totally different side of Anquetil: he could hardly believe how distrustful and suspicious he could be. After Jacques had got back into condition again, they both flew to the Isle of Man for a racing trip, during which time their good relations were re-established and they discussed how much they would need each other in the forthcoming Tour. During the Tour itself Jacques had been totally self-confident and relaxed. After Van Looy retired from the race nobody really believed that he could be beaten. Nobody had dared to attack him and he underlined his crushing superiority in both time trials.

Anquetil himself was questioned about how his win had affected his popularity with the public and how they had reacted to the trade teams. He said that the French had obviously identified themselves with the national teams and, of course, their own regional teams. No longer did the public have some sort of idea where a rider came from by the colour of his racing vest. These previous jerseys were certainly regarded as more attractive and tasteful, rather than multi-coloured strips advertising a couple of different products. He blamed his bad reception the previous year largely on the press, which had been kinder to him in 1962. So, he was reasonably satisfied with his popularity. On an average day, he said, he would receive about 100 letters and, since it was obviously impossible for him to reply to them all, his father-in-law acted as his secretary. He always found it tiring to be mobbed by autograph hunters, and you could never get away without signing at least 50 of them. It was just too much.

Because of the effects of the tape worm Jacques was in poor form, and this remained with him for the rest of the season. The World Championship, held at Salo in Italy, was won by his friend Jean Stablinski, while Jacques and most of the French team played a spoiling role to make sure that the winning break stayed clear. Jacques' finished in fifteenth place – clear proof of his continuing lack of form. He did not even finish the Tour of Lombardy, and he rode none of the big, end-of-season time trials except the Baracchi Trophy.

Jacques had become accustomed to not winning this event and did not really prepare seriously for it. On the way to the event he even went sight seeing in Venice. His partner was Rudi Altig, who was still something of a rival as far as time-trialling was concerned: three stage wins and the green jersey in the Tour de France had considerably increased the German's reputation and he kept his good form until the end of the season. He had, nevertheless, grown very fond of Anquetil and had eventually come to realise that the man who he had known in the Tour of Spain – a worried, anxious, suspicious, and distrustful person, was not the real Anquetil. In Bergamo, before the start of the Baracchi, he joked to the journalists: 'Jacques will never ride this event again, because today I am going to make him suffer.'

And so it proved. With 50 kilometres still to go, Jacques was completely 'cooked' and could no longer go through to do his turn. Altig encouraged him; he insulted him; he even pushed him by the saddle. For Jacques the mist that appeared before his eyes became a thick fog; all he could see was Altig's back wheel. At speeds of 30 m.p.h. and more, he was gritting his teeth and was just able to cling on. He could no longer see the road. When he felt the wind on his left cheek he moved to the right to get into the German's slip-stream; when he felt the wind on his right cheek he moved to the left.

The pain and suffering were such that he became only vaguely aware of what was happening. Eventually, he felt two big bumps and fell off into the middle of a crowd of people. Only later, when he fully came round, did he realise that the first bump had been on to the track itself and the second was him riding on to the grass in the centre of the arena. The two men had been timed at the entrance to the stadium, but still had to ride a lap of the track. Anquetil, however, had been quite unable to turn sharp right. In a daze, and totally unaware of the blood streaming down his face from his crash, he was carried to the infirmary. From there he was taken back to the hotel; it took a full two hours for him to recover. In the meantime, Altig rode his lap of honour alone because, amazingly, the two men had won the event, having recorded the fastest time at the entrance to the track.

Jacques had never been so humiliated before, but he was the last one to take things laying down. Two weeks later the two men rode a similar event in Baden-Baden. This time Anquetil was properly prepared and was not willing to show any mercy. After the start he came through to open up a lead of five lengths over Altig. Rudi tried and tried and tried to close the gap, but was unable to, and after ten kilometres of going flat-out the German was totally exhausted. Anquetil finally allowed him to rejoin, and then rode the rest of the race at the front. Rudi was unable to come through to do his turn once. He was humiliated in front of his own crowd and Jacques had got his revenge. It was curious that this lesson Jacques gave to Rudi was to seal a very close friendship that was to last for the rest of Anquetil's life. Perhaps it was because, at last, Rudi was forced to admit that Jacques was the master.

It had been a long, hard season for the Frenchman – one of almost non-stop suffering, although most people had not noticed. Jacques was far too proud to complain or make excuses, but he had won his third Tour de France, and, at last, his first Baracchi Trophy. So, a three week trip to New Caledonia before the end of the year was most welcome. Jacques was accompanied by Jean Stablinski, Jean Graczyk and their wives. They contested some races on the road and on the track, did a little hunting, and soaked up the sun. Then it was back to Jacques' skiing lodge for Christmas.

Tour de France 1962: Jacques Anquetil, and team-mate,
Rudi Altig, temporarily in the yellow jersey, while
World Champion, Rik Van Looy looks on

Chapter Thirteen

Anquetil's fortunes were to see a considerable improvement in 1963. He said that at the age of 29 he felt more confident than ever before; he even thought he was less susceptible to the cold and the rain. He certainly started off well by winning the Paris–Nice and the National Criterium – success in two stage-races and the season had hardly begun. He paid a quick visit to Spain to ride a hilly time trial of less than eight kilometres at Arrade. The winner was the Spaniard, Sargadey, one second in front of his country-man, Bahamontes, who was, in his turn, one second faster than Anquetil. Whilst such a tight result may not have proved a great deal, it demonstrated that Spain was able to produce a whole host of good climbers, most of whom were unknown outside of their own country and that, after being off-form for a few years, the 35-year-old Bahamontes was again a force to be reckoned with. It also showed that Anquetil was continuing to make progress on the climbs.

A few weeks later he crossed the Pyrenees again for the start of the Tour of Spain. The current crop of Spanish riders did not seem to be very strong away from the mountains and there were no other foreign stars from outside Spain. The organisers of the race were very pleased to have him because victory by a top star would give more credence to their event.

Everything was going well for Anquetil, and he looked like making up for his disappointment of the previous year. Then came the time-trial stage, and Jacques was beaten by the Spanish rider, Velez. 'Who's he?' they said. 'How did he beat Jacques? Is something wrong with him?' Although the answer was a resounding 'Yes' – he had some sort of debilitating stomach upset – he was determined that nobody would know.

That evening all of the teams in the race happened to be staying in the same big hotel. Jacques came down to dinner dressed in a suit, as was his custom, and calmly sat down at the table. Trying to take dinner was rather a pointless exercise, but he could not afford to let anyone know this. So, Géminiani sat next to him with a pile of serviettes. Jacques tried, but he just could not keep any food down. As he pretended to wipe his lips he vomited into the serviettes. In this way he unobtrusively brought up all of his dinner, and used no less than eight napkins in the process.

Géminiani stayed with him in his room as he turned and sweated on his bed, totally unable to sleep. At about three in the morning, the fever started to leave him and he suddenly felt ravenously hungry. A whole chicken was rapidly consumed, along with a couple of bottles of beer. On the road the next day he was stronger than ever. Once again, he had succeeded in bluffing everyone to the extent that people even started to wonder if he had been soft-pedalling in the time trial.

In adversity Anquetil always managed to surpass himself: no other champion in the history of the sport had ever been able to dig so deep into his reserves. Many have claimed that he was an exceptionally lucky rider, and this may well have been true as far as broken bones were concerned, but this did not stop Jacques from having some extremely bad days, just like anyone else. The difference was that not only did he hide his suffering, he also managed to produce something to convince people of the very opposite. Most of the riders were aware of this amazing side of his character, but he managed to hide it from the journalists so the public never believed, or noticed, his bad days; all the public saw was a ruthless, calculating man, for whom everything, seemingly, was easy – a sort of cold perfection.

Jacques duly won the Vuelta, beating the Spaniards, Colmenajero and Pacheco, and, in doing so, became the first man in history to win all three major Tours. He hoped to follow this up by doing 'the double' (winning the Tours of France and Spain in the same year). Certainly he was riding more strongly than ever before and looking for new challenges and new 'doubles'. After his failure in the 1958 Paris–Roubaix, he really believed that he was incapable of winning a major single-day event and, although he continued to express the desire to put on a French national champion's, or a world champion's jersey, deep down he never really believed that he would, but Jacques thought that by continuing to win the Tour de France he should be just as popular as if he had won a dozen classics.

His professional career had lasted ten years and seemed as if it would go on for a long time yet. He had been careful with his efforts, but, at the same time, he had kept the number of necessary sacrifices to a minimum. He was critical of riders who drank only during the off-season. They were making a mistake, he argued. If you wanted to drink, then it should be all year round, or not at all. However, he did not admit to the fact that he only drank very moderate amounts and always encouraged the belief that he drank to excess. It was his way of trying to destroy the morale of his rivals.

The man who was seen to be as cold as ice and as hard as steel was, in fact, modest and decent. He regularly visited the old lady in his village of Quincampoix who used to bandage him up as a kid when he fell over, and also Madame David in Sotteville who gave him his lunch and fussed over him so much during the three years he was at technical college. Then there were the annual reunions with the friends from his youth.

It took a lot of courage to announce, cynically, that you rode simply for the money, but Jacques was too honest to say anything else. He always said what others only dared to whisper and, in years to come, this trait would get him into hot water, and permanently stain his character.

Jacques was at the start of the Dauphiné Libéré alongside most of the hopefuls for the Tour de France. Victory in such a prestigious event was important, although most of the riders were there mainly in order to come to form for the *Grand Boucle*. It was assumed that this race, in which the Spaniards always seemed to do well, would be too hilly for Jacques, but things went much more easily than in the previous year. Everaert and Stablinski, Jacques' team mates, won stages. Perez-Frances, the Spanish climber, won one (as did a couple of obscure Belgians) and Van Looy won two. Jacques won the time trial, of course, and finally put on the leader's jersey the day before the finish.

Then the journalists got to work. 'Tour fever' was building up and there had been plenty of pointers in this week of racing in the mountains. After Anquetil, the next four places were occupied by Spanish riders, one of whom was Bahamontes. He had been a wonderful climber in his day, but, at the age of 35, nobody had expected him to do so well. Poulidor had tried an offensive in the mountains, but had failed miserably and was only prevented from retiring by sharp words from Antonin Magne. Van Looy was clearly feeling strong, even if he did not manage a high overall placing.

It had seemed an easy win for Jacques. It was his first major success in the event and he had won 'a la Tour de France', which is to say that he stayed with the leaders on the climbs, and won the race in the time trial. When he announced to the press that he was not certain about starting the Tour de France nobody knew what to make of it. Was this just another big bluff? Nobody knew and nobody will ever know, but what we do know is that he had a medical check-up before he finally announced his participation, and he confided to his team manager that he was still haunted by the memory of the terrible time he had gone through in the Baracchi Trophy. He was scared that such a thing could happen to him in the Tour.

The national championship at Rouen was won for the third time by Jacques' team mate, Jean Stablinski. Anquetil contributed to his victory by neutralising Poulidor for most of the race before outsprinting him for third place. With Guy Ignolin in second place, the St Rapha team collected all three medals.

The head of the St Rapha company told Géminiani that they had taken on Anquetil specifically to ride the Tour de France. Without him the team would be nothing and the whole affair would be a disaster. He ordered Raphaël to put pressure on Jacques to make him ride the Tour. Géminiani told his paymaster that it simply did not work that way with Anquetil, and any attempt to force him to start the race would automatically make Jacques dig his heels in and definitely refuse.

On the Tuesday before the start of the Tour Jacques was ordered to appear in front of Max Augier, general director of the St Rapha company, at their head office in Paris. Also present were Daniel Dousset and Dr Dumas. Anquetil had met Augier twice before, and had not taken to him at all. Jacques was examined by the doctor who passed him fit. Augier had been warned by Géminiani that, under no circumstances, should he order Anquetil to ride. So, Augier turned on the charm and gently explained his point of view. Jacques saw an entirely new side of the man and, after explaining that he was not a robot, he finally agreed to start.

Géminiani had previously prepared the ground by telling Jacques that the Spanish riders had been dominating all the races but he had beaten them all in Spain. When Anquetil finally said yes to the Tour, Géminiani pretended not to believe him. 'Are you really sure?' he said. 'Is that your final version?' After this, of course, wild horses would not have kept him away from the race. 'Gem' understood Jacques very well indeed.

Nevertheless, on the Friday before the start, Anquetil was in a restaurant in Paris and told the journalists that he was still not sure whether he would ride. He just could not resist one final game of bluff, but those among them who knew him well were finally convinced when they saw him go to the barbers to have his hair cut short.

For the first time in many years the race started in Paris, but it was lost in the middle of the huge metropolis. It simply did not have the same disruptive effect as it did on a provincial town where it caused enormous traffic problems and you simply could not miss it. Charly Gaul was no longer a danger, so Jacques' main rivals seemed to be Van Looy, Poulidor and, perhaps, even Bahamontes. Géminiani loudly announced that Jacques was in exceptional form, way above the class of Poulidor who could not put up with the pressure so well. After two consecutive wins by Anquetil the organisers wanted, and needed, a more open race, so they had reduced the distance of the time trials and even reduced the time bonuses for winning them. Jacques was not entirely unhappy with this new arrangement as it gave him the chance to prove that he was an all-round rider and not just a specialist against the watch. However, even though he had agreed to start, he remained worried that he was overdoing things

For Van Looy it proved to be a successful Tour. He won four stages and the green jersey. He was clearly very strong, but, being far too heavy for the mountains, he was completely out of the picture in the overall race. In the early part of the event, though, Anquetil found Van Looy's incessant attacks very tiring and started to wonder if the Belgian's main objective was to make him lose the Tour; but Géminiani's confidence stimulated him: it really was something he needed. Once, when Anquetil had gone clear, he found Bahamontes sitting on his wheel and was loath to continue his effort. 'Gem' then leaned out of the car window and screamed at him through his megaphone: 'In the name of God, Jacques, give it everything. Never mind about Baha; you've dropped all your other rivals!' That evening Anquetil said, 'Thanks, Gem. You were right.'

Poulidor made exactly the same mistake as he had in the Dauphiné. He attacked on the Col de La Forclaz in Switzerland, but went far too early and into the wind. He exhausted himself and took the most terrible 'packet', and, with it, lost all chance of a high overall placing.

Tour de France, stage eleven: in the foothills of the Pyrenees with the peloton still together. Anquetil with José Perez-Frances (Ferrys), race-leader Gilbert Desmet (Wiels) with Raymond Poulidor on his wheel, and Francisco Gabica (Kas)

After Poulidor dropped back on this stage to Chamonix the fans were thrilled to see the battle between Anquetil and the 35-year-old Bahamontes. The contrast in the style of the two riders was so noticeable that it was almost laughable – Jacques stretched out over the bike and the Spaniard sitting almost upright. As they climbed the Forclaz together Federico winced at the creaks and groans coming from Anquetil's bike. Such things clearly did not bother Jacques, but Bahamontes had always been very fussy with his machines and very demanding of his mechanics. The Spanish champion had experienced a few lean years, but was now fully back on form and had improved his sprinting, his descending, and his time-trialling ability.

The two of them dropped everyone else in their own private battle. Federico was a nervous impulsive climber who climbed in fits and starts, bounding away, and then easing up a little. Jacques was the opposite – the same steady pace, but he was always able to pull the Spaniard back. On that stage to Chamonix, Bahamontes attacked fifteen times, but Anquetil always managed to get up to him and eventually beat him in the sprint to take the stage win.

At the finish in Paris there was not a lot in it: Anquetil beat Bahamontes by 3 mins 35 secs, with Perez-Frances third at ten minutes. Jacques had won both short time trials, but this time he had won the race in the mountains. In fact, he had won two mountainous stages to Bahamontes' one. There were loud cheers for Jacques and for Federico, two magnificent champions who had made the Tour interesting, and exciting. Poulidor could only finish eighth, so it was he who was whistled at the Parc des Princes. It was an unusual experience for Raymond, and he said how much it had hurt, and that then he understood what Jacques had had to put up with.

After the criteriums it was back to serious business as most of the top men rode the two-day Paris–Luxembourg as preparation for the World Championships. Altig won, with Poulidor third and Anquetil sixth.

And so to the World Championship: this was to be a race that nobody would quickly forget. There were no major hills to speak of, but, as usual, the distance and the aggressive riding made it a hard event. Jacques had judged things well and was, perhaps, stronger than even he realised. With just one kilometre to go he was in the lead, and clear; then he made the fatal mistake of turning round. He saw the big bunch chasing behind, so he sat up and allowed himself to be caught. The peloton drew level with him as they were just beginning to start the final sprint. The Belgian crowd went wild with delight as Van Looy looked to be sprinting towards his third world title when, just a few metres from the finish, his team mate Beheyt got his wheel in front to be first across the line. But this was not right! This was the wrong man! Van Looy was mad with rage, but had to bite his lip as the crowd screamed for the blood of the winner. In the changing rooms Van Looy roared with rage as Jacques tried to calm him down. They had always got on well together as they were never really direct rivals. 'But I paid him! I paid him!' Rik shouted – something he could certainly not say in public.

When the Belgian eventually calmed down he asked Jacques, 'Why on earth did you sit up in sight of the finish? We were all chasing flat-out and were making no impression on you at all. If you had not looked round you would have won the race with ease.' With victory in sight most riders would have ridden themselves into the ground, but Jacques had convinced himself that he just was not capable of winning a world title. Seeing the bunch behind him was his excuse to himself for not winning.

After what had turned out to be one of the most controversial World Championships in the history of the sport, André Darrigade had a different tale to tell. He said that as the sprint started Tom Simpson gave Van Looy a huge shove. This not only propelled the Belgian forward, but also brought the Englishman almost to a standstill and it was a miracle that nobody behind him crashed. Van Looy took Beheyt from the right-hand side of the road to the left, blocking Darrigade's path, thus forcing him to brake to avoid hitting them both. After the finish the excitable André was persuaded to see Anquetil, who said to him: 'Calm down, André, you cannot change anything. The Belgians bought off the Dutch team and even I have had a non-aggression pact with the Emperor since the Tour de France. In return for which, Poulidor will be prevented from winning anything!'

Stories and anecdotes about Jacques Anquetil are legion. Many have been recounted by Géminiani and many by the journalist Pierre Chany. Both were present at Géminiani's restaurant in

Clermont-Ferrand on the eve of a minor race known as the Ronde d'Auvergne. It was an evening full of good humour, good food and alcohol, so the reader might be excused for wondering if a degree of exaggeration has crept into the story. After the aperitifs, the dinner, the wine, the brandy, the coffee had all been consumed, Van Looy threw in the towel at midnight and went to bed as the race was to start at eight in the morning. Anquetil and Géminiani continued with whisky, champagne, fried eggs and goodness knows what else.

By now Jacques had become somewhat loquacious and decided to phone Marcel Bidot for a chat – at two in the morning. He said he had something to discuss with him about a forthcoming event and would he please drive over. Poor Bidot took him seriously and jumped in his car to drive the 300 miles to join him. Jacques finally went to bed some time after 4 a.m.

Now, the one thing that Anquetil hated most of all was getting out of bed, so after just a few hours sleep no amount of persuasion could get him up. Eventually, he was literally pulled out of bed by his feet. Still bleary eyed and grumbling, he punctured early in the race and said to Géminiani, 'That's it. I'm going back to the hotel.' Raphaël replied, 'No, don't be daft. Look at that blue sky. It's a wonderful chance to get rid of some of that poison from your body!' Jacques had to admit that he was right and, as the leading group was whittled down, he was still there with them. Within sight of the finish he jumped away to a splendid victory. The following day he won again at Quillans and Tom Simpson quizzed Géminiani: 'What have you done to Jacques? I've never seen him so strong in all my life.' He was indeed an incredible man.

The season ended for Jacques with the Baracchi Trophy, partnered by Poulidor. Raymond had just won both the Grand Prix des Nations and the Grand Prix of Lugano, but Jacques had started neither of them. Poulidor was looking forward to achieving a famous 'triple', and who better than Jacques as a partner? After the half-way point Anquetil pretended that he was going through a bad patch and left all the work to Raymond. At the finish it was announced that they were the winners, which did not seem to please Jacques very much. Later it was announced that they had been beaten into second place by Velly and Novales, by a mere nine seconds. As this was announced, a smile returned to Anquetil's face.

He had always felt it unfair that the press had played such a part in making Poulidor so much more popular than he was. The only way he could think of redressing the balance was to outshine Poulidor and, as was to be proved three years later in the world championships, it was much more important to him that Poulidor should lose than that he should win. He never admitted it to anyone, but by now it was quite clear that Jacques' jealousy of Raymond's popularity was reaching alarming proportions.

At the end of the season Anquetil was named winner of the Super Prestige Pernod – his second success in this season-long competition.

With just a few contracts on the winter tracks, Jacques and Janine flew off to the West Indies again for a holiday in the sun. While he was there he was saddened to hear that his former *soigneur*, Pons, had been killed in a road accident. A week later he was devastated when he learned that his father had died in a similar fashion. They flew back for the funeral at Quincampoix immediately. As they stepped off the plane in France, Jacques said to Janine, 'I know full well that I will not live to be as old as he was.' Ernest Anquetil had died at the age of fifty-seven.

Chapter Fourteen

There was every sign that this amazing champion would be even stronger for the coming season. Indeed, he was looking for a newer and bigger exploit as he hoped to achieve a new 'double', this time by winning the Tour of Italy and the Tour de France in the same year – something that only Coppi had ever been able to achieve. But there were also signs that his main rival, Raymond Poulidor, was reaching maturity and many people thought that 'Pou-Pou' would be around for many years to come, whereas Anquetil had made it plain that he would retire in 1968.

However, in an interview at the start of the season, Jacques maintained that he would be quite happy to win either the Giro or the Tour. If he had to choose just one, then he would prefer it to be the Italian Tour: he had been beaten in 1959 by an exceptional Charly Gaul, by the narrow margin of 28 seconds, and then felt robbed of victory in 1961. He said that he would work for Altig in the Tour if he proved to be the stronger, but thought this unlikely as he considered that both Stablinski and Geldermans were better stage-racers than the German. He would certainly go for victory in another major stage-race if the opportunity presented itself, but that was certainly not his main objective for the season. He considered that Bahamontes had ridden incredibly well in the previous year's Tour, especially at the age of 35. He went on to say that he would never be tempted to ride Bordeaux–Paris as most of the 600 kilometres are meaningless and he would certainly not want to ride all night at 30-odd kilometres per hour. He would prefer to win Paris–Roubaix, but there was so much chance attached to this race designed for acrobats.

The first main pointer to form of the year was again Paris–Nice and this time the race visited Corsica. Raymond beat Jacques by three minutes in the time trial, but it was up a mountain. The message was clear, however: Anquetil was still the master on the flat, even if Poulidor had closed the gap, but Poulidor was the better climber. The latter retired from the race whereas Jacques went on to finish sixth.

It was back up north to Belgium for the semi-classic Ghent–Wevelgem. Jacques was not too sure where the finish was so he asked a Belgium rider. 'About a couple of kilometres up the road,' came the reply. Jacques thought it might be an idea to attack and nobody was able to close the gap that he opened. It was a total surprise to everyone, and his most important single-day win so far, but it was almost as if he won by accident.

Many people thought that if a strong rider like Anquetil rode all the classics then, according to the law of averages, he must win something one day, and here was the proof. Even those who were opposed to him had to admit that he was certainly capable of winning virtually anything he chose, and were mystified when he did not. To add to the frustration of the French fans, France was going through a very lean period as far as the classics were concerned. Jacques was the one man able to carry off a few, and the fact that he failed to do so hardly added to his popularity.

Jacques started the three-stage National Criterium with a bang by winning the first stage. The following day the snow came down, and he and the whole of his team climbed into the broom wagon. He was very vulnerable to the cold – no doubt, with the modern thermal clothing he would have coped very much better. There was, of course, the added risk of crashing, leading to injuries which could curtail the season. The fact that he never had one really serious crash in his life must, in part, have been due to prudence as well as luck. So, it was a little ironic when he crashed in the Paris–Roubaix, and in the Circuit du Provençal.

As Jacques was preparing for the Tour of Italy, Poulidor was in the Iberian peninsula winning the Tour of Spain. He clinched victory in the final time trial and, at the end of three weeks of racing, had a mere 33 seconds in hand over the Spaniard, Otano. It was just what he needed to boost his morale to face Anquetil in the Tour, although many experts still claimed that he was too 'placid' to win the Tour de France. For his part, Jacques was determined to reply in kind and went to Italy very well prepared. Before the start somebody reminded him of what he had previously said: 'There is no point in me achieving the double, because they will expect even more of me the following year.' Anquetil smiled and did not deny it, but explained that his sponsors always wanted publicity and, if he started the Tour after having won the Giro, then he would be in a more relaxed frame of mind.

So, he started the Giro in determined mood and, on the fifth day, won the time trial at a staggering average speed of more than 48 k.p.h. to put on the leader's pink jersey. It was a very hard blow for the Italian riders, all of whom were determined to prevent him winning the race overall, but rather more enjoyable for Jacques' team mates, one of whom said, 'It's just wonderful. Jacques pulls something special out of the bag and it's we who win the money.'

Géminiani drove the team car behind Anquetil in this race against the watch and alongside him was the famous Pinella di Grande. He noted that Anquetil had much shorter thighs than Coppi, but pushed much bigger gears. Coppi never moved forward in the saddle in moments of intense effort, but Anquetil's back was parallel with the top tube. Jacques changed down before a bend so that his exit was quicker. The bottom line was that the two men belonged to two different schools of thought and two different eras: in Coppi's time, the time trials were longer and slower, and it was Bobet who was the first to use a 54-tooth chainring in such a race, in the 1951 Tour. Géminiani replied that if time trials were held over 120 kilometres, Anquetil would win by 15 minutes so that stage-racing would be pointless.

According to Pinella, Coppi always doubted himself. Géminiani replied that on the day before a time trial Anquetil, too, was haunted by the spectre of defeat, but always managed to hide his feelings.

The mechanic, Louis Debruyckere, joined in the conversation to say that Jacques never asked for anything special for a race against the watch. 'He left everything up to me,' he said. 'He told me not to change the cranks or the gears on the spare bike as it would mean too much work for me. He said that it was already a light bike with light tyres so that would do for him – but, of course, I did not listen to him.'

Anquetil's team discussed the wisdom of letting an Italian take over the race leadership in order to take the pressure off Jacques, but it was considered to be too risky. This was what Bobet had done previously, in 1957, and he had lost the race by a whisker. So Anquetil remained an easily recognisable target and the Italian attacks were incessant; the fans pushed their own men on the climbs, while Jacques was punched in the back and spat on.

Later in the race, on a long descent, covered in dust and gravel, Géminiani's car had a puncture in the rear wheel. They were going quite fast and the vehicle became increasingly difficult to control, but Raphaël was determined to follow Jacques in case he needed any sort of service. Sure enough, they caught up with Anquetil at the side of the road, holding a rear wheel in the air to indicate a puncture. After giving him another wheel, Géminiani then had to change his own as the tyre was nearly off the rim, but the ever-resourceful 'Gem' put Debruyckere on a spare bike to chase Jacques down the mountain.

On the stage from Montepulciano to Livorno, a long break nearly resulted in an unknown Italian, Renzo Fontona, taking the pink jersey. He would have done, but for the unanimous reaction of the peloton: the top Italians such as Zilioli, Adorni and Pambianco were not disgraced by being beaten by Anquetil, but being beaten Fortona was another matter! So, they all combined to bring him back. They need not have worried too much as on the stage from Cuneo to Pinerolo, although Jacques did not attack, most of them weakened, including Fortona who dropped to sixth place and out of the picture.

By the time the race reached the beautiful little town of Santa Margherita Ligure, where the riders had a rest day, the Italians had been forced to admit Anquetil's superiority and had all virtually thrown in the towel. The press and the fans, however, found that attitude totally unacceptable, and pinned their hopes on the new generation of riders such as Franco Bitossi. He had won four stages, including the one from Cuneo to Pinerolo after having been away for 130 kilometres. He had even beaten Coppi's 1949 time for the stage by nearly an hour. Many others thought that the 22-year-old Gianni Motta was showing even more promise.

After the finish in Milan, where Jacques emerged winner of the Giro, finally beating Zilioli by 1 min. 22 secs, he and his team were all nervous wrecks. In spite of their dominance most of them were so exhausted as to be on the point of cracking. There was, however, a lighter side to this ferocious battle. Jacques had become quite neurotic about Poulidor and his popularity. When he was looking through the result sheets, early in the race, he spotted the name of Polidori. 'That's close enough for me,' he thought, and ordered his team to allow him no freedom. Every time poor Polidori moved, he discovered one of Anquetil's team mates on his wheel. He put up with it for a full ten days before riding alongside Jacques and saying, 'Hey, what gives? You know I'm not going to beat you, so how about calling the hounds off?' The man in the pink jersey gave a big grin, apologised and said he would do as requested. Polidori moved up quite a few places on general classification after that.

Back in France the Dauphiné Libéré, the hard stage-race in the Alps and the traditional pointer to pre-Tour form, proved that both Bahamontes and Poulidor were in good condition while, once again, the Spanish were able to provide a never-ending supply of excellent climbers, the best of whom seemed to be Julio Jiménez. There was every sign that France could anticipate an excellent Tour, with Anquetil the obvious favourite. Géminiani said, 'Coppi won the Tour by a knockout, but Jacques is a defensive fighter and will win on points.' Others put it in a more cynical way when they said that in past years Anquetil had 'accepted' victory and that this year he would be 'condemned' to win. Poulidor was more than ever expected to be his main rival, but would need to attack Jacques incessantly – something that was hardly in his character. On the other hand, Raymond was more likely to be the fresher man as he had enjoyed a much easier time in the Tour of Spain than had Anquetil in Italy.

Géminiani had the job of reassuring Anquetil before the start of the Tour. He pointed out that Raymond had never beaten him against the watch, had never dropped him in the mountains and had always managed to have at least one bad day to ruin his chances. It was just what the man who was going for his fifth win wanted to hear. He was always reassured by Géminiani's logic, his wit and his enthusiasm. However, there was another worry gnawing away in his mind: an astrologer working for a Paris newspaper had predicted that Anquetil would not finish the Tour, indeed he would meet his death on the 14th stage. Hundreds of

Poulidor fans sent him cuttings of the article. He tried to forget it, but, as the fourteenth stage approached, he grew increasingly apprehensive and said to Géminiani, 'If you ever meet this bloody woman, punch her in the face for me.'

Very few people realised just how fragile and delicate Jacques' morale was; he needed a climate of security. Left to himself, he became sad and worried – he needed company. Darrigade's good humour and gaiety were like a drug to him while Janine maintained his morale. The Belgian, Hilaire Couvreur, as well as Jean Stablinski, helped to keep his spirits up during a race and when his *soigneur*, Robert Pons, was replaced by Julien Schramm he had yet another man who could lift his spirits. Finally, Géminiani was able to 'move the pendulum' just as he had done in previous years with Bobet: both men needed a morale stimulant.

A few weeks before the Tour started Jacques rode the Boucles de la Seine. First run in 1945, it had always been a hotly contested event. Based on Paris, it followed the twists and turns of the River Seine before finishing back in the French capital. It had since developed into a selection race for the French national and regional teams in the Tour, but, with trade teams, this no longer applied. Consequently, the contest was beginning to lose its much of its significance and the race was to disappear a few years later. Eyebrows were raised when Anquetil stopped at the feeding station, claiming that he needed to rest and relax after his hard campaign in Italy.

There were minor worries with Jacques' team, as well. Altig had not been in top form and was hoping to shine in a particularly hard event to prove to Jacques that he could be relied upon. The opportunity arose when he travelled with his team mate, Shay Elliott, to the professional race on the Isle of Man. The Irishman agreed to help him win the event which did something to restore his morale.

It was to prove to be a very 'tight' Tour, the closest that had ever been seen. Every second gained or lost was important. Poulidor lost fourteen seconds after a crash on the first stage to Lisieux. However, he surprised Jacques in one stage before the Alps, opening a gap that Anquetil was only able to reduce to 34 seconds by the finish. The next day Poulidor finished the stage in second place while Jacques punctured and lost another 47 seconds.

On the following stage, to Monaco, Anquetil was first across the line to take the time bonus of one minute. It was a little curious that, in a Tour which would later prove to be one of the most memorable of all time, the passage through the Alps was of little significance, apart from the fact that Bahamontes was allowed to win the most mountainous stage while Jacques controlled the rest of the riders.

Two days later the Norman won the time trial and, with the bonus, put 46 seconds into Raymond. Anquetil was now laying second overall, with 'Pou-Pou' next a further 31 seconds down. The two men had been within a minute and a half of each other for most of the event. Then the race stopped for a rest day at Andorra, the tiny independent state in the Pyrenees. There, the hosts laid on a *mechoui* – a sort of barbecue. Jacques fulfilled his obligations and was photographed with Géminiani, tucking into a large portion of grilled lamb. Anquetil refused to ride his bike, as was customary on a rest day, and, next day, was too nervous to warm-up before the start. When Géminiani took Jacques to the starting line on this fourteenth stage, he had the impression that he was leading a condemned man to his execution. His team leader was a very superstitious person and was fully expecting to meet his Maker as the astrologer had predicted.

The stage started with the Col d'Envalira, and immediately Bahamontes and Poulidor attacked. A gap of 500 metres opened up as Jacques began to suffer. It was unbelievable, impossible, unreal. Rostollan stayed with his leader whose face started to pour with sweat as his eyes glazed over. He was shouted at, encouraged and even pushed – for which he received a fifteen-second penalty. Jacques was on the point of giving up and had even released his toe-straps when Géminiani drew alongside him. 'Jacques!' he shouted. 'In the name of God, if you're going to die get to the front and die there. A man like Anquetil does not die in front of the broom wagon.' Jacques was seized with a fit of giggling.

He crossed the summit, cheered up by Géminiani's levity and was informed that he was four minutes down on Bahamontes and 3 mins 50 secs behind Poulidor. In the heavy mist he took a newspaper, stuffed it down his jersey, and embarked upon the descent. The visibility was down to just a few yards so Jacques was guided by the lights of the cars in front. Louis Rostollan said later: 'It was totally crazy the way he went down that mountain. I really never expected to see him alive again.'

About 50 riders had crossed over the Col d'Envalira before Anquetil and he had passed about 30 of them by the end of the descent. At the front, a group of fifteen men had formed with almost 140 kilometres still to go to the finish. This leading group contained the yellow jersey, Georges Groussard, and four of his team mates including the green jersey, Jan Janssen. Also present were Poulidor, Jiménez and Bahamontes. The whole group were determined to stop Anquetil rejoining.

Jacques, for his part, found himself with a group of seven – none of them were team mates, although they were all chasing as hard as they could. At the head of the race Poulidor and his Mercier colleague, Poulot, were doing long, hard turns in order to keep the pace as high as possible. So, too, were the five men of the Pelforth team who had their two jerseys to protect. The team managers had their eyes glued to their watches as the time checks came through: 1 min. 20 secs, then 1 min. 40 secs. Then it was 60 seconds; 55 seconds two kilometres later; another twelve kilometres and back to 1 min. 5 secs. They flew through the town of Foix and then, fifteen kilometres later, the junction was made. Anquetil breathed a sigh of relief as all 22 men came together.

The pace dropped a little as the riders continued on their way to Toulouse. With 28 kilometres still to go, Antonin Magne drew alongside Poulidor and said, 'One of your wheels is buckled; you'll have to change bikes.' The operation was done swiftly and smoothly, but the Mercier mechanic was a rather strong man and a little too enthusiastic. He pushed Raymond so hard that he fell off into the ditch. Poulidor's team mate, Poulot, waited for him, but he was of little help as he was 'cooked' after his previous efforts. Maurice de Muer, the *Directeur Sportif,* of the Pelforth team urged his men to greater efforts. They had previously tried to distance Anquetil, but had been unable to do so. Now was their chance to get rid of Poulidor, another dangerous rival. Anquetil, however, was not the sort of man ever to take advantage from the misfortune of a rival and never once shared in the work.

The twenty men were only 200 metres ahead when Poulidor finally got going, but his heart was slowly filled with despair as gradually they disappeared from sight: by the finish of the stage he had lost 2 mins 37 secs. The day that had started so well for Poulidor, and so badly for Anquetil, had seen a complete reversal in the fortunes of both of them. It was a highly dramatic stage and the journalists had a field-day. It was claimed that Jacques' *defaillance* was due to the *mechoui* and they all insisted that at the top of the climb the Tour was definitely lost for him. None of them pointed out that when a climb is situated at the start of a stage, it rarely has a decisive influence on the result at the finish. At the finish in Toulouse, the first two across the line were the Belgian sprinters, Ward Sels and Gilbert Desmet.

Antonin Magne had a long talk with Raymond to restore his morale and to decide what needed to be done. In a magnificent gesture of defiance, Poulidor went away on the Col de Portillon the next day for a wonderful stage win. At the end of the thirteenth stage Poulidor had been 21 seconds down on Anquetil; after the fourteenth stage the gap had grown to 3 mins 2 secs, and now, at Luchon, it had fallen to a mere eleven seconds.

The following day the 36-year-old Bahamontes stayed away all day, over four major mountain passes, and overtook them both on general classification to come within 35 seconds of the yellow jersey, still worn by Groussard. It was continuing to be an exciting Tour with action every day, but there was more to come.

The 42-kilometre time trial was duly won by Anquetil from Poulidor, but only by 37 seconds. As in the previous year, the time bonus in a time trial remained minimal, so that although Anquetil was now in the yellow jersey, his lead over Raymond was a mere 56 seconds, with Bahamontes third at 3 mins 31 secs. The tension eased a little as the next two stages ended in bunch sprints. Then came the leg to Clermont-Ferrand, with its finish on top of the Puy de Dôme.

The French had been glued to their television screens as live pictures had been transmitted to them. On the road to Clermont-Ferrand they watched Poulidor go clear, with a small group containing Georges Groussard, the former yellow jersey. Anquetil was obliged to chase very hard, with Altig, and was able to catch them just before the start of the final climb. As the gradient increased the weaker riders disappeared and a group of five was formed when the climb started in earnest. There was the Spanish climber, Jiménez, Bahamontes anxious to take advantage of this last climb to pull back some time, Anquetil and Poulidor closely watching each other, and, finally, the Italian, Adorni.

Adorni was the first to crack as the lightly-built Jiménez danced away into the lead, with Bahamontes after him. Anquetil and Poulidor climbed steadily, each at the limit of his capabilities. Jacques was determined to prove that he was the master of the situation, and a combination of pride and will-power helped him to keep his bike half a wheel in front. Most of France was now watching this exciting battle which was to last for nearly an hour. Anquetil's style was as beautiful and as well balanced as ever, but he was suffering badly, though if anyone knew how to hide it, he did.

This was his arch-enemy he was up against – the man who, unjustly in his eyes, was the more popular rider. Jacques surpassed himself as never before; he suffered more than he had ever done in his life, but he would not yield; he would not. Poulidor got his wheel in front, then took half a length on him. Anquetil fought back and gave it everything he had. The cameras zoomed into Jacques' face: it was a mask of agony. But still the pedals were going round so smoothly. His style was perfection, as always.

Then, suddenly, he conceded a length; two lengths; five lengths. This was unbelievable! Anquetil giving ground to Poulidor! Raymond tried to accelerate but he was already at his limit – 20 metres, 50 metres, 100 metres. Jacques was definitely gone and Poulidor was winning the Tour de France!

Few were really interested as Jiménez won the stage, ten seconds in front of Bahamontes. Few were interested as Adorni caught and passed Anquetil. Only the clock was important. As Raymond crossed the line everyone counted the seconds. It seemed like an eternity, but, in fact, it was only 42 seconds before a semi-conscious Anquetil arrived.

He hardly noticed the insults and whistles directed at him from some of the crowd as he slumped across the bonnet of a car. He had just one question for Géminiani: 'How much?'

'Fourteen seconds,' came the reply.

'Well, that's thirteen more than I need.'

That evening the debate raged in France. Poulidorists said, 'Raymond has pushed Anquetil to the limit; he's never been so tired before. He will certainly beat him on Sunday afternoon in the time trial to Paris. Fourteen seconds? No problem!' 'No,' said the Anquetilists. 'He's never beaten Jacques against the watch. The yellow jersey will finish in grand style by winning the final stage, and Poulidor will probably fall off!'

The next day the newspapers fanned the flames as their sales went through the roof. The fact that Jean Stablinski won the stage to Orleans was of little importance apart from the fact that, as his right-hand man, it was seen as a good omen for Jacques.

If any Frenchmen had made previous plans for that Sunday, they cancelled them. Those not privileged to be on the route were in front of a TV set, either at home or in a bar. The morning stage to Versailles was won by the Belgian World Champion, Beheyt.

A short break for lunch, and then down to the real business. What a Tour! 'Pou-Pou' at fourteen seconds and Federico Bahamontes at 1 min. 33 secs. There had never been a Tour as tight as this before. The *lanterne rouge* was Anquetil's team mate, Anatole Novak, and as he launched himself into the final 27 kilometres to Paris a huge roar went up. In just a couple of hours the 1964 Tour de France would be won and lost. But by whom?

Eventually Poulidor started, to be followed, a minute later, by Anquetil. There were no shortage of time checks and they showed that although Jacques was in the lead, 'Pou-Pou' was closing the gap, and closing it and closing it! Just five kilometres to go and Raymond was three seconds down. Three seconds! If he beat Jacques by one second he would get the time bonus and win the race! But Jacques was calm, so calm and well informed. It was now or never – just one final supreme effort, and he would go down in history as the first man to win five Tours de France.

There was a huge roar of approval as Poulidor caught his minute man, Bahamontes, on the Parc des Princes track. Just a few more seconds and Anquetil would arrive. When he did it was jubilation for the Anquetilists and groans from the Poulidorists. The gap was 21 seconds and Jacques had won.

When the two men rode a lap of honour together with their arms round each other's shoulders there was nothing but heart-felt applause. If Raymond looked just a little rueful, Anquetil looked radiant, as well he might. He was later to say that this time trial was one of the best exploits of his career, and one of his best memories.

One metre from the line – the fantastic finale to the
1964 Tour de France

It was an emotional climax to a wonderful afternoon and a fabulous Tour. None of those present at the Parc des Princes would ever forget it. As the two Frenchmen climbed on the podium Anquetil gave a little grin and murmured in Poulidor's ear, 'You really made me sweat this time, Raymond.' From Jacques this was quite a compliment!

Next year's Tour must surely be for Poulidor. France went bike crazy as the sales of cycles shot up. The French cycling federation was bombarded with requests for racing licences as large numbers of young men felt inspired enough to take up competition.

In the middle of August, Géminiani caused a big stir when he announced that St Rapha would not be sponsoring a team the following year. Anquetil's initial reaction was to look for a place on an Italian team, but Géminiani had other ideas. Along with Roger Rivière, he had done some car rallying for Ford France, so his contacts with the company were already well established. When he spoke to Monsieur Chemin, one of the main directors of the company, about the possibility of sponsoring a cycling team the latter was immediately interested. Things moved rapidly and Géminiani informed the press that the new contract would be signed in the middle of September and Ford had made no demands as to which races Anquetil should ride, although they made it plain that they would prefer him to ride the Tour. Most of the St Rapha team would be retained with the exception of Rudi Altig who was finding it increasingly difficult to fit in with Jacques' plans. He considered himself to be a star in his own right and found Jacques' selfishness in a stage-race somewhat hard to bear. Moreover, he had come in for his own share of criticism, particularly for not helping Anquetil on the Col d'Envelira.

The national championships were run in the third week of August in Brittany. Two days before the event Jacques made his customary excuses. This time, he said he was off form because he had eaten too much seafood; he would, therefore, be helping his friend, Stablinski, to win his third consecutive French title. Few people were really fooled as to his true intentions, which were to stop Poulidor winning. The plan worked to perfection: Jean put on the red, white and blue jersey for the third time in three years, after Anquetil had spent the race neutralising Raymond Poulidor's attacks.

The last main race before the World Championships was again the two-stage Paris–Luxembourg. On the second stage a group of fifteen escaped, and quickly gained two and a half minutes. The gap grew considerably when the main bunch was stopped at a level-crossing. Both Anquetil and Poulidor were worried that they were being made to look ridiculous, so they joined forces to bring the escapees back. Quite clearly, on this occasion, personal pride was stronger than personal rivalry.

In the World Championships, at Sallanches, Henry Anglade was away for most of the race along with three others. Finally, he was accompanied only by Taccone of Italy before Tom Simpson got up to him. As the main bunch closed in on them, Taccone weakened to be replaced by Adorni. The front group swelled when first Poulidor and then the Dutchman, Jan Janssen, joined them. These two attacked on the final hill and it was goodbye to the hero of the day, Anglade. As expected, the bespectacled Dutchman was the fastest in the sprint with Adorni second, Poulidor third and Simpson fourth. In the meantime the main bunch had closed to within six seconds and Anquetil finished in seventh spot.

It had been a good day for the French, but they only had a bronze medal to show for their efforts. However, it had been an unfortunate day for the Belgians as their best man, Beheyt – the previous world champion – could finish only eleventh. For Van Looy it was a catastrophe.

Without the presence of Anquetil the Grand Prix des Nations was a very uninspiring race won by a little-known Belgian, Walter Boucquet. The only real star in the race, Ferdinand Bracke, also from the other side of the Belgian border, lost any hope of final victory when he crashed and then punctured.

Bike fans were more inspired by another event run against the watch on the same weekend. The Grand Prix Parisien Libéré was contested by teams of six riders and, as Anquetil disliked such events, his St Rapha team had an opportunity to show what they could do without him. The race was held over 131 kilometres on a course between Beauvais and Compiègne to the north of Paris. The St Raphas totally dominated the event, catching the Belgian Groene Leeuw team for five minutes and the Mercier team for ten. However, few riders were really happy: it had been a long, hard season and Anquetil was not the only one who complained of being tired. Many of the top riders had raced the previous day in Brussels and had been obliged to travel overnight.

The race did establish, beyond any doubt, that there was considerable talent in Anquetil's team, but they had never really been permitted to demonstrate it. Altig was particularly critical when he said that Jacques' selfishness was quite frightening. He had hoped to do something in the Tour when the race passed through Germany, but Anquetil would not hear of it. Nevertheless, Rudi insisted that, in private life, Jacques was the most charming person possible and the two men remained close friends until Jacques' dying day. The other members of the team protested from time to time, but none of them could deny that they were all making a good living.

Generally speaking, the latter part of the season was run off in a dream. The criteriums attracted record numbers of spectators, and Jacques and Raymond were acclaimed wherever they went, but Anquetil rode none of the late-season time trials, not even the Baracchi Trophy.

With the spotlight off Jacques, the headlines were grabbed by Gianni Motta who won both the Tour of Lombardy and the Baracchi Trophy. In the latter event Poulidor was teamed with Anglade, but they could only manage seventh place. Van Looy was unhappy about being pipped on the line in Paris–Tours by his young countryman, Guido Reybroeck. It was hoped that Anquetil would shine, as he usually did, in the Criterium des As behind the Dernys, but it was not to be: Peter Post dominated the whole field and broke all records.

It had, none the less, been a terrific season for Jacques. It also marked a turning point in the history of the sport. Due to excellent TV coverage, road racing was no longer a sport where the spectators caught only the briefest of glimpses as the riders flashed by.* Now, with the aid of mobile cameras, people could follow the action, as it happened, from their armchairs and they could almost feel part of the race itself. Just as there had always been a marriage between the press and bike racing – they had both

---

* Ironically, since the BBC's television coverage of cycling has always been minimal, Anquetil was named Sportsview's International Sportsman of the year.

needed each other – it was now becoming evident that TV was to play an even more important role in the promotion of racing. Inevitably, modern technology was later to have a profound effect on the way the races were to be run. To keep the interest of the viewer, the issue had to be in doubt until the very last moment because, quite simply, television loved close finishes.

The year that had been so exceptional was finally to finish on a sad note when the Swiss, Hugo Koblet, one of Jacques' boyhood heroes, was killed in a car crash. Only much later was it fully established that it was suicide.

Tour de France: a moment during the critical stage from Brive to the Puy de Dôme. Anquetil leads from George Groussard, green jersey Jan Janssen, and Eddy Pauwels

Chapter Fifteen

Before the start of the 1965 season Anquetil gave an interview in which he spoke about his private life. He had sold his small hotel in Rouen in 1963 and bought a farm the following year, although as he refused to say exactly where it was there remained some element of doubt about that – running such an enterprise was time consuming, and Jacques had certainly had a busy enough season as it was. Asked about a motor manufacturer sponsoring a cycling team, he did not think it at all strange: he himself was a car enthusiast with a passion for driving, and said that one of his greatest exploits had been in 1963 when he had left Forli in Italy at five in the evening and arrived home in Normandy the next morning. Of the 1,400 kilometres, he had driven 900 and Janine had driven 500. The following day he had ridden the national championships at Rouen.

Once again, he said that he would not be riding the Tour de France and was evasive when questioned about the Bordeaux–Paris. Jacques had had two very successful seasons – two Tours de France, a Tour of Spain and a Tour of Italy. He had regained some of his popularity, but, in general, the public still preferred Poulidor. In the country they were usually behind Raymond, while in the cities and in Belgium, Holland, and Italy it was Anquetil who was the favourite. Jacques expressed his disappointment about this to Géminiani who replied in his expansive way: 'They're not happy? OK, so we'll give them more. If that's not enough we'll give them still more, and we won't stop until they are satisfied.'

If the Tour and the Giro were not enough then, obviously, it would have to be something quite sensational. Géminiani understood Anquetil well enough to realise the futility of saying, 'You should do this' or 'You should do that'. If Jacques said no, then that was the end of the affair. But Raphaël knew how to plant a seed in Anquetil's mind, how to water it and how to keep it growing. 'You know Jacques,' he said to him, 'a man who could pull off a feat – something like winning the Dauphiné and then going straight on to win the Bordeaux–Paris the next day – could count on being popular for the next twenty years.'

Anquetil said nothing – he was quite aware of just how subtle 'Gem' could be; he was never at any time taken in, and he was amused by his scheming – but Géminiani continued to return to the subject from time to time.

One day Jacques said to Janine: 'This crazy idea of Gem's. You don't think I could do it, do you?' Janine replied, 'It's not so crazy as you think. Nobody else could, that's for sure. But I know you could.' That was enough to encourage him. 'Oh yes? Well, if you really think so, then OK.'

The next time Géminiani brought the subject up Jacques wearily said 'OK. OK. Make sure of all the arrangements. Make sure that we can get from one side of France to the other in a few hours, and we'll do it.'

An approach had to be made to Ford and when the project was properly explained to them, they were all for it. If such a feat were to be realised it would bring even more publicity. The Ford directors entered into the spirit of the thing and suggested that Jacques drove his Ford Mustang from the finish of the first race to the start of the second. 'Gem' rolled his eyes in horror and promised to do a feasibility study, the outcome of which must already have been obvious to most. Seven hours to do 400 miles through the mountains did not really bear thinking about.

Another project was much more realistic and Jacques, with Géminiani as co-driver, started the Monte Carlo rally in January. There was no shortage of journalists and photographers to record the event, but the Ford Mustang, with its long wheelbase and excessive wheelspin, was hardly the ideal car for the snow in the mountains. They lasted three days before they were 'beaten by bad weather'.

Away from racing Jacques was charming and relaxed. Anyone who visited his house said that it was a marvellous experience. One such person was the journalist, René de Latour, who paid a visit to his house by the river. Jacques was smoking a pipe and said, 'I like the smell of tobacco, but I don't inhale.' The charm was turned on and the drinks came out.

'No,' said Jacques, 'I won't be riding the 1965 Tour de Poulidor.'

'What do you mean?' asked the journalist.

'What I mean,' came the reply, 'is that the Tour de France is designed for Raymond and against me. It will not be a straight fight and I will be at a disadvantage. They have reduced the amount of time trials.'

'Yes,' said Janine, 'he's not bluffing. He does think the Tour is made for Poulidor and against him, and when he gets an idea in his head …'

It was interesting that Janine always backed up every word he said, as if he needed constant reassurance.

Anquetil went on to add that his main dream was to become World Champion and that he would definitely retire in 1968. He also talked of the farm that he had bought – it was not very far away but, again, he would not say exactly where. The methodical Jacques was planning for the future, but made no mention of the Bordeaux–Paris.

The journalist could not wait to get to Poulidor's house to get his reaction. Raymond gave a huge grin and said, 'Bloody Jacques. He always says something controversial about the Tour, but it's usually a couple of weeks beforehand. This year he's a bit early. He forgets that the progress I've made in time trials has brought me up to his level. All I want is for him to be there.'

The total distance of the time trials was exactly what it had been the previous year and as it had been in 1964. Although time bonuses for time-trial wins had been reduced, there was certainly no evidence to support Anquetil's view that the cards had been stacked against him. But Janine's claim that he had convinced himself that they were may well have been true.

Nevertheless, Jacques left an element of doubt in the minds of the journalists about the Tour de France. After all, the Tour de France without Jacques was a little like Hamlet without the Prince. They all knew that he liked to play verbal games and keep people guessing. At 31 he was stronger than ever and, for the moment, he was determined to take one race at a time. He kicked off the season with a masterful win in the Paris–Nice, in front of Altig, Zilioli and Poulidor, sealing victory mainly in the time-trial stage.

Altig, too, shone in this 'Race to the Sun'. No longer a member of Anquetil's team, he was now the leader of the French Margnat–Paloma squad. He finished only 33 seconds down in the time trial, and managed to win three stages to finish in second spot overall.

From there Jacques went on to win the Mont Faron hill climb for the first time in his life. Then it was the National Criterium and now people were really seeing a new mature Anquetil. Always at the front, always dominating, he stamped his authority on the race, leaving no hope for anyone. He won it by 41 seconds from Poulidor, but again he owed his overall victory to the time trial as Raymond won the hilly stage. It was beginning to appear as if he was operating on a higher plane, even more inaccessible to the public, a sort of inhuman dominator. But many were beginning to see in his coldness a certain sadness.

He rode all the usual spring classics. In the Tour of Flanders he retired in the heavy rain. The event was notable for the fact that the top ten finishers agreed to submit to a drug control and none of them were found positive. He finished well down in Paris–Roubaix which was won by an emotional Van Looy. Perhaps Anquetil saw these races mainly as a way of coming to form as it appeared that Jacques felt that he had no duty to shine in these races since they were unpaid.

At the beginning of May Poulidor again crossed the Pyrenees to ride the Tour of Spain. Once again he put on the leader's jersey that Van Looy had been wearing for several days as a result of winning the time trial. A few days later he lost his lead to his Mercier team mate, Wolfshol, who had gained a lot of time in a long break. Obviously Poulidor was not allowed to attack his German colleague who was now leading the race by nearly seven minutes.

This Tour of Spain became a most memorable race. Poulidor's victory in the final time trial was not enough to regain the leadership as he could only beat Wolfshol by 33 seconds, but the real battle of the day was between the German and Van Looy. The Belgian was clearly a danger-man after the time bonuses he had accumulated as a result of winning no less than eight stages. Wolfshol caught Van Looy in the time trial, but could not drop him. The battle raged for 40 kilometres, and it was a magnificent finale to a wonderful Tour.

Wolfshol said, afterwards, that he would devote himself to helping Poulidor in the Tour de France. Van Looy was clearly still a force to be reckoned with as he had a Paris–Roubaix victory to add to his eight stage wins. Less fortunate was Rudi Altig, who was put out of action after breaking his femur.

But the end of May was approaching – the supreme test – and Jacques was making the final preparations for what was to be the greatest challenge of his life. The seven-day Dauphiné Libéré should not be too difficult, providing the weather was not too bad, but the hardest bit would be the Bordeaux–Paris to follow.

Jacques had never ridden this 'Derby of the Road' before and, much more importantly, neither had Géminiani. Raphaël got a lot of advice from Raymond Louviot who had been associated with the event for twenty years, as rider and as manager. It was indeed a very special race, so special that Jacques and 'Gem' were to receive quite a shock.

When Jacques went down to Macon for the start of the Dauphiné Libéré, his two team mates for the 'Derby', Jean Stablinski and the Englishman, Vin Denson, went down to Bordeaux to get in a week's training. Anquetil was hoping for an easy race – although Poulidor must be beaten, whatever it took. The journalists claimed that Raymond had made so much progress that he could now be considered to be on an equal footing with Anquetil. This made Jacques see red. He had won eight major stage-races and what had Poulidor won? For his part, Poulidor was praying that Jacques would not achieve this incredible double and was determined to stop him from winning this Alpine stage-race.

The race was a battle royal between the two rivals. On the leg from Roanne to St Etienne Anquetil was second, three seconds behind the Belgian, Desmet, but Poulidor was third. When Jacques went away over the mountains on the stage to Oyonnax, Poulidor went with him. Jacques won the sprint to take the stage, the time bonus and the leader's jersey, with Poulidor just a handful of seconds behind. The event was cursed with bad weather, which caused Jacques to suffer considerably, but it did not prevent him from attacking two days later. After four major climbs, Anquetil crossed the line first again to take another time bonus, but Poulidor finished alongside him.

On the road to Grenoble it was freezing cold and Jacques was suffering so much that he was dropped on a major climb. In a do-or-die effort he rejoined on the descent to save his jersey. The 38-kilometre time trial on the penultimate day again saw Anquetil victorious but only by thirteen seconds from Poulidor. It looked as if the journalist's assessment of the quality of the two riders was not far short of the mark. When Anquetil finished the race in triumph, in Avignon, he had a lead of 1 min. 43 secs on Poulidor. The difference had been accumulated by time bonuses and in the time trial: Raymond had given Jacques no presents at all.

After the arrival in Avignon there was no respite for Anquetil as he embarked on the second race of the day: seventeen minutes to receive his bouquet, his prizes and to salute the public; back to the hotel where he had just 35 minutes for a bath and a meal; into the car again, and a police escort enabled them to drive at high speed to the airport at Nîmes where, on the tarmac, an executive jet was waiting for them. It was, in fact, a government aircraft that had been especially laid on by the President of the Republic, General de Gaulle, one of Anquetil's greatest fans.

The flight took 40 minutes. Then it was by car to the hotel to meet Stablinski and Denson. He took a meal with them, choosing kidneys in red wine from the menu. Denson went white at the very idea, but Stablinski grinned – he knew Jacques too well. Anquetil did try to sleep, but was totally unable to. Press reports claimed that he slept for an hour and a half, but this was totally untrue. Any sort of sleep would have been most beneficial, but he was far too excited, even if he remained outwardly calm. He would soon be paying a heavy price for the energy that he had dispensed during the day.

The start was given at one in the morning: it was cold and damp, and everyone was well wrapped up. The pacing motors were to be picked up at Châtellerault and there was an unwritten agreement that nobody attacked before then. As the small group of riders rode gently along, with only the lights of the following cars to show them the way, Anquetil's eyes became heavy. He was beginning to realise what he had let himself in for.

He felt most uncomfortable in the cold and the wet so, after putting up with it for a while, he said to Stablinski, 'I'm not going on. This is ridiculous.' Jean replied, 'I've ridden the race several times and the way you feel is perfectly normal, but it won't last for long.'

Géminiani drove alongside and Jacques grumbled: 'You and your bloody daft ideas. I'll never listen to you again.' Raphaël gave him words of sympathy while trying to keep a straight face.

Vin Denson put an arm round his leader's shoulder and asked how he was. The reply was that he felt just awful, that he was not going on, he was going to retire and that was it! The Englishman was rather alarmed at this: it would be a very good pay-day for him if the exploit succeeded.

'Look, Jacques,' he said, 'Jean and I have been in Bordeaux all week training for this. We both feel tired as well, but we know it'll pass. It'll be the same for you.' But Jacques was only half-listening. He felt one overwhelming desire – to close his eyes, just for a little while. If only he could stop for five minutes, just five minutes, he knew that he would be alright after that. Just five little minutes. 'No!' said Géminiani. 'We'll all be stopping soon for a change of clothes, a quick wash and then we'll pick up the motors.'

The dawn came up, cold and grey as the chilling light rain continued to fall. The race came to a halt – bikes were to be changed as well as clothes. Anquetil was dead on his feet and flopped into Géminiani's car. 'That's it,' he said. 'Finished. No more', and through the window he said to the mechanic 'Don't take my bike off the car; I'm packing right here.' When Anquetil had made up his mind about something, nothing would change it.

Jacques did not get the reaction he expected from Géminiani and heard only gentle words: 'OK, kid. I quite understand. I only ask one thing of you: shake my hand, for it will be for the last time. I just cannot stand a pansy.'

'WHAT!' screamed Jacques. 'Me? A pansy? Here, give me that bloody bike. I'll show you if I'm a pansy!' In a blind rage he was back on his machine and out of the saddle sprinting to pick up his Derny. But Géminiani was even quicker: he told the pacer, Jo Goutourbe, that he was about to pace a volcano ready to explode.

As his anger dissipated, the pain and the suffering returned. He knew that he had been conned by his team manager, but decided to keep going for as long as he could before he retired. The big town of Tours was not far away; he should at least be able to make it as far as there. Meanwhile, Denson had gone after an early attacker while Stablinski stayed faithfully by Jacques' side. The Breton François Mahé had gone clear and established a lead of more than six minutes, but this was nothing at this stage of the race.

The sun came fully up, the Derny motor bikes continued their eternal droning and Jacques continued to suffer. A lot of the time was taken up with eating – small amounts at a time until the final kilometres of the race when only liquids were consumed.

Tours was reached and the race crossed the River Loire. There was no end to Jacques' suffering and as Géminiani finally began to comprehend exactly what he had let his man in for, he was overcome with anguish, and remorse. Through Orleans they went, and along the long, straight tree-lined roads. As the sun was coming from the right, the trees shut off the sunshine for a split second. This was repeated thousands and thousands of times, and it was torture to Jacques' red eyes.

Across the wind-swept plains of Beauce the agony continued, and the famous cathedral of Chartres appeared in the distance. Jacques, however, was in a world of his own and saw nothing but the back wheel of his *velomoteur*. He continued to suffer; he had never endured anything like this in his life before. Yet he was still there as other riders started to retire. Mahé was gradually brought back, so the main danger-man was now Tom Simpson who still looked surprisingly fresh and perky. Tom had won the event two years previously and was determined to win today.

Anquetil started to feel a little better, but was dreading the hills of the Chevreuse valley which he knew so well. If he could survive them, surely he must get to Paris; he started to come round more and began to believe in his chances. He started to feel even stronger, and suddenly things were becoming very easy. He felt as if he was on a training ride, he was riding with virtually no effort. The crowds on the hills were enormous, and all cheering for him and, yet, when he tried his heart out all he got from them was whistles. It was all so unreal: was it a dream? Simpson kept attacking but it was easy enough to pull him back and Jacques had the impression that the Englishman was beginning to weaken. Now Jacques was starting to 'float' along. He really could not feel the pedals.

Bordeaux–Paris: Jean Stablinski, Jacques Anquetil and Tom Simpson

By now there was no possible question of him not winning, but where should he attack? On the last hill, of course, where else? It was about time Simpson was put in his place and shown who the real boss was. It was about time to show everyone else, for that matter. Jacques went hard on the Côte de Picardie, less than ten miles from the Parc des Princes track. Simpson could not respond and Stablinski stayed with Tom to keep an eye on him.

When Jacques emerged from the tunnel on to the pink cement of the Parc des Princes track he was shaken by the noise from the crowd. They all seemed to be hysterical. Anquetil had always craved for his talent to be acknowledged. Here at last, after all these years, he was finally being given the sort of reception he deserved.

He completed his lap of the track and was then immediately enveloped by a mob of journalists. As he put his foot to the ground, tiredness overwhelmed him. He absolutely hated being crowded, but he was too happy and too tired to resist. Just under a minute later, Stablinski beat Simpson in the sprint for second place.

Vin Denson arrived in the middle of all the hubbub. His pacer was a certain Monsieur Champion who was returning to his home town of Paris where he was a policeman. Vin had told him to ease up as he wanted to take the special prize for the fastest lap of the track. Denson was inspired by his captain's win and duly won the prime. It was a total triumph for the Ford France team, but the Englishman was especially pleased. As was his custom, Anquetil gave his prize money to his team mates, with the lion's share going to Denson. On top of the prime he won, he also received a bonus from his sponsor. It was his biggest pay-day ever.

Jacques was not really an emotional man, he was ashamed of showing his feeling. Never in his life did he raise his arm in a victory salute – it was his pacer who raised his arm in triumph. So, only Janine fully realised how touched Jacques had been by his reception from the Parisians. These had been amongst the very hardest moments in her life, too. She had been beside herself with worry learning how much her husband was suffering during the race. After this incredible day, as the car drove away from the Parc des Princes, Jacques could not hold back his tears. But, he was a professional racing cyclist – this was his living – and the next day he was riding a race in eastern France.

It remained the high point of his career and, also, one of the high points of cycling itself. No more would Jacques have to endure the humiliating whistles at the start of an event. Jacques was a superman and Jacques had proved it. He won criteriums everywhere. He flew to the Isle of Man and won the Manx Premier race. He rode an evening criterium at Caen, then won the Forli time trial the following afternoon. Baldini had retired and was now the *Directeur Sportif* for the Molteni–Ignis team. So it was the young Italian hopeful, Gimondi, who finished in second place.

As the end of June approached, everyone's thoughts were, once more, centred on the Tour de France and this time it was obvious that Anquetil would not be taking part. So, most people thought that it would be child's play for Poulidor. Some of the experts were more careful, however. Without Jacques' iron grip on the race it would be a different event.

At the end of the third stage it was Gimondi, the winner of the previous year's amateur Tour de l'Avenir, who put on the yellow jersey. Poulidor won the time trial in Britanny; Gimondi lost the overall lead and then regained it again. After the Pyrenees Poulidor was now in second place at three minutes, and on the stage which finished on top of the Mont Ventoux, Raymond closed to within 39 seconds of the young Italian leader. With two time trials to come, France started to prepare to celebrate Poulidor's first win in the *Grand Boucle*. The first was up the Mont Revard and the second was on the final stage to Paris, but, to everyone's surprise, Gimondi won them both, and finally ran out the overall winner by 2 mins 40 secs. Poulidor made no complaints or excuses – quite clearly the Italian had been the stronger – and he was later to say: 'the Tour was never the same without Jacques.'

At the end of August, Anglade won his second French championship in magnificent style. Again the winner of this prestigious event was chased home by Anquetil and Poulidor – this time Raymond taking the silver medal and Jacques the bronze.

The World Championships were held at San Sebastián in Spain. Anquetil had made it quite clear to Marcel Bidot, the French team selector that the team should contain just the one leader. Although he did not actually put it into words, he was the uncontested number-one Frenchman so the team should have been built around him and Poulidor should not have been selected. Obviously, this would have been unacceptable to Raymond's fans, and, with his two second places and two fifth places in the past four appearances, his record was far better than Jacques'. So Bidot was forced to manage a somewhat disunited team.

From the very start a group of seven minor riders, including three Spaniards, attacked. With less than 40 kilometres gone, the German, Altig, and the Englishman, Simpson, set off in their pursuit. When they joined the leaders it was to be the winning break. Stablinski and the Irishman Elliott tried hard to join them, but were delayed by mechanical problems – the neutral Spanish service vehicles were not really up to standard so both riders were unsuccessful – and Jan Janssen and Henri Anglade both made an effort, but neither were on form.

Anquetil and Poulidor remained in the shelter of the bunch, watching each other, and falling further and further behind. Eventually, for the first and only time in their careers both men abandoned a World Championship. As the finish approached, Simpson and Altig had shed all their companions, and, as Altig was by far the best sprinter, most people were expecting a German victory.

How quickly the fans had forgotten that only three months previously Rudi had been in hospital with a broken hip. With the aid of crutches he had taken his first step on the day the Tour de France had started. He had ridden just the Tour of Luxembourg as preparation for the title race, so it was little short of a miracle that he was still in at the kill of this championship which had lasted for 267 kilometres. It was certainly no disgrace when he was outsprinted by Simpson for the title.

The rest of the top riders hardly covered themselves in glory. Most of them retired. Stablinski was the only Frenchman who had made any real sort of effort and was the only French finisher, in tenth place at nearly six minutes. Only sixteen riders completed the course.

The journalists dipped their pens in vitriol. They claimed that this must be the end of the national teams formula. Not only had Anquetil and Poulidor disgraced their country, but there had been difficulties with the Belgian, the Dutch and the German teams as well: Van Looy had eight Belgians working for him, but he could not even finish the race; Jan Janssen knew that De Roo would be riding against him; and the third top Dutchman, Den Hertog, had openly admitted that he was only there to help his trade-team captain, Anquetil. It was no secret that the German, Wolfshol, would be riding for Poulidor and the third top German, Junkerman, openly declared his sympathy for Van Looy!

Anquetil made amends, to some extent, by winning the Criterium des As run off behind Dernys in Paris. Then, after virtually a four-year lay-off, he returned to time-trialling. First it was victory in the Grand Prix des Nations, beating Altig by 3 mins 9 secs and Poulidor by 4 mins 58 secs, then the Grand Prix of Lugano, where he beat Gianni Motta into second place.*

The Paris–Tours was run according to a rather strange formula in 1965: derailleurs were banned from the bikes. Those who wanted to change gear were obliged to dismount and move the chain manually from one sprocket to another, and those who did, including Anquetil, usually had a photographer on the spot to

---

*His speed in the Grand Prix des Nations was an astonishing 47.669 k.p.h. – faster than the Hour Record. Jacques said this was not possible, so the course was remeasured: he was found to be correct.

record the event. It reminded people of racing back in the 1930s when many riders were unconvinced of the advantages of the new-fangled and unreliable gears. To add to the controversy in 1965, the race was won by the Dutchman, Gerben Karstens, at record speed, albeit with a strong following wind.

Anquetil finally won his second Baracchi Trophy, partnered by his friend and team-mate, Jean Stablinski. It was a victory that gave him a lot of pleasure since it helped to wipe out the painful memory of 1962.

It had been quite a year and it was only fitting that, for the third time in his career, he won the Super Prestige Pernod – all the more so, perhaps, because in the previous season, despite his historic double in the Tour and the Giro, the trophy had gone to Poulidor. In 1965 Jacques felt he had something to prove and, as always when he was in that frame of mind, he did just that.

Chapter Sixteen

This was Anquetil's fourteenth season at the top and he had had more luck than most professionals could dream of. In 1958, and again in 1962, he had had a couple of debilitating illnesses, but even they had only lasted a matter of weeks. He suffered very few accidents, and no broken bones, indeed the researcher will be very hard put to find a photograph which shows a plaster or bandage on one of his limbs. His policy of economising his efforts in the interest of prolonging his career seemed to be paying off. The fact that, compared with other riders, he took drugs sparingly (even if it was on a regular basis) seemed to have underlined, in his own mind, his theory that if these products were strictly limited, then they would do him no harm in the long run.

He had pulled off three famous doubles – in 1963, 1964 and 1965 and, finally, he had won the hearts of much of the French public. This had been his greatest battle of all. He had left the 1965 Tour de France clear for Poulidor to win, but Raymond had been unable to do so. Here was positive proof that 'Pou-Pou' was not in the same league as he was. Poulidor was only two years younger than Jacques, and at his age Jacques had won five Tours de France, two Tours of Italy, one Tour of Spain, three classics and countless time trials. Poulidor could not match this: despite winning the Tour of Spain, a national championship, two classics and victories in many other top-class races, not to mention numerous podium positions, Anquetil's record continued to put him in the shade. 'Pou-Pou' did eventually win the Paris–Nice twice, but only after Anquetil had retired; he almost always played second fiddle while Jacques was racing. The rare exception to this was in the French classic, the Criterium National, which Poulidor ended up winning five times to Anquetil's four. Clearly the Norman was the boss, even if Poulidor remained the more popular in the eyes of the French public.

With such overwhelming proof of his superiority, Jacques believed that, at the very least, he had the right to be as popular as Raymond, but things did not happen that way. Raymond gained an enormous amount of sympathy for his bad luck, whereas Anquetil's elegance was taken for snobbishness. If the Mercier rider gave every impression of innocence, then Jacques seemed machiavellian. If the Norman was sophisticated, then the man from Limoges exhibited a natural simplicity.

The French actor, Claude Brasseur, summed it up best when he said, 'The man in the street always has little set-backs, but this never seems to happen to Jacques. When he is on form he wins without trouble. When he is off form he still wins, but by small margins. Coppi was vulnerable, but won stages in the Alps; Jacques Anquetil can only finish second or third, but still keeps his yellow jersey. Seeing him untouched by misfortune, he is seen as an exceptional being – admired, but not loved.'

'The man in the street' had loved Coppi's kind and gentle character. They had adored his victories which had always been overwhelming and glorious. Poulidor was popular because he, too, had his share of 'little set-backs'; people could identify themselves with him – indeed, he was one of them. Too many agreed with Antonin Magne when he said, 'Jacques is out of the ordinary. An athlete who has the mind of a businessman and, like a businessman, sometimes without humanity – cold, and hard.'

Anquetil was enraged by what he considered to be such unjust criticism. His successes had been due to very hard training and the ability to suffer more than anyone else could. If he was blessed with natural class, good luck and excellent health, then he could hardly be criticised for it. If he was unable to achieve Poulidor's popularity, it was because he really did not fully understand what the public wanted. Even if he had realised, he would have refused to be anybody but himself. He came to consider that his only course of action was to prevent Raymond from winning too much.

Jacques started the 1966 season well by winning the Tour of Sardinia. Géminiani, who knew precisely how to restore his morale, would say to him in the morning, 'Oh, Jacques, I must tell you, I've found this little restaurant where they do the most fantastic fish.'

'Oh, yes?' Jacques would say.

'Yes and they've got this local wine which is just superb.'

'Oh, great, great.' And Jacques would ride the whole day as happy as a sandboy. The next day it would be repeated.

'Oh, Jacques,' Géminiani would say. 'I must tell you. You know how you like venison? Well I've just been told about this famous place just around the corner from the hotel. The venison there melts in your mouth, and their wine cellar is supposed to be one of the best in the country.'

'That's wonderful. Make sure to book a table tonight so that we don't miss out!'

When Jacques got back to France he was upset to see that the papers were full of Poulidor and little mention of his win in Italy. He was to make his frustration evident in their first confrontation of the year in the Paris–Nice, which visited Corsica for a couple of days. When the time trial started he was wearing the leader's jersey. His mechanic had made a mistake by putting his saddle up instead of down and fitting longer cranks to his bike. Unusually, he did not warm up before the start, so he did not notice these differences. The course was quite a hilly one, more suited to Poulidor, who beat him in this chrono to take the jersey as well as the stage. Janine knew about the changes to his bike, but he forbade her to say anything as it might seem as if he was making excuses.

Many of the fans were wild with joy at Poulidor's success while Anquetil plotted revenge. The final stage was the most eventful in the history of the race. So much has been said about it, so much has been written, so much has been denied and so much has been confirmed that the whole truth of the affair will always be in doubt. When the stage started Anquetil's team mates co-operated with the Italians in attacking the Mercier team in general, and Poulidor in particular. The French Peugeot team sided with the Merciers and things got rough. The English Mercier rider, Barry Hoban, was put in a ditch.

The Italian, Adorni got clear and Poulidor was obliged to go after him to protect his jersey. Then it was Motta's turn: Raymond had to make another big effort. Then, after he had been brought back, Anquetil attacked, but Poulidor got up to him. He went again, but the race leader neutralised him. Then he went again and again until, finally, after thirteen attempts, Anquetil got clear. An exhausted Poulidor gritted his teeth and sought to limit the damage, but Jacques won the stage into Nice by 1 min. 24 secs to take the overall victory as well.

In the hall of his hotel Antonin Magne came face to face with Géminiani. Hot words were exchanged, the journalists fanned the flames and microphones were shoved under Poulidor's nose. Raymond was reluctant to say anything apart from a diplomatic 'Anquetil remains the master of cycling and has proved that he is clearly better than me.'

This satisfied nobody and he was given no peace. 'You must defend yourself, Raymond. What happened today was scandalous. You must give your side of the story.' Eventually, a weary Poulidor gave in, knowing the journalists would pester him until he did say something. 'What was done to me and my team today was not very Catholic,' he said. 'Jacques is a loyal adversary and, if he is true to himself, he will admit that what his team did was wrong.'

If anybody had failed to understand the inference that Anquetil had 'bought' the Italians, the journalists soon made it clear. Jacques was furious. 'This interview,' he said, 'on which he cast doubt on my morality and the value of my victory, is not worthy of a champion. I will not find it easy to forgive him.'

The Anquetil–Poulidor war had reached a new intensity, with France even more divided between the two champions. There was an unconfirmed story going around that one convinced Anquetil fan was married to a passionate Poulidor supporter. Eventually, the argument over the merits of the two champions became so serious that the only way to settle their differences was in the divorce court!

On 2nd May Jacques was at the start of the Liège–Bastogne–Liège, the oldest race on the calendar. It was a very hot day and Jacques fancied his chances. He gave rather curious instructions to his team mates: if he went clear and any of them were in the chasing group, then they must either retire, or drop back. He did not want anybody to claim that he owed his win to anybody else.

Reading the faces of those around him on the hill at Wanne, he saw that they all seemed to be at their limit. A first attack got rid of everyone except Motta, Merckx and Gimondi. On a second hill he dropped this trio, as well, and continued to increase his lead until the finish where the gap was more than five minutes. Felice

Gimondi told the reporters that when Anquetil had attacked the second time they had all been ready for him, but there was simply nothing they could do; he was simply too strong for them. Right up until the finish they had worked very hard together, but the gap had kept growing and growing.

It was the sort of performance that Coppi used to produce, and one which everyone knew Jacques was capable of, although no one knew just why he didn't produce this type of effort more often. Whilst giving interviews to reporters after the race, an unknown man tapped him on the shoulder and said, 'Excuse me, Mr Anquetil, you've got to do a pee.' Jacques vaguely thought that perhaps it might have something to do with the new drug controls in Belgium, but did not take too much notice of this rather casual approach. After an hour he left to drive to Valenciennes where he had arranged to have dinner with Jean Stablinski and his family.

The next day the bombshell came – Jacques had been disqualified from the race for refusing to take a drug test. He was furious, and said that in Belgium it was well known that such controls were for minor riders and foreigners, but never for Belgian champions. He protested that he had not been approached officially, that the controls themselves were inefficient and unsatisfactory. It was left to the Press to point out that if the ban was ratified, then it would be the Belgian, Van Schil, who would be declared the winner. Eventually the Belgian authorities gave way and he was finally credited with a superb classic win.

His next big event was the Tour of Italy. On the very first stage the race broke up on the hills above the Italian Riviera. There was the usual regrouping on the descent, but the front group was never caught and stayed clear to finish with a lead of 3 mins 15 secs. This leading group contained all the favourites except Anquetil, despite the fact that he had tried very hard to get up to them and had dropped all his team mates in the process.

'For Anquetil the Giro Is Finished', read the headlines and later events were to prove this to be the case. The Tour of Italy was always a very 'tight' race and, although a three-minute deficit should not have been insurmountable, he was beaten against the watch by Adorni and dropped on the climbs by Motta. He eventually finished third at Milan.

Although most people drew the conclusion that his strength was now on the decline, they were looking forward, nonetheless, to seeing Jacques return to the Tour de France as another Anquetil–Poulidor fight was expected and, this time, it must surely be Raymond's turn. Events in the Paris–Nice had, for many people, proved that Jacques would stop at nothing to beat his rival.

Unfortunately, the Tour did not come up to expectations. The two men spent the whole time watching each other. A couple of unknown riders won the two mountain stages in the Pyrenees; Poulidor won the time trial and then the two men went back to watching each other.

As they both fell further and further behind the race leader, the organisers of the post-Tour criteriums were again expressing anxiety, and started to talk of cancelling their events. Jacques said to Raymond that they were both beginning to look silly, so they should call a truce and work together to make up some lost time – after all, the criteriums were a major source of income for them both – but, when Jacques' team mate Lucien Aimar went away in a break on the road to Turin, Anquetil would obviously not chase. The group finished the day with a considerable lead and Aimar put on the yellow jersey.

So, Poulidor attacked the next day in the mountains, but Anquetil helped to protect his young protégé's lead. The following day Jacques retired, but, by this time, the race was virtually over. 'Pou-Pou' had proved that he was the stronger of the two, but Anquetil had the double satisfaction of seeing his team mate win and seeing Poulidor lose. Raymond could hardly claim to have ridden a glorious Tour as Altig beat him in the final time trial, and the Dutchman, Jan Janssen, took second overall. Poulidor was third.

Then it was off to the World Championships in Germany, held on the hilly motor-racing circuit of the Nurburgring – it was clearly going to be a race for the strong and the fit. The French team manager, Marcel Bidot, told Anquetil that Poulidor had agreed to co-operate with him in the interests of a French victory, and asked him to do the same. Jacques said in private that Marcel was even more stupid than he had thought.

Early in the race it was the young Italian, Felice Gimondi, who went clear to grab a lead of 35 seconds. However, Anquetil brought

Anquetil and Poulidor on the Galibier. Anquetil cannot lead: his team-mate, Jiménez, is ahead on the road, and pride prevents him from following Poulidor, so they ride shoulder to shoulder

The home-made banner reads: 'Anquetil, Poulidor – honour your reputation'

up Motta, Zilioli, Merckx, Van der Bossche and Poulidor. This front group gradually dwindled until only the two Frenchman and Motta were left. As the race was reaching its closing stages, Rudi Altig, who had had an awful morning constantly vomiting, was now feeling like a new man and chasing hard with Lucien Aimar. How much the winner of the Tour was helping the German is impossible to say – some reports said he was; some said he was not. That they were able to join the front group just before the finish was mainly due to the fact that both Frenchmen at the front were sitting up and watching each other. Jacques was very well aware that Altig would outsprint them both, and, for him, the only important thing was that Poulidor should not to win.

The German duly took the gold medal, Jacques the silver and Raymond the bronze. Anquetil had always so much wanted to be World Champion and this time he had thrown it away. Some said that it was not the action of a rational man and Jacques refused to take his place on the podium. He also refused a drug test and this time he was backed up by the whole of the French team.

Not surprisingly, the French journalists were bitterly disappointed that two of their countrymen had come so close to a gold medal, but France had been robbed of a victory that would have meant so much. The French fans wanted to see a Frenchman win, no matter who, so had Jacques stopped this from happening?

Roger Bastide smelt a rat and was at pains to reveal that, before the race, Jacques and Janine Anquetil had stopped at Altig's house in Cologne, and that, after the race, Janine warmly congratulated Rudi for beating her husband. He also pointed out that immediately after his victory Rudi rushed to thank Lucien Aimar, who was Anquetil's trade team-mate, for his help in getting up to the leaders. It was never explained why Jacques did not take his place on the podium, but his excuse that he was held back by the crowds did not seem very credible.

It is hard to believe that anyone would 'sell' a World Championship, especially Jacques, who had always said how much he wanted to win it. However, few doubted that Anquetil's main objective was to prevent Poulidor winning and Altig was certainly more likely to achieve this than he was.

Jacques could only finish third in the Grand Prix de Lugano time trial won by Adorni, but in the Grand Prix des Nations it was a different matter. The race had always meant so much to him: it had made him famous, started him out on a very lucrative adventure and he considered that his whole career was based on this very race. He won it for the ninth time – three times more than anybody has ever done.

However, the season was far from over: the Super Prestige Pernod was still up for grabs, and Anquetil had young pretenders, Gimondi and Merckx, on his heels. Gimondi could win this un-official world championship if he won the final event, the Tour of Lombardy, and if Anquetil wasn't highly placed, but after finishing second in the official Worlds, Jacques had no intention of letting this title slip. Despite a puncture at a crucial part of the race, he put in a fantastic effort to catch up with the leading group which included his main rivals. At the finish Gimondi just outsprinted Merckx, with Poulidor third, but Anquetil was only one place behind. This was enough for him to clinch his fourth and final win in the Super Prestige Pernod, which was so often won by the most complete rider of the season.

When it came to major one-day races – the kinds of events that pundits thought were his weakness – he had proved that he was still up there, still able to compete against the very best if he chose to do so. As far as the major Tours were concerned, however, the writing was now on the wall.

*1966 – Anquetil winning the Grand Prix des Nations for
the ninth time. This was the event on which his reputation
was founded after his first victory in 1953*

Chapter Seventeen

This was to be the year when Jacques started to abstain from some of the classic races, and finish even fewer of them. He remained obsessed with Poulidor's standing and it was beginning to be thought that Raymond would take the number-one spot in terms of results, as well as popularity. Géminiani was talking about an attempt on the Hour Record, but Anquetil dismissed the idea. He said he was too old, the record was already held by a Frenchman, Roger Rivière, and, anyway, it required too much special training which meant renouncing too many contracts.

These paid appearances on the road and the track had always been Anquetil's main source of income. He had been the highest-paid rider at such events for a number of years, mainly due to his victories in the Tour de France and the Tour of Italy. There was now no great incentive to make big efforts to win major races. It was clear that he was not the man he used to be in the major Tours and was resting on his laurels.

This lack of ambition threw Géminiani into a series of rages. He had the best French rider of all time, but one who still did not live up to his potential. They had gone to the Vigorelli track in Milan two years earlier to conduct some trials in great secrecy. They were accompanied by Jean Stablinski, and the journalist Pierre Chany, and there had been some crazy idea of using a derailleur, but this had soon been abandoned. They reached the conclusion that a successful attempt was only possible with a larger gear, perhaps even as big as 52x13. These trials were taken so seriously that on one unofficial attempt Anquetil had taken some stimulants. However, Italy is not the ideal place to keep anything secret for very long and the tests were abandoned when the Italian journalists started to penetrate the track; but 'Gem' would not give up the idea of a proper attempt in September 1967, and embarked on the long process of convincing Jacques.

The Ford-France team had been disbanded and Anquetil and most of the riders now belonged to the new Bic team. If Jacques had entertained any thoughts at all of riding the Tour de France, they were quickly dismissed when it was announced that it was to be run on a national-teams formula. Anquetil and Poulidor in the same team was beyond anybody's imagination and, by now, most Frenchmen were pinning their hopes on Raymond.

Anquetil again started the season by riding the Tour of Sardinia, but treated it more as a training race, then went on to the Paris–Nice. This year the National Criterium was a one-day event in Rouen, but Jacques had a heavy cold so he announced that he would not be riding. Géminiani was staying at his house for a couple of days at the time and, as the alcohol flowed on the evening before the race, he calmly said, 'Oh well, Jacques, this time tomorrow we'll be celebrating Poulidor's success.' There was a deathly silence as the full impact of Raymond winning in Jacques' home town sank in.

'You really don't think anyone else in the team can beat him?' asked Anquetil.

'I'm afraid not, Jacques, and I doubt if the locals will be pleased. Why they might even be saying that you're scared of him.'

'Right,' said Anquetil. 'Get my bikes ready for the morning. I'm off to bed to get some sleep.'

The next day the town of Rouen was happy when Jacques Anquetil beat Poulidor to win the race and the Press said that the story of his cold had just been another of his big bluffs. It was his fourth win in the event. Much later, Jacques was to admit that Poulidor had brought the best out of him in the race: 'If he had not been there I would not have won.'

After the Flèche Wallonne in Belgium it was the Tour of Italy again. Although he was one of the main players, few people really expected him to be successful. After winning the time trial he proved that he was still a man to be respected, but could only finish third overall behind the man who many Italians believed was going to be the new *Campionissimo*, Felice Gimondi. Anquetil had now ridden the Giro six times and he had never finished lower than third.

By now it was the middle of June and France was beginning to be taken over by Tour fever. As expected, Marcel Bidot picked

Poulidor as team leader, backed up by Lucien Aimar, winner the previous year, plus one of the best team men of them all, Jean Stablinski. These latter two riders were, of course, Jacques' team mates in the Bic formation and Anquetil was far from happy to see them both being put at Poulidor's disposal. Jacques, the old despotic king felt that he was being sidelined, pushed totally out of the limelight and ignored. He felt enraged when the spotlight was fixed firmly on Poulidor and the media would talk about nothing but him.

Anquetil came to an agreement with the newspaper *France-Dimanche*, a 'scandal sheet' if ever there was one, to write a series of articles which would appear during the Tour de France itself. He promised they would be sensational. Jacques' brief excursion into journalism was a reflection of his own character – his taste for provocation and the extraordinary came through clearly. He was extremely blunt and said what most others only dared to murmur. In short, it was an exposé of the whole professional cycle-racing scene: yes, he took drugs on a regular basis; yes, all the other riders did as well; yes, he had bought off riders in his time, but it was nothing – just common practice.

It was total madness. All in the racing world who had loved and respected him felt betrayed, and wanted to hang him. The whole affair was very serious indeed, and people were beginning to express doubts about his sanity.

Unfortunately, all this coincided with the death of Tom Simpson on Mont Ventoux during the Tour. His death was judged to be due to heart failure brought on by several different causes, but, when a small quantity of amphetamine was discovered in his stomach during the post-mortem, the Press had a field-day. 'Simpson Dies Of An Overdose' screamed the headlines. 'Drugs Kill Major Tom.' Such is the power of the Press that to this day most people, cyclists included, believe this distorted, over-simplification of the truth. Anquetil is certainly partly to blame for the myth, and he was most unwise in not considering the possible consequences of his revelations.

There was an uproar in the racing world. Many people shunned Jacques and there was certainly no question of him being selected for the World Championship, especially after the fiasco at the Nurburgring the previous year.

171

The Tour ended in triumph for the French team. Roger Pingeon had taken the lead after Poulidor had had a bad day and lost all hope of winning. Poulidor and the rest of the French team worked hard to keep the jersey on Roger's back and, just to underline what might have been, Poulidor won the time trial on the last stage to Paris.

After the finish Bidot took his men for the traditional celebratory dinner at an expensive Parisian restaurant. Anquetil, Géminiani and the rest of the Bic team also got together for a dinner of their own on the other side of Paris, at the Green Parrot restaurant. It had been agreed that the Bic riders in the French team would leave Marcel Bidot a little early, and finish the evening off with Géminiani and co.

Anquetil had been genuinely surprised at the trouble he had got himself into over the *France-Dimanche* articles. He had always found it difficult to put up with criticism at the best of times, but now he was under attack from all sides. When Stablinski and Aimar arrived at the Green Parrot he turned on them like a wounded tiger. He said that supporting Poulidor was an act of betrayal and even held Stablinski personally responsible for Poulidor's win in the time trial! 'You're a bunch of bastards!' he screamed. When Stablinski got over his initial shock, he, too, lost his temper. The two men were all for going out into the street to settle the affair with a bout of fisticuffs, when Géminiani intervened and pulled them apart. The party finally broke up with bitterness and acrimony as 'Gem' told Anquetil how stupid, ridiculous, and unreasonable he had been.

Two days later Jacques apologised to Jean, but too much had been said, the wound was too deep and, in spite of an association that had lasted ten years, things were never the same between the two men. The following year Jean Stablinski joined Poulidor's team.

In the meantime, Géminiani got to work on Jacques: he had made himself unpopular; he'd made a fool of himself and the sport, as well; his obsession with Poulidor was, by now, totally irrational and he must, at all costs, bring it to an end; he still had the ability to ride a couple more seasons so he must re-establish himself; he had to bring off an outstanding exploit: he must go for the Hour Record.

Three days before the attempt at the Velodromo Vigorelli in Milan, Jacques held a well-publicised dress rehearsal on the track at Besançon in eastern France. There was certainly no question of him breaking any records there – the track was far too slow and it was also a very windy day. However, 45.775 kilometres in these conditions was very impressive indeed. People began to wonder if a new record might be on the cards, even though Anquetil was nearly 34. He then announced the sensational news that he would indeed be using a gear of 52x13.

With all the publicity, there were a lot of famous names present to witness the attempt. Rivière said that he was now too old to succeed. Van Steenbergen said that he had come to see a miracle – it would certainly be miraculous if he succeeded on that gear. The stadium was packed to capacity as Jacques launched himself into a very fast start, but his great experience had taught him not to overdo it. Then, as expected, he eased slightly before finishing very strongly to beat the record by 146 metres.

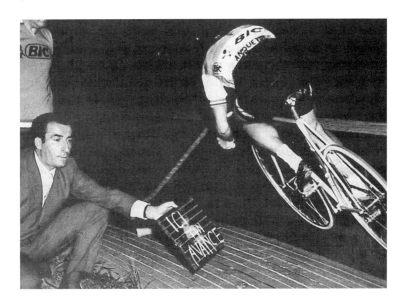

Anquetil during the Hour Record, encouraged by Géminiani

The Italian crowd were hysterical and those near enough tried hard to touch him, as if to confirm he really was flesh and blood, and not some sort of god, for this was an exploit that could be compared with his 1965 'double' of the Dauphiné Libéré and the Bordeaux–Paris. Once again he had amazed and astonished everyone. He had vindicated himself completely and underlined that he was not a doddery old king, faded around the edges, but still the complete monarch.

The Italian doctor appointed by the UCI introduced himself and asked if he could conduct the required drug test. Géminiani protested that there were no facilities available at the track and that his man could hardly be expected to produce a urine sample in public. The doctor refused to travel the 30 kilometres to Anquetil's hotel and, though he stayed late at the track, the test did not take place: the record was not ratified.

Once again, a great exploit ended in chaos and confusion, but this time there was no appeal. Jacques said that he knew that he had beaten the record and that was all that mattered to him; he was not too bothered that it did not appear in the record books. Nevertheless, in an attempt to vindicate himself he conducted his own private drug test when he returned to Rouen, and was found to be 'clean'. Géminiani's attempts to blame the doctor convinced nobody as Anquetil had publicly admitted, only a few months previously, that he regularly used stimulants. On the other hand, Anquetil's fans pointed out that Rivière had admitted to taking stimulants in his previous record-breaking rides. In those days there were no tests so the record had been ratified.

In the eyes of most people, refusing a drug test is equivalent to an admission of guilt, although with Jacques Anquetil it was never possible to be entirely sure. Of course, he had admitted as much, although, as Jean Bobet pointed out, Anquetil's seeming frankness was questionable, since he had been receiving money from *France-Dimanche* for his disclosures.

Drugs were first used in the sport at the end of the nineteenth century, but they were relatively ineffective. They started to be used widely in the six-day races and were often administered by the *soigneurs*. It was only after the war that they started to be used regularly by the road riders, and it was not long before these stronger drugs were realised to be dangerous. Everyone in the sport refused to talk about the subject and pretended that there was no problem. Their use became so widespread that virtually all the riders took them; nobody could imagine that it was possible to win a major race without them.

Jacques Anquetil, although he never tested positive, was almost certainly no exception: Pierre Chany, in his book *The Man of 50 Tours*, talks of the day when Anquetil came to an agreement with Baldini, before the start of the Grand Prix Forli in Italy. Just to see what would happen, both men agreed to ride the race without the use of stimulants and compare notes afterwards. The result was that both men were about one and a half kilometres an hour slower than they would normally have been, yet it has to be said they still dominated the race. Both of them, however, suffered more than they would otherwise have done, and both swore that they would never do it again.

You could certainly race without drugs, Anquetil said, but you could not race anything like so often. The top riders did not need to race so often, Jean Bobet claimed, but the real truth was that the racing calendar had became so full of events, and the pressure on the riders to compete so great, because those who controlled the sport knew that those stimulants would help the riders get through what was then felt to be a long and arduous season. The public may well have believed that taking drugs was a form of cheating, but the riders did not see it that way. For them drugs were something that made a very hard job a little easier.

To allay public fears the cycling authorities did, eventually, introduce drug tests. These, however, were ineffective; they were mere window-dressing: it was not that the tests, themselves, were ineffective, but that all too often positive results were quite simply ignored, or the penalties that were administered were too trivial to serve as a deterrent. Occasionally, lesser-known riders were sacrificed to reassure everybody that the measures were working, but the champions were often left alone. If Anquetil objected to drug testing it was because he was so bitterly opposed to the cycling authorities'pretence of righteousness. Instead of doing something to solve the problem, they hypocritically insisted that there was no appreciable problem. Anquetil was virtually the only man prepared to speak frankly about the problem that infected the sport, and he was vilified for it.

Perhaps the attitude of cycling's governing authority to the drugs problem began to change in the 1970s, but their response was never really convincing even after the revelations that followed in the wake of the 1998 Tour de France. The affair is far from finished, but only now do we begin to have some idea of the extent of their earlier indulgence. Anquetil was a product of those times – he regularly used stimulants, albeit in small doses – however, he also chose to be candid about it in an attempt to expose the whole rotten system. For that we owe him a debt.

One day General De Gaulle, looking through the lists drawn up by his senior officials of those who were due to be awarded the Légion d' Honneur, noticed Anquetil's name missing from the list. He asked why, and was informed that it was because his name had been linked to drugs. The General was horrified that a man who had brought such prestige to the country should not receive its highest award. His name was immediately added to the list and he received the award at the Elysée Palace from the hands of the President himself.

For the first time in his professional career Anquetil was not selected to ride the World Championships. It was true that he had not ridden in 1956, but this was a matter of choice since he preferred to concentrate on the pursuit title. His non-selection was hardly to his liking and he took great delight in dominating the whole of the French team when he won the Criterium of Censeau. In the title race itself, the best that the French could manage was André Foucher's twelfth place.

As the season drew to a close Van Looy proved that he was still a force to be reckoned with as he won his second Paris–Tours. In the Baracchi Trophy Anquetil teamed up with the young Bernard Guyot. Although they finished in a respectable second place it was due more to the efforts of the younger man. 'Guyot murdered me,' Jacques said.

In November Jacques Anquetil became President of the French Professional Cyclists Union, taking over from Louison Bobet. It was an organisation whose principal aim was to protect the interests of the minor riders.

Chapter Eighteen

By the beginning of 1968 Jacques started to come to his senses and admit just how ridiculous his feud with Raymond Poulidor had been. He was obliged to admit that Raymond could often beat him in a time trial, especially on a hilly course and when, at long last, friendship began to grow between the two men, Jacques finally admitted how stupid it had all been. So many years when they could have been such good friends and the fact that they were not was due entirely to his intransigence. One of the favourite pastimes of racing cyclists is card games. Anquetil quickly came to realise that Raymond had a gift for cards, indeed he was virtually unbeatable.

For several years Jacques had been quite adamant that 1968 would be his last season and now that he had made his peace with 'Pou-Pou', and it was obvious that he was no longer as strong as he used to be, the public warmed more towards him. This new-found popularity was most welcome and a sign that the fans were starting to see him as human. He may well have found it torture to speak to strangers, he may well have detested public interviews, but nobody could ever have hidden their discomfort better than he. His strong voice and assertive manner certainly gave the impression of him dominating the situation. This, allied with the intelligence he used in making and controlling a race, led to a belief that he was an intellectual.

The very nickname, 'Maître Jacques', was very much more of a compliment than most English-speaking people realise as 'Maître' is the title given to advocates and QCs in France. But Jacques was no intellectual: his tastes in music were more for pop and jazz, but never anything classical and, strangely, perhaps, in a country where artists are greatly appreciated by a whole cross-section of society, his taste in art was limited to the cartoons of Pellos. He may well, on occasions, have had a quiet and reflective nature, but he did need people around him – he was quickly bored with his own company. When you practise the profession of racing cyclist you tend to live in a bubble – your horizons restricted to lots of training, lots of travelling, boring hotels and card games. Most professionals take to hunting during the winter, but this did not really interest him although it was something he did occasionally. Skiing was rather more to his taste and, now that air travel was becoming more commonplace, the West Indies was becoming one of his favourite winter haunts, but usually with his friends as well as his wife.

For the first time ever, he invited a journalist to his luxurious seventh-floor flat in Cannes which overlooked the sea. He said how much he regretted that Stablinski had moved to another team, but that the two of them remained friends. Uniquely, in his career, he had no precise plans for the season: he would not be riding the Tour of Italy nor the Tour of Spain, but a few classics, perhaps. He could not make up his mind about the Tour de France as he knew that he could earn just as much money out of it as a commentator. He still had a secret desire to ride the Tour, but would not be pushed into it by Géminiani, and there was no question of him riding in Bidot's team. Perhaps he was forgetting that the rules clearly stated that if he was selected for the national team then he would be unable to ride for any other.

In the Paris–Nice there was a prize for the fastest descent of the Mont Faron, with the time being taken on the finishing line at the end of the stage. His team mate, Lucien Aimar, said to him, 'Stay with me on this descent, which I know so well (he lived just down the road), and we'll work together to the finish. That way we must take the prime.' After the finish Jacques said, 'Lucien was quite mad. I nearly hit a rock and I nearly went over the edge. All that for an unimportant prime, just for the fun of it. At my age I'm still acting like a kid – it's simply not on.' In spite of himself he always found it very difficult to refuse a challenge and he got an enormous amount of satisfaction from conquering danger. He was to finish the race in tenth spot overall.

As the season progressed he was able to relax more. He proudly showed the press around his new house and farm, and explained that during the course of a day's work with the tractor he lost two kilos in weight which was only slightly less than during a ride in the Grand Prix des Nations. He admitted that he had only trained 50 kilometres in the previous week, but, now that he was a serious farmer, he needed to take advantage of the warm spring weather to do his sowing. The farm covered a total area of 1,000 acres which meant that he had to drive perhaps two kilometres back to his magnificent house. His previous house by the river had been called *Les Elfes* so he decided to call his new residence *La Domaine des Elfes*.

He was also able to enjoy his racing more and, since he was still able to win a few races and there was certainly no shortage of lucrative contracts on offer, he decided to prolong his career for another twelve months. Finishing second in the Mont Faron hill-climb was quite an exploit for a non-climber near the end of his career. He remained an excellent criterium rider, but when he only managed fifth spot in the Grand Prix Forli many people thought that he was virtually finished.

He started the National Championship race and, after helping Lucien Aimar win, he retired before the finish. After all the speculation, he did not start the Tour de France but finished 24th in the Paris–Luxemburg which, by that time, had established itself as the main warm-up race for the World Championships. He was, of course, a natural selection for the title race as the scandal which had been attached to his name twelve months previously had all been forgotten. Quite simply, Poulidor and Anquetil were still the two best riders that France had. This was certainly a reflection on the paucity of French talent at the time. Even on the decline, Anquetil could still pull something special out of the bag and finish eleventh place in the world title race.

By now the two main stars on the international scene were Merckx and Gimondi. The former had the greater potential, but it was the Italian who had, at the end of 1968, achieved the better results. So, when he and Anquetil lined up together in Bergamo for the start of the Baracchi Trophy, it was expected that Felice would be doing the lion's share of the work. This rather special pairing had only been agreed some five days previously and Jacques, having had a very light season, was rather short of racing miles, especially compared with the Italian. The heavy clouds looked as if the forecast rain would materialise, and everyone knew how Jacques hated the wet.

From the very start of the race the pair went straight into the lead and stayed there. The rain had already started to fall and, as it became heavier, all hopes of them breaking the race record disappeared. When the Italian started to weaken Jacques got stronger and stronger, and, eventually, Gimondi was unable to come through and Anquetil had to tow him for the final few kilometres. It was a fine and popular win, and everyone was happy. Just as, some eleven years previously, the Baracchi Trophy had marked Coppi's last major win, in 1968, it was to be the scene of Jacques Anquetil's last great triumph.

At the end of the season he was in dispute with the Bic company and was in the process of moving to an Italian team. There had previously been rumours that the Dutch Willem II team were after him and, possibly, even Mercier, as well. He asked Lucien Aimar if he wanted to join him in Italy and Lucien agreed immediately. The two men got on very well together, even if they came from opposite ends of the country. They had been sharing hotel rooms together during the season and had had interminable conversations about nature, and the world in general, but Lucien was the current National Champion, and Bic were not prepared to let him go; the only way to retain him was to accept Anquetil as well.

Although Jacques had devoted less time to his bicycle, he had nevertheless been quite busy with his sand quarry and with his bicycle factory. He had also been expanding his farm and buying more cattle. The enterprise was being mainly run by a childhood friend and even his young stepson, Alain, had given a helping hand.

One rainy day in November Janine's family were in the house when Jacques suddenly said, 'I can't stand all this awful rain. Let's all go to the West Indies.' He then rang some friends with the same proposal. In all, he offered to pay the expenses of no less than eleven people, but this gay, busy life never managed to overcome his secret torments, and his persistent worries and fear of illness, and death. Janine wondered if perhaps they were too happy. Was Jacques afraid that it was all going to come to an end? She never really knew.

PART FOUR – ABDICATION

Chapter Nineteen

By now all eyes were on the Belgian, Eddy Merckx. The Anquetil era was coming to an end and Eddy was the young prince, waiting to take over from the ageing king about to abdicate, and he was impatient. The two men were photographed together many times, and the journalists made a big thing about Eddy catching Jacques in the time trial of the Paris–Nice. However, it was not quite what it seemed as it was a hilly time trial, the type that Anquetil had never really shone in. What was not emphasised was that although he was caught, he still finished fifth on that particular stage, was third in both the other time trials, and finally finished third overall. Not bad for a 35 year old in his final year of racing.

There were the usual rumours that Anquetil might start the Tour de France, even in 1969, and Géminiani did nothing to dampen the speculation. But Jan Janssen, winner of the previous Tour, was now the official leader of the Bic team and Anquetil would never have consented to work for him in the Tour. He was present at the Tour, as a radio commentator. His prediction of an anti-Merckx coalition was somewhat wide of the mark and the young Belgian was not only incredibly strong, he was also thirsting for revenge after his unjust disqualification from the Tour of Italy. His win in the *Grand Boucle* was so overwhelming it is most unlikely that Jacques could have influenced the race in any way. It was after his magnificent Tour de France that Eddy Merckx was finally 'crowned' the new king. In fact, he went a step further and became the uncontested emperor of the sport.

Merckx could hardly have been more different from Anquetil: he wanted to do nothing but win, and win. There was no question of saving his strength, of marshalling his forces, of prolonging his career. He was totally obsessed with the sport, interested in nothing else and only knew how to ride aggressively. Many have wondered what might have happened if the two men had met when they were both at the height of their form. Most believe that the Belgian would have forced Jacques to race much harder, and would have brought the best out in him. Perhaps one of the real tragedies of the Frenchman's career was the fact that from 1961 onwards – his best years – there was nobody who could offer him a real challenge: Poulidor was simply not in his class, no matter what the fans and the journalists may have claimed. So, he did what was necessary, and no more. Roger Rivière was a different matter for he normally beat Jacques against the watch and his injury robbed the sport not only of a great champion, but also of a wonderful potential spectacle when competing against Anquetil.

Jacques was already almost semi-retired, and now basking in the glory of a long and fabulous career. He did manage fourth place in the Criterium des Six Provinces stage-race and followed this with his last major win on the road – the Tour of the Basque Country. Then came his usual clutch of wins and places in criteriums all over France, and a lowly 40th place in the World Championships behind the surprise Dutch winner, Ottenbros.

It was farewell to the Parisian fans when he rode an omnium against Merckx on the Velodrome Municipale in the French capital. He beat the new 'master' of cycling by five matches to four and, many years later, this rather uninspiring track was named after him. Then it was his final contract of all on the track in Brussels on 27th December, and it was all over. Some said that it was a deliberate snub to his home country to finish his career abroad, but it was more likely that it was the last contract of the year that was available and, anyway, there were not many winter tracks in France. Right up until the day of his last race he remained the best-paid French rider of them all.

Away from his bicycle, it had been an especially busy year for Jacques. He bought the small chateau adjacent to his farm. Built in brick, in nineteenth-century style, it had once belonged to the writer, Guy de Maupassant. When the purchase was being transacted the solicitor expressed surprise that he needed so large a house with twelve bedrooms, but Jacques made it clear that he wanted to entertain on a grand scale. In front of the house he constructed a swimming pool, converted the attic into an observatory with a powerful telescope, and, as usual, left all the decisions about furniture and decoration completely up to Janine.

He also had big plans for the farm: he spent considerable sums on expensive equipment and invested in new stock to improve the breed of his cattle. He was proud to show the journalists around his new estate. He had bought extra land so that he now owned more than 1,000 acres. He explained that he had renovated a house on his land and his retired uncle was living there. He possessed five vehicles including a large Mercedes and a Willys jeep. He had known his friend Georges Louzé since the age of seven and had appointed him to run the farm, while his stepson Alain also was employed on the estate. In the stables there were five ponies. He had set his brother up in business at Elbeuf as a butcher while his mother was now living at Igoville.

It was, he explained, only eighteen kilometres to Rouen and just over 100 to Paris, but he also owned a sand quarry about 50 kilometres away so he was expecting to be kept quite busy. He said that when he was six years old he cut his finger and his father slapped him hard, telling him that next time he must remember to be more careful, and, since then, he had always been.

He now had the time to sit back and reflect on the past. It had been an incredible career: the youngest ever National Champion; the youngest winner of the Grand Prix des Nations and the Grand Prix of Lugano; the first man to win five Tours de France; the first Frenchman to win the Tour of Italy; the first man to win all three major Tours; nine Grand Prix des Nations, five Paris–Nice, two World Hour records with a gap of eleven years between them. It was fantastic, but it should still have been better.

Jacques had had only three *directeur sportifs*. His relationship with Francis Pélissier was frankly disastrous – it was a bit like mixing oil with water – and he learned very little from the former champion. Jacques had spent a very long time getting his style and position right. He did it alone and unaided, and most experts came to recognise it as 'cycling perfection'.* But all Pélissier could tell him was: 'You ride like a potato. You're too high on your bike;

---

*In his later years Anquetil became very friendly with Bernard Hinault and, after they had discussed the matter in some detail, they came to the conclusion that Jacques would have benefited from a different position.

your toe-clips are too short; your position is too hunched up, and you do not use your ankles.' Although Jacques always respected Pélissier for his long and brilliant career – he was, after all, one of the most important figures in the history of the sport – he never fully recovered from what he considered to be the insult of Pélissier following Koblet, rather than him, in the 1954 Grand Prix des Nations.

After this, his second team manager, Paul Wiegant, could only have been an improvement. Whilst he may have been a good and competent manager, it is rather doubtful if he was a big influence in Anquetil's life. After Wiegant had deliberately given him false time checks in the Grand Prix des Nations, Jacques would never trust him again. Even so, Anquetil's initial reaction was to prefer him to Géminiani – he thought that anybody would be better than Raphaël. Géminiani was to push him to ever greater exploits, but to do so he had to use all of his guile and methods of persuasion.

It may have been a successful relationship, but it was also a stormy one as the man from Clermont-Ferrand went into wild rages at Jacques' lack of ambition and disinterest in panache. 'Anquetil never satisfied me,' he said. 'He won eight major Tours without ever once being first over a major climb.' For someone whose career was never affected by a major injury, his record in the classics was quite abysmal. He was the best *rouleur* of all time, beyond all question. His class was out of this world, his courage was unimaginable, but two classic wins was nothing compared with what he should have achieved.

Then there was the national team manager, Marcel Bidot (whose official title was *Directeur Technique*). Anquetil certainly respected him, but, at the same time, thought he lacked personality and was too serious. In a long stage-race you needed to relax and joke a little, and Géminiani filled this role admirably.

The unofficial title of *Campionissimo* is, of course, reserved for Italian riders and it is difficult to say exactly how you qualify for the title. There have only been four in the history of the sport (Italy has been waiting 40 years for another). Perhaps you could say that you need to win five major Tours and five classics to qualify. If this is the case, Merckx would have qualified twice over, Hinault would have qualified as well, but Anquetil (and Induráin, for that matter) would not.

Jacques' career spanned a remarkable period of change and upheaval: the Fourth Republic had been the most unfortunate in French history, particularly noted for its instability in a country already known for its political volatility. Ill-judged colonial wars had ended in disaster and shame, leaving the country to be rescued by its wartime leader-in-exile. He did great things to restore the confidence and prestige of his country, but his nerve cracked during what proved to be the country's biggest civilian turmoil since the French Revolution: Charles de Gaulle resigned less than a year after the 'Events of 1968'.

The whole sport of cycling also altered during Jacques' time, with the introduction of *extra-sportif* sponsors and the appearance of TV. The former saved the sport by its large injections of cash, and the latter changed the face of it, not always for the better. But change it did, from being one of the least observed sports into one of the most closely observed. At the same time the fans discovered that, off the bike, their heroes were human beings after all. And yet, Jacques was different: he continued to baffle people. Now that he had withdrawn from the public eye, he found it much easier to preserve his privacy living the life of a lord in his own private fiefdom.

The year was rounded off in a particularly pleasant way when Daniel Dousset held a party in his restaurant to celebrate the sixteen years during which he had been associated with Jacques. All those invited brought their wives and the list included: Poulidor, Pingeon, Altig, Baldini, Jan Janssen, Gimondi, Merckx, Darrigade, Aimar, and Stablinski.

Many times Jacques had been asked to sum up his own career and he identified three achievements that he considered his most outstanding: first, there was his 'double' in 1965 as the Dauphiné Libéré was the hardest stage-race in France, after the Tour, and Bordeaux–Paris the hardest single-day event on the calendar. For many years after, Anquetil had spoken of the terrible hours he had endured in the race: they were, quite simply, the worst moments that he had ever known in his career. Second was his Hour Record of 1967, achieved at the age of 33 after being at the top for fourteen years. Finally, he was proud of victory in the 1961 Tour which had been such a strain on him, both physically and mentally. He admitted that he had been hurt by the whistles from the crowd, but he blamed the Press for that. He would never forgive or forget the piece in *L'Equipe* about the 'yellow dwarves'.

His best team mates, whom he also considered to be friends, were: Darrigade, Stablinski, Everaert, Rostollan, Mirando, Thielin and Cazala. His hardest adversaries were: Van Looy, Baldini, Poulidor, Bahamontes and Gaul.

And the person who helped him most, and influenced him most, was Janine. It was, perhaps, her experience as a nurse which helped her to understand him so well.

Chapter Twenty

Jacques could now enjoy life to the full. No more sacrifices. In fact, he never really touched his bike again, but he was not the sort of person to do nothing, and running the farm kept him busier than he had ever been in his life. In the beginning the neighbours were a little contemptuous and cold towards this presumptuous young man who had seemingly bought all this land for purely materialistic reasons. Photos of him taking delivery of cattle from Britain wearing a snazzy three-piece check suit and mucking out cowsheds in suede shoes were hardly likely to help his credibility. Most Frenchmen who worked the land were more akin to smallholders than farmers, so they had little respect for someone who paid someone else to run his farm for him. Working the land meant getting your hands dirty, not driving around your estate in a big car.

However, Jacques was prepared to learn. He gave up on cattle and concentrated on crops, thus spending long hours on his tractor, and no longer looking like the dandy he had always been. He was never happier than when driving a tractor, never more delighted than when his crops started to shoot up, and never more enthralled than when walking through his woods at night observing the wild animals. Anquetil had always been a 'night' person and, apart from spending all night amongst the trees, he would also spend long hours studying the night sky. It seemed something of a paradox that a man who had needed company to restore his morale, now admitted that he was able to combine a love of solitude with a love of the land.

He started to read extensively – mostly scientific works since fiction did not interest him at all. He had big reunions with his boyhood friends, numerous *fêtes de familles* and loved to invite all his friends from his racing days. With twelve bedrooms he could accommodate a large number of guests. He was a charming, delightful and wonderful host, and a very generous man. Perhaps, at the same time, this excessive hospitality continued to give him the feeling of being in control of the situation. His wife had always done her best to give him this impression, possibly because he always needed to feel on top of things.

Although he never used his bikes, he still maintained his own private cycle museum, which might seem rather strange for someone who, previously, had always shown little interest in his racing machines, preferring to leave their preparation – even the choice of gears – up to his mechanics. He had never demanded much of them: he never even asked them to wash his handlebar tape, for instance. On the other hand, he always took great pride in his own personal appearance and usually visited the hairdressers on the day before a time trial.

His chateau at Neuville Chant d'Oisel became a haven of peace and tranquillity. Jacques was never so happy as when he was at home. He liked to travel and to be involved in bike racing, and he always spent a month in his skiing chalet at St Gervais, but could never get back home soon enough. He did, however, join the organisation of Paris–Nice, work as an adviser to the French Cycling Federation and write a column for *L'Equipe,* the organising newspaper of the Tour de France. He was also a radio commentator whose insight enabled him to sum up a race better than anyone. These paid commitments to the sport were, so it was said, a welcome source of income. With the château, the extra land and expensive farming equipment, Jacques was thought to have considerably extended himself financially. To maintain his lifestyle and lavish hospitality he needed some extra revenue. There were others, however, who viewed this somewhat sceptically, saying that Anquetil was always 'a real Norman' – the French equivalent of an English man accusing somebody of being 'a real Scot'.

He saw a lot more of Poulidor because he now considered that their years of rivalry was a period when they should have been friends, and now he wanted to make up for lost time. However, Raymond was not in the least interested in Jacques' farm. He had suffered too much as a child on the land ever to want to go back to it; he planned to go into the real-estate business.

Anquetil, like all former champions, was always happy to be interviewed and talk about the old days, and, now that he no longer had any need to bluff, his observations were all the more interesting. He said that he admired Bobet, but he never really liked him. Louison was the type who would take advantage of the misfortune of other riders while he, Jacques, never did. His brother, Jean Bobet, was a totally different kettle of fish.

He went on to say that he believed he had been a stimulus for Poulidor, just as Raymond had been for him. He thought that he had brought out the best in his rival in stage-races, but admitted that 'Pou-Pou' was usually very good in one-day events.

Poulidor said that when he was young Anquetil was his idol and neither of them was very happy with their rivalry which had been built up so much by the press, but the crowds often enjoyed seeing one of the top men fail. The more Jacques tried to prevent him winning, the more popular he, Raymond, became. He went on to say that he considered himself to be better than Jacques in a hilly time trial, his equal in a one-day race, but he was always dominated in a Tour – Jacques always seemed to have fewer crashes and fewer punctures; he had the ability to go to the limit, and, perhaps, even beyond, which Poulidor never could. He thought Anquetil was one of the most stylish bike riders of all time, and that it was a natural thing. The way he could easily turn a 54x13 – he was a phenomenon!

There was an interesting story told by Robert Chapatte, the TV commentator and former Tour de France rider. Both he and Jacques were in Mexico in 1971 to report on the Hour Record attempt by Eddy Merckx. Most people thought that with a man of Merckx's class the whole thing would be a formality, especially at altitude: all he had to do was turn up and ride. Eddy duly broke the record and was immediately whisked away by the Mexican police to the privacy of a trackside cabin. Only Chapatte and Anquetil were allowed to enter. Merckx was stretched out on the bed, his face contorted in agony, quietly groaning.

'Well, Eddy,' said Jacques, cheerfully, 'how do you feel?'

No answer. The Belgian just continued to groan and whimper. Jacques gave it a minute or two, and asked again.

'Terrible,' said Merckx. 'I've never suffered as much as this in my life before.'

'Where does it hurt so much?' asked Jacques. Eddy pointed to the muscles on the back of his legs all the way up to his buttocks.

'But why does it hurt so much? Didn't you train over the distance on the track and know exactly what to expect?'

Eddy shook his head.

'Then you're a real fool! When I beat the record the last time at Milan I took the precaution of a trial run four days beforehand. You should have done the same thing.'

'Ah! I didn't know … It's a pity!' said Eddy. He tried to get up, but was totally unable to.

'How you managed to break the record under those circumstances is beyond me. But I have to tell you that although your success was magnificent, it was also unjust! Do you understand me?'

'Yes I do,' Eddy whispered. 'But the main thing is that I've broken the record.'

'Well, maybe you did,' Anquetil replied. 'But think what you could have done with proper preparation; you would certainly have beaten the 50-kilometre barrier.'

Eddy gave him a rather bitter smile. 'I've got to give it to you – you're still quite a fellow!'

Eventually, the two men got the Belgian to admit that he had started far too fast. Nobody believed that he intended to ride the full 60 minutes. It seemed obvious that he wanted to get the attempt behind him, and it was only pride that kept him going. They both tried hard to get him to say a few words into the microphone, but all he could do was groan in pain. Eventually, Jacques lost patience and exploded: 'It hurts! It hurts! Of course it hurts! Why don't you be honest and say you stole the record. You have no right to it! In the name of God there must be someone in that team of people you brought with you who could make you prepare in a proper way!'

Chapatte felt he must be dreaming all this. Here was Merckx, the greatest cyclist the world had ever known, who had produced the ride of his life and was still suffering untold agonies, and Anquetil was castigating him as if he was a child, even to the point of telling him his record was 'unjust'. It was a totally surreal scene, but the fact that he could do it, and get away with it, gives some idea of the respect in which Anquetil was held.

His personal life, however, was not to be as smooth as might have been expected. Anquetil was a strange, unusual man and he still baffled most people. No champion had ever burst on to the sporting scene so quickly. The life he had led had been somewhat divorced from reality. After being treated as a king for so many years, he perhaps finally took himself to be a king. Or perhaps Janine removed too many of his responsibilities; perhaps she – the ex-nurse, five years older than him – had 'mothered' him too much, agreed with him too often. Her comment that the last thing Anquetil needed was a wife younger than himself was perhaps indicative of how much he came to rely on her and that, after his retirement, he needed her less. Or, perhaps, he had just been too lucky, and had known too few set-backs. Whatever, for all that Anquetil remained one of the most respected men in the racing world, odd rumours about his private life began to circulate.

It was well known that Janine could have no more children so, when people started talking about Jacques becoming a father, everyone started to wonder how. A miracle operation, maybe? The baby was born and christened Sophie, but the circumstances of the birth were so shocking that at first few believed them. The truth was that Sophie's mother was, in fact, Annie – Janine's daughter by her first marriage – so the baby was Janine's grand-child.

Jacques' wife agreed to bring the child up as her own daughter, at least for a while. Neither he, nor Janine, would ever talk about their differences in public, but, not surprisingly, the couple's relationships soured and they eventually separated. Jacques continued to live in his manor and Janine moved to a small flat in Paris. The fact that Anquetil had managed to keep his personal life so private was an achievement, in itself. Claims of incest are clearly wide of the mark as Annie was his stepdaughter and no blood relation.

We have no right to judge him for his private life any more than we are at liberty to criticise his prolonged use of drugs. In that respect he acted no differently to any other rider, apart from the fact that he refused to be hypocritical about it. Whether or not these stimulants were at the root of his later health problems is very hard to say, but it certainly remains a possibility. It has been suggested that the prolonged use of some drugs can result in the premature onset of cancer. The examples given are Bobet, Nencini and Anquetil, all well known for using stimulants, and who all died in their fifties from cancer. Nothing has been medically proved, but the question remains. Jacques believed that he was safe because he took such small quantities, and claimed that it was more by way of helping him with a heavy racing programme, rather than improving his performance.

In 1976, and then a second time in 1978, he was diagnosed as having an oedima of the lungs. It is possible that this was an hereditary complaint: two of his father's brothers had died of congestion of the lungs, which was the reason why his grandmother had forbidden his father to take up cycle racing. A heart condition was later diagnosed, and he was obliged to take anticoagulants for the rest of his life. When his stomach cancer was finally identified, it was far too advanced to be treated with any hope of success. An earlier diagnosis may well have saved him, but Jacques, being Jacques, preferred to put up with the pain rather than make a fuss.

1987 – commentating during the Tour de France

Chapter Twenty-one

In 1984 Anquetil's life took a new direction when Dominique, fifteen years his junior, moved into the château of Neuville Chant d'Oisel. She had known him for many years, but had always found him unapproachable. In fact, Dominique had previously been married to Alain, Janine's son and had a little boy by the name of Steve. She was captivated by Jacques' sophistication, by his dynamism, his enthusiasm and his passion for life. In short, he was a joyous and wonderful companion.

Anquetil, himself, was beginning to suffer from stomach pains, but dismissed them as being due to overeating – at that stage they seemed insignificant compared to the suffering he had endured during his racing career. His favourite flowers were lilies, but Dominique, an energetic young woman, insisted on planting 300 rose bushes by the side of the drive which led to the big house. She encouraged him to dig out a lake to the rear of the building in order to entice the ducks and other birds away from the swimming pool. But, by now, Anquetil, the man who could never stand his own company, had acquired a taste for solitude as well as for nature. He showed Dominique how to identify the signs of the wild animals in the woods and opened up a whole new world for her. Many times they would get up in the middle of a moonlit night to watch the foxes, the badgers, the hares and the wild boars through binoculars from the bedroom window.

Jacques could still not resist a challenge and remained captivated by the thrill of competition. When he took part in Paris–Dakar, the famous motor rally across the desert, she was desperately worried and secretly relieved when a mechanical failure caused his premature retirement. 'It was wonderful, Dominique,' he said. 'The crowds, the atmosphere, driving across the desert at high speed, there's really nothing like it. The only thing I did not appreciate was the 5.30 a.m. starts.'

He was overjoyed at the news that Dominique was pregnant; perhaps this would be the son that he had always longed for. To celebrate the event they took a winter holiday in Guadaloupe. Jacques was never satisfied with easy adventures, but, when he went swimming one evening in a lagoon where sharks had been reported, Dominique was beside herself with anxiety. When he eventually returned he had a big smirk on his face, laughing at the fact that she had been so worried about him.

They had previously been on a trip on a twelve-metre yacht and he was amused when they ran aground, was fascinated when they flew over a volcano and loved it when the plane had difficulty landing at St Barthelemy. He always enjoyed travelling, while at the same time missed being away from home. Dominique worried each time they parted, but Jacques said to her, 'If I die, it's not too serious. In my lifetime I've lived five or six times more than most people have.'

He had always found fame hard to bear as he was always mobbed wherever he went.* It was perhaps for this reason that he so much appreciated the peace and tranquillity of his estate in Normandy. Curiously, when he was in the house he only seemed to be able to live with noise, whether it be from the radio, the TV or the record-player. It took Dominique a lot of patience to get him to turn the music down, and she often wondered if he missed the noise of the crowds.

When Christopher was born Anquetil was the proudest man alive. He absolutely adored him. He could not bear to be parted from him and took him everywhere. The baptism of the child took place in the grounds of the chateau and was a very big affair – all of the family, together with a large number of friends from his racing days with whom he had never lost contact. Bernard Hinault, with whom Jacques had become very friendly, became the child's godfather.

The following day the specialist from the hospital at Rouen discretely informed Dominique of the results of the tests that Jacques had recently undergone. What they had hoped was no more than an ulcer was, in fact, cancer of the stomach. She gently

* Janine has also revealed how he had always found the Press difficult to deal with, no matter how much journalists tried to give the opposite impression.

broke the news to him and he was overcome with a wave of sadness. 'I'll no longer see my children, the flowers, the trees which I planted or the little animals,' he said. 'Imagine what that means to me.'

A few weeks later he fulfilled his obligation as a commentator on the Tour de France. Although he received one and a half hours treatment every evening, few people were even aware of his illness. He believed that he could beat his cancer and, on 8th August, he underwent a four-hour operation in the clinic at Rouen. The surgery seemed to be successful, and he was at the World Championship in Austria where he had the pleasure of seeing a Frenchman, Richard Vivien, winning the amateur title.

The couple went to Colmar in eastern France in order to fulfil an engagement, but he had a relapse, and was rushed to a local hospital from where he was flown back to Rouen. All hope had now gone and, as the cancer spread to his spinal column, he endured the most terrible pain. He was still strong enough to settle his affairs and to make sure that his children were well provided for. His divorce with Janine came through at the end of September. He was even allowed to go home, but only for a couple of hours. This one last look at his estate gave him the most enormous amount of pleasure.

However, he had a steady flow of visitors and well-wishers. He told Poulidor that what he had suffered on the Puy de Dôme was nothing compared to this. Darrigade made the long trip from south-western France a few times. He had not seen as much of Jacques as he would have liked since his wife had been so shocked at the circumstances of Sophie's birth. On his bedside table was a bottle of holy water and a picture of the Pope – Jacques' religious faith had never deserted him. He faced death with courage and dignity, but, as the end approached, he asked his friends not to visit him as he was feeling so tired. It was also, perhaps, to avoid causing them distress at seeing him so weak. On the day before he died he received a visit from his aunt and his mother whom he had always loved so dearly.

At seven o'clock in the morning of 18th November 1987 he smiled at Dominique, squeezed her hand and peacefully died.

The funeral service was held in the magnificent cathedral at Rouen. Despite its size, it proved too small to accommodate the many thousands of mourners, so the service was relayed outside by loudspeakers. The list of stars from the cycling world was, perhaps, the greatest assembly of talent of all time. The only time the world had ever seen anything like it had been at Coppi's funeral, some 27 years previously. His body was laid to rest next to that of his father in the village of Quincampoix, where the great adventure had all started so many years before.

A Chapter of Quotations

There has been so much comment on Jacques Anquetil. So much
has been written and so many attempts have been made to
understand his enigmatic personality. Perhaps many observers
feel a sense of collective guilt that he did not achieve the acclaim
he deserved. In an attempt to dig a little deeper into his character
there follows a series of quotes from those close to him, distant
witnesses, and from the man himself.

Maurice Dieulois:	He spoke at length of the victories of others, but never those of his own.
	Jacques was the sort of person from whom it was difficult to hide things.
	It was difficult to get him to change his mind. He never admitted his mistakes.
	He really loved being a farmer and was even prepared to plough his fields at night.
Robert Chapatte:	If Anquetil was 'complicated' as many claimed, it was only because he managed to keep his private life from public view. Glory was only valuable for the material assets which it brought.
André Darrigade:	It was in adversity that Jacques became unbeatable.

Raymond Poulidor:	His supporters respected me more than mine respected him. I was upset when they insulted him.

You had the impression that the bike adapted itself to him.

Jacques impresses you with his calm. The riders liked him more than me. You cannot drop him when he does not want to be. I would never go in his car because he drove too fast. One of my most passionate supporters was in a wheel chair. One day he went to Jacques' house just as he [Jacques] was about to leave for Paris. He apologised for his departure, but said that Janine would make him comfortable and he would be back in a couple of days.

I rarely suffered as much as I did on the Puy de Dôme.

In the 1965 Criterium du Dauphiné Libéré there were the two of us and there were the others. At one point he was 100 metres down on me for over 30 kilometres without giving up. He caught me one kilometre from the finish and beat me in the sprint.

In the 1965 Tour de France I lost all of my motivation without Jacques.

Not a day passes without me thinking of him. When he died part of me went with him.

Antoine Blondin:	Jacques the Conqueror.

Federico Bahamontes:	Jacques was not a good climber, but stayed with the best because he knew how to suffer.

198

Jean Stablinski:	Jacques was both easy and difficult. All you had to do was to get him to the time trial in good condition. He never gave an order or criticised a team mate, but he was always worried. Training with him was incredibly hard.
	Anquetil had always benefited from a much stronger team than Poulidor.
	I was like his big brother giving him advice, his professor of the races. Anquetil's exceptional memory never let him down. He never complains to a team mate – that's why they all love him.
Lucien Aimar:	He always wanted to be right.
Jacques Goddet:	Jacques knew that I did not approve of his way of life.
	No one has the right to penetrate into the life of a champion.
	He always knew how to tolerate critics.
	He was gifted with a divine power.
	Jacques was enormously kind and pleasant. He was total harmony, sublime, a phenomenon. He blended with his bicycle like a musician with an instrument.
His doctor:	He had an above average quality of muscles and an exceptional ability to concentrate.

Raphaël Géminiani:	I adored him.
	In terms of strength, he was the greatest rider in history, but his moral behaviour robbed him of any charm. At his best he was a super man, but his ferocious selfishness and glacial temperament made me feel indignant.
	He was a stil, a jet engine and a computer.
	Jacques did not have an enormous love for competition. He preferred events where nothing was left to chance. But he loved the atmosphere and he loved winning. He never drank before a race.
	He sometimes rode 200 kilometres accompanied by whistles.
	Jacques ate practically nothing at the *mechoui* in Andorra in the 1964 Tour de France.
	Jacques has a special kind of charm. He acts like a teenager and laughs like a kid. He always amazes me and makes me feel enthusiastic, but he does not conform to normal rules. He is more intelligent than most, he has incredible strength and enormous pride. A man who is totally unknown to the public.
Pierre Chany:	Jacques never lived like the rest of the world. After the 1953 Grand Prix des Nations, he no longer belonged to himself. When he retired he gave the impression of having been every-where and done everything. In fact, he was still a kid who knew nothing of life. After his retirement he discovered another world.
	Anquetil is the anti-Christ of the religion of cycling.

Janine Anquetil:	He had a deep desire to preserve his private life from the curious. Prior to 1957 he had led an unstable existence, without warmth. He had moved rapidly from adolescence to manhood. The last thing he needed was a wife younger than himself.

When I left my first husband we drove to Paris in a newspaper van lent to Jacques by friends.

To win a time trial was a point of honour. He was always fussy and irritable beforehand, and looking for alibis and excuses. He usually went to his friend Noyés, a hypnotist in Paris. He believed in him as he had once cured him of tonsillitis.

He was afraid of death and afraid of wasting time. He always wanted to go faster and live life to the full. After his retirement he slowly withdrew from the world.

Anquetil, himself, had the following interesting observations to make:

I have a terrible appetite, but eat as little as possible during a race.

There is no stage-race where you are not obliged to surpass yourself.

I do not want to end up like Bartali, with no money.

Sporting humiliation is a man looking at his trophies while accepting free drinks.

I took all my important decisions alone. I have always rejected orders.

I beat myself to death on the Puy de Dôme in order to be insulted.

Outside my own small circle, all human contact is impossible. Everything is exaggerated.

I have no obligation in the classics because nobody pays me.

I told my team mates that Johnny Halliday pays his orchestra and they work for him. My team mates are my musicians.

I always had a desire for social advancement, but was never going to make it by normal work.

I renounced everything, including the classics, to win the Tour de France.

Bordeaux–Paris is like trench warfare. The night, the rain, the mud. Soldiers launched on forced marches. There is no question of pity or fraternity because men are up against each other, and our turn will come. The rider who has been knocked out is both someone else and ourselves at another time. We can describe their feelings because we, too, have suffered at another time the same fate.

It is not in my nature to be aggressive, hence my record.

Because of my rivalry with Poulidor, anonymous letters have threatened me with a violent death.

The 1966 Paris–Nice was a lamentable affair.

Postscript

The little cemetery in the churchyard at Quincampoix is now full and a new one has been opened on the edge of the village. Jacques' tomb is made from black marble and is the shape of an open book. A picture of him is engraved in grey marble and a copy of his red ribbon for the Légion d'Honneur and the blue ribbon for the Medaille de Merité are both slowly fading in the weather. The grave containing his paternal grandmother, Ernestine Anquetil, who died in 1941, and his father, was finally filled up after his mother, Marie, died in 1995 at the age of 91 in the house of her other son, Philippe. She had meant much more to Jacques than anyone else on this earth.

Philippe never became a boxer as his father had hoped: he is now a financial adviser for an insurance company. He has his own office in Sotteville and sells flowers with his wife in the market on Sunday mornings. His two daughters, Laurence and Béatrice, also live in Normandy. The latter was Jacques' favourite and he was her godfather.

Janine Anquetil maintains close contacts with all of the family and they all come together, including Jacques' brother, Philippe, for the annual reunion held on 18th November, the date of Jacques' death. Her son, Alain, now works as a company representative in Nantes while her daughter, Annie, has married and lives in Corsica. There are several other members of the family living on what the French call the 'Island of Beauty', so Janine now spends much more time there than she does in her flat in Paris.

Never has a nation been more determined to remember one of its champions. Since his death, the Velodrome Municipale, in the Vincennes woods in Paris, has been renamed the 'Jacques Anquetil

Velodrome'. There is little evidence that he competed very much on this track, but it is the only remaining one in the city. For some years there has been a cycle reliability trial in Normandy called simply 'The Jacques Anquetil'. There have been roads named after him and, in 1996, there was a big reception at what is known locally as 'Château Anquetil' to inaugurate 'Jacques Anquetil Hill', just a stone's throw from Jacques' beloved estate. In the grounds itself there is a small marble monument. It simply depicts Jacques riding out of the saddle on his bike, wearing his Ford–France jersey, with his signature beneath.

The following year, 1997, marked the tenth anniversary of the death of the legendary Frenchman, and the opportunity was taken to commemorate the man and his career: in his honour, the Tour de France started from Rouen where a shy Christopher Anquetil was presented to the media. His retiring manner, his blond hair and his pale face reminded everyone so much of his father. Sophie Anquetil was a little less in evidence, but she does look rather like her mother, Annie.

Many magazines and newspapers brought out souvenir editions retracing his career. They contained many interviews with his boyhood friends, all of whom still seem to be alive. So, ironically, we are more than ever aware of the details of his youth. In Rouen, itself, Jacques remains their most famous son and the many parts of the town named after him are a testament to the fact that he will never be forgotten there. Not surprisingly, most 'Rouennais' have an opinion on this controversial character.

Dominique still lives in the château and occasionally lets it out for functions. It was said that some time ago she did try to sell the famous house, but, being unable to find a buyer, was obliged to make the place generate some sort of income.

Six flag-poles provide the backdrop to the Anquetil memorial in front of the gates, and a huge concrete yellow jersey is set in the ground. The magnificent trees at the entrance to the grounds are floodlit (although, sadly, some of these were lost in the storms at the end of 1999). The climb up the Jacques Anquetil Hill starts at the level of the River Seine and lasts a full three and a half kilometres before finishing at the gates of the Château.

Further to the north, the house where Jacques grew up is still to be found in the Rue Maurice Ducatel in the hamlet of Le Bourguet. Urban development has meant that Quincampoix and the hamlet are now one. Indeed, all Ernest Anquetil's orchards have been replaced by a small housing estate. Even the shed where Jacques proudly put his car, which he won in the 1953 Grand Prix des Nations, has been converted into a small house. The hayloft of the house itself has been converted into extra bedrooms; there is a satellite dish on the side of the house, but, sadly, no longer any roses round the door.

Perhaps of most interest is Jacques' house by the River Seine, further to the west at St Adrien. It was here that he lived for most of his racing career and it was here that so many photographs of him were taken. It was recently flooded and it is sad to see it in such poor condition.

At first sight it is rather a pretentious house with what appear to be false wooden beams. So it is all the more surprising to learn that the house dates back some hundreds of years. A visit to the interior gives a totally different picture, with a rabbit warren of small rooms, delightful stone fireplaces and a superb sun lounge looking out on the river. On the top floor a partition can be drawn back to make one very big room which Jacques used for his famous dinner parties and which could be converted into his own small private, cinema. The jetty for his motor boat is still there, but Jacques never seemed to allow anyone to take pictures of his swimming pool. It was claimed that Jacques and Janine grew tired of their privacy being invaded by journalists coming up the river in boats trying to photograph them unawares, and this was one of the reasons that persuaded them to move.

The factory chimneys on the other side of the river, and the constant roar of traffic past the front door, make the location far less attractive than it was 30 years ago, but the interior remains totally fascinating. Jacques' house was originally bought by an English couple; it is not known whether or not they realised exactly how famous its previous owner had been.

Bibliography

Books

Anquetil, J., *Je Suis Comme Ça*, Voici, 1964
Anquetil, Janine and Chany, P., *Anquetil*, Hatier, 1971
Bastide, R., *Caids du Velo*, Solar, 1971
Bidot, M., *L'Epopée du Tour de France*, Olivier Orban, 1975
Chany, P., *La Fabuleuse Histoire du Cyclisme*, de la Martinier, 1995
Chapatte, R., *Le Cyclisme, La Télé et Moi*, Solar, 1966
Chapatte, R., *Alors Chappate Raconte*, Calman-Levy, 1975
Dazat, O., *Seigneurs et Forçats du Velo*, Calman-Levy, 1987
Géminiani, R., *Les Routiers-Flingeurs*, Calman-Levy, 1973
Joly, P., *En Brulant les Etapes*, Calman-Levy, 1966
Ollivier, J-P., *Jacques Anquetil - La Véridique Histoire*, Glenet, 1994
Penot, C., *Pierre Chany – l'Homme aux 50 Tours de France*,
        Cristel, 1996
Sevin, B., *Anquetil – Jusqu' au Bout du Courage*, Lafon, 1987
Terbeen, F., *Les Confessions du Maillot Jaune*, Pac, 1979

Magazines

Miroir du Cyclisme, 'Les Vainqueurs du Tour de France', 1987
Miroir du Cyclisme, 'Jacques Anquetil – Album Souvenir', 1987
Cyclisme Magazine, 'Special – Anquetil', 1969
Ouest France, 'Anquetil – Champion de Légende', 1997
Paris-Normandie, 'Jacques Anquetil', 1997
Paris Match, 'Jacques Anquetil', 1987

The richest sources of material are the weekly illustrated sports magazines, *But et Club, Le Miroir des Sports*, and *Miroir-Sprint*. The latter two are no longer in print, but have been superceded by the monthly *Miroir du Cyclisme* and *Cyclisme Magazine*.

Appendix

Jacques Anquetil's Palmarès

1951

1st G. P. Maurice Latour
1st G. P. Pont-de l'Arche
1st G. P. l'UC Darnétalaise
1st G. P. Bernay
1st G. P. Cycle de Caen
1st G. P. Pont-Audemer
1st Championship of
    Normandy (ttt with Le Ber,
    Levasseur, Quinet, Dieulois)
1st Overall *Paris–Normandie*
    Trophy for Young Riders
    (comprising series of races)
Plus seven other regional
    victories

1952

1st G. P. de France (tt)
1st G. P. de France trial (Caen)
1st French Amateur Road-
    Race Championship
1st Road-Race Championship
    of Normandy
1st Championship of
    Normandy (with Le Ber,
    Dieulois, Laroche, Anny)
1st G. P. Le Harvre
1st G. P. Commercants de
    Gaillon
1st Prix Talbot
8th= World Amateur Road
    Race Championship

Bronze medal with French
team in Olympic Road Race
(12th place individually)

1953

Independent
1st Prix Noël Ernault
1st G. P. Paul Brand
1st Prix du Pont-de-l'Arche
1st Prix des Cafés Nadi
1st Road Race Championship
    of Normandy
1st Championship of
    Normandy (ttt with Le Ber,
    Levasseur, Billaux, Brière)
1st Championship of France
    (ttt with Le Ber, Levasseur,
    Leneutre, Brière)
1st G. P. du Pays de Caux
1st G. P. de Pierrecourt
1st Prix de Godefroy
    Commercial
1st Prix de Doudeville
1st Prix de Rouen
1st Tour de la Manche
1st Du Harcouët stage of Tour
    de la Manche
1st Overall Maillot des As de
    Paris–Normandie (13 events)

Professional
1st Grand Prix des Nations (tt)
1st G. P. Lugano (tt)

1st Criterium, Haye–Pesnel
1st Omnium France–Italy
(Velodrome d'Hiver, with
Andrieux, Darrigade,
Hassenforder)
2nd Trophy Baracchi (ttt with
Rolland)
3rd Circuit de l'Aulne

1954

1st Grand Prix des Nations (tt)
1st G. P. Lugano (tt)
1st Criterium Pornichet
1st Criterium Plonéour-
Lanvern
1st Time trial stage Paris–Côte
d'Azur (7th Overall)
2nd Trophy Baracchi (ttt with
L. Bobet)
2nd Criterium des As
2nd Criterium la Grand-
Combe
2nd Criterium Châlons-sur-
Saône
2nd G. P. Rouen
3rd G. P. Geneva (tt)
3rd G. P. Guéret
5th World Road-Race
Championships
9th Criterium National
11th Paris–Tours

1955

1st Grand Prix des Nations (tt)
1st G. P. Geneva (tt)
1st Bol d'Or des Monédières
1st Criterium des Essarts
1st Criterium Brive
1st stage 6, Tour du Sud-Est
(9th Overall)
1st Pursuit Championship of
France

2nd Trophy Baracchi (ttt with
Darrigade)
4th Prix *l'Echo d'Oran*
4th Criterium Daumesnil
5th French Road-Race
Championship
5th G. P. Catox à Marseilles
6th World Road Race
Championships
14th **Paris–Roubaix**
15th **Paris–Tours**

1956

World Hour Record 46.159
kms (Vigorelli, Milan)
1st Grand Prix des Nations (tt)
1st G. P. Geneva (tt)
1st Criterium Rouen
1st Criterium Sallanches
1st Criterium Caen
1st Circuit de Trégor
1st Criterium Bellegarde
1st Criterium Nantua
1st Criterium Château-Chinon
1st Fourth Stage 'Three Days
of Anger'
1st Pursuit Championship of
France (beating Andrieux)
2nd World Pursuit Championship (beaten by Messina)
2nd Roue d'Or Daumesnil
(with Darrigade)
2nd Criterium Barsac
2nd Criterium Plonéour-
Lanvern
2nd Criterium la Châtre
6th Prix *l'Echo d'Alger*
8th National Criterium
12th **Milan–San Remo**

1957

1st Tour de France
  1st Stage 3A (ttt)
  1st Stage 3B
  1st Stage 9
  1st Stage 15B (tt)
  1st Stage 20 (tt)
1st Grand Prix des Nations (tt)
1st G. P. Geneva (tt)
1st Paris–Nice (winner of tt
  stage)
1st G. P. Europe (at Ravenne)
  (ttt with Darrigade and
  Forestier)
1st Roue d'Or de Daumesnil
  (with Darrigade)
1st Prix Langon
1st Criterium d'Alger
1st Criterium Hoeit (Belgium)
1st Paris Six-Day (Velodrome
  d'Hiver, with Darrigade and
  Terruzzi)
2nd Genoa–Nice
2nd Criterium Saint-Denis de-
  l'Hôtel
4th Boucles de la Seine
4th Trophy Baracchi (ttt with
  Darrigade)
6th **World Road-Race
Championship**
7th Criterium National
10th **Paris–Tours**
13th French National Road-
  Race Championship
18th **Paris–Roubaix**

1958

1st Grand Prix des Nations (tt)
1st G. P. Geneva (tt)
1st G. P. Lugano (tt)
1st Four-Days Dunkirk
  (winner tt stage)
1st G. P. Marvan (Belgium)
  (winner Stage 2A, ttt with
  Darrigade, Forestier, Elliott,
  Meneghini)
1st Roue d'Or de Daumesnil
  (with Darrigade)
1st Prix de Villaréal (Spain)
1st Criterium Château-Chinon
1st Criterium Decize
1st G. P. Rousies
1st Criterium Roanne
1st Stage 5A (tt) Paris–Nice
1st Paris Six-Day (Velodrome
  d'Hiver, with Darrigade and
  Terruzzi)
2nd Stage 8(tt) **Tour de France**
(retired with pneumonia before
start of Stage 23)
2nd Trophy Baracchi (ttt with
  Darrigade)
2nd Prix Montceau-les-Mines
2nd Criterium Bourges
3rd G. P. Forli (tt)
3rd Boucles de la Seine
3rd Criterium d'Alger
8th French Road-Race
  Championship
8th Paris–Vimoutiers
10th Paris–Nice
10th **Milan–San Remo**
12th **Paris–Tours**
12th National Criterium
14th **Paris–Roubaix**

1959

1st Four-Days Dunkirk
  (winner tt stage)
1st Criterium des As
1st Roue d'Or de Daumesnil
  (ttt with Darrigade and
  Graczyk)
1st G. P. Lugano (tt)
1st G. P. Geneva (tt)

1st Criterium Château-Chinon
1st Trophy Logines (ttt with
    Darrigade, Elliott, Graczyk,
    Vermeulin)
1st TT Stage Paris–Nice–Rome
    (5th Overall)
2nd **Tour of Italy**
    1st Stage 2 (tt)
    2nd Stage 8 (tt)
    3rd Stage 12
2nd G. P. Forli (tt)
2nd G. P. Bourcefranc
3rd **Tour de France**
3rd Trophy Baracchi (ttt with
    Darrigade)
3rd **Ghent–Wevelgem**
6th National Criterium
9th **World Road-Race
    Championship**
13th French Road-Race
    Championship

1960

1st **Tour of Italy**
    1st= Stage 11 (tt)
    1st Stage 16 (tt)
    2nd Stage 2 (tt)
    3rd Stage 14
1st G. P. Lugano (tt)
1st G. P. Forli (tt)
1st Criterium des As
1st Criterium Château-Chinon
1st Criterium Romans
1st Criterium Saint-Gervais
1st Criterium Evreux
1st Criterium d'Avenières
1st Criterium Sallanches
1st Time Trial Stage Tour of
    Romandie (8th Overall)
2nd Roue d'Or de Daumesnil
2nd Criterium Ploerdut
3rd Criterium National

3rd G. P. d'Alger
3rd Trophy Logines (ttt with
    Darrigade, Elliott, Graczyk,
    Vermeulin)
8th **Paris–Roubaix**
8th French Road-Race
    Championship
9th **World Road-Race
    Championship**
14th **Tour of Flanders**

1961

1st **Tour de France**
    1st Stage 1B (tt)
    1st Stage 19 (tt)
    2nd Stage 9
    2nd Stage 21 (final stage)
    (Leader from Stage 1B to finish)
1st Paris–Nice
    1st Stage 6a (tt)
1st National Criterium
    (Montlhéry)
1st Grand Prix des Nations (tt)
1st G. P. Lugano (tt)
1st G. P. Forli (tt)
1st Criterium Bain-de-
    Bretagne
1st Criterium Toulon
1st Criterium Caen
1st Criterium Annemasse
1st Criterium Moulin
1st Stage 6A (tt) Tour of
    Romandie (10th Overall)
2nd **Tour of Italy**
    1st Stage 9 (tt)
2nd Ronde de Montélimar
3rd Mont-Faron
4th French Road-Race
    Championship
4th Ronde d'Aix-en-Provence
4th Criterium Cenon
4th Nocturne Maurs

4th Criterium des As
4th Criterium Château-
Chinon
5th Trophy Baracchi (ttt with
Stolker)
6th **Flèche–Wallonne**
9th Genoa–Nice
17th Tour of Lombardy

1962
1st **Tour de France**
1st Stage 8B (tt)
1st Stage 20 (tt)
3rd Stage 2B (ttt)
3rd Stage 13 (tt)
1st Trophy Baracchi (ttt with
Altig)
1st Gold Cup des Monédièrs
1st Criterium Vichy
1st Criterium Laval
1st Circuit de L'Aulne
2nd G. P. Forli (tt)
2nd Criterium Saint-Claud
2nd Prix de Visé
2nd Criterium Evreux
2nd Roued'Or Daumesnil (ttt
with Stablinski)
4th Prix d'Ussel
4th Prix Sigrand à Nice
4th Manx Trophy (Isle of Man)
6th Criterium Château-
Chinon
6th G. P. Lugano (tt)
9th Criterium des As
12th Dauphiné Libéré
12th French Road-Race
Championship
15th **World Road-Race
Championship**

1963
1st **Tour de France**
1st Stage 6B (tt)
1st Stage 10
1st Stage 17
1st Stage 19 (tt)
1st **Tour of Spain**
1st Stage 1B (tt)
1st Stage 12B (tt)
(Leader from Stage 1B to finish)
1st Criterium National
1st Paris–Nice
1st Stage 6A (tt)
2nd Stage 7
1st Dauphiné Libéré
1st Stage 6A (tt)
3rd Stage 2
1st Criterium Vergongen
1st Ronde d'Auvergne
1st Criterium des As
1st Criterium Château-Chinon
1st Criterium Sallanches
1st Criterium Oradour-sur-
Glane
1st G. P. Ferrière-la-Grande
1st Criterium Quillan
2nd Trophy Baracchi (ttt with
Poulidor)
2nd G. P. Forli (tt)
2nd Prix de Dortmund
2nd Criterium Vichy
3rd French Road-Race
Championship
3rd Course de Côte d'Arrate
4th Criterium Ploerdut
4th Ronde de Valognes
4th Tour la Haute-Loire
4th Tour du Var (winner of
second stage)
6th Paris–Luxembourg
6th G. P. Felletin
6th Bol d'Or des Monédières

12th **World Road-Race Championship**

1964
1st **Tour de France**
  1st Stage 9
  1st Stage 10B (tt)
  1st Stage 17 (tt)
  1st Stage 22B (tt) [Final stage]
1st **Tour of Italy**
  1st Stage 5 (tt)
  1st Stage 10
1st **Ghent–Wevelgem**
1st Criterium Bain de Bretagne
1st Criterium Oradour-sur-Glane
1st Nocturne de Maurs
1st Criterium Castillon
1st Prix de Commentry
1st Prix de Saussignac
1st Prix de Quiberon
1st Criterium Evreux
1st Criterium Alençon
1st Criterium Graignes
1st Stage 1 Criterium National (Retired Stage 2A)
2nd Criterium Laval
2nd Prix de Braine-le-Comte (Belgium)
2nd Criterium d' Eu
3rd Criterium des As
6th Paris–Nice
  2nd Stage 3 (ttt)
7th **World Road-Race Championship**
7th Paris–Luxembourg

1965
1st **Bordeaux–Paris**
1st Paris–Nice
  1st Stage 6A (tt)

1st Criterium National
  1st Stage 2B (tt)
1st Dauphiné Libéré
  1st Stage 3
  1st Stage 5
  1st Stage 7B (tt)
1st Grand Prix des Nations (tt)
1st G. P. Lugano (tt)
1st Trophy Baracchi (ttt with Stablinski)
1st G. P. Forli (tt)
1st Criterium des As
1st Mont-Faron (tt)
1st Isle of Man Trophy
1st Criterium la Limouzinière
1st Criterium Soissons
1st Criterium Gouesnon
1st G. P. Vichy
1st Criterium Châteaugiron
1st G. P. Felletin
1st G. P. St Hilaire-les-Places
1st Criterium Arras
1st Criterium Meaux
1st Criterium Vitré
1st Roue d'Or (Cipale)
1st Tour of Campazar (Spain)
2nd Ronde de Seignelay
2nd Criterium Saint-Brieuc
2nd Circuit de Guerlesquin
2nd Bol d'Or des Monédières
2nd Circuit de l'Aulne
3rd French Road-Race Championship
3rd Boucles de la Seine
3rd Stage 2 Midi Libre (14th Overall)
4th Tour of Sardinia
4th Ronde d'Auvergne
4th Criterium Quillan
7th Circuit du Provençal
8th Tour of Lombardy
16th **Paris–Roubaix**

1966

1st Paris–Nice
  1st Stage 8
  2nd Stage3
  2nd Stage 6 (tt)
1st Tour of Sardinia
  2nd Final Stage
1st Liège–Bastogne–Liège
1st Grand Prix des Nations (tt)
1st Criterium Saint-Hilaire-
  du-Harcouët
1st Criterium Boulogne
1st Circuit de la Toulouvre
1st Criterium Ussel
1st Criterium Pléaux
1st Roue d'Or (Cipale)
1st Stage 6B (tt)Tour of
  Catalonia (2nd Overall to
  team-mate, den Hartog)
**2nd World Road-Race
Championship**
2nd Criterium Baden-Baden
2nd Tour de Campanie
3rd **Tour of Italy**
  2nd Stage 13 (tt)
  2nd Stage 19
  3rd Stage 16
Tour de France
  2nd Stage 14 (tt)
  2nd Stage 16
  3rd Stage 11
  (Abandoned Stage 19)
3rd Bol d'Or des Monédières
3rd G. P. Puteaux
3rd G. P. Lugano (tt)
4th Tour of Lombardy
4th Criterium Brest
5th G. P. of Holland
13th **Flèche–Wallonne**

1967

World Hour Record 47.493
  kms (Vigorelli, Milan – not
  ratified)
1st Criterium National
1st Tour of Catalonia (Spain)
  1st Stage 6B (tt)
1st Criterium Auxerre
1st G. P. Fabriano (Italy)
1st Criterium Censeau
1st Criterium Brettes-les-Pins
1st Criterium Flers-de-l'Orne
1st Roue d'Or (Cipale)
2nd Trophy Baracchi (ttt with
  Guyot)
2nd Tour l'Hérault
2nd Criterium des As
2nd Pursuit Championship of
  France (beaten by Grosskost)
2nd Omnium Championship
  of France (beaten by
  Grosskost)
3rd **Tour of Italy**
3rd Stage 8 (tt)Paris–Nice
  (16th Overall)
4th Criterium Château-
  Chinon
7th A travers Lausanne

1968

1st Trophy Baracchi (ttt with
  Gimondi)
1st Prix du Petit-Varois
1st Ronde d'Aix-en-Provence
1st Criterium Saint-Claud
1st Criterium Montbéliard
1st Circuit d'Aulne
1st Criterium Soissons
1st Criterium Maël-Pestivien
1st Criterium Armentières
1st Criterium Périers
1st Criterium La Rochelle

2nd Mont-Faron (tt)
2nd Criterium Limouzinière
2nd G. P. Baden-Baden (ttt
   with Altig)
2nd Stage 4A (ttt) Paris–Nice
   (10th Overall)
3rd Criterium Valenciennes
3rd Criterium Ambert
4th Liège–Bastogne–Liège
5th G. P. Forli (tt)
11th **World Road-Race
Championship**

1969
1st G.P. Eibar
   3rd Stage 4B
1st Criterium Curac
1st Circuit des Mégalithes
1st Criterium Rouen
1st Criterium St Thomas de
   Conac
1st Criterium La Clayette
1st Criterium La Gacilly
1st Criterium Vayrac
1st Criterium Sarregnemines
1st Criterium Bourg
1st Criterium Châteaugiron
1st Criterium Flers
1st Criterium Londinière
3rd Paris–Nice
4th Dauphiné Libéré
   3rd Stage 1A (tt)
4th Criterium des As (Le
   Havre)
7th French Road-Race
   Championship

Jacques Anquetil's last race
was on 27 December 1969 at
the Antwerp Velodrome. He
won the Team Omnium (with
Merckx, Altig and Ottenbros)

Track
Apart from those track events
previously listed, such as
some Six-day races, Anquetil
won numerous events both on
indoor and outdoor tracks –
pursuits; omniums; madisons;
points races.

Other competitions and awards (selected)

Super Prestige Pernod
1st   1961
1st   1963
3rd   1964
1st   1965
1st   1966
2nd   1958 (competition, at this
time, restricted to French riders
only)

World Cup for Teams
1st   1965 (Ford-France)
2nd   1961 (Helyett)

Trophy Emile Gentil (for outstanding achievement)
1st   1953
1st   1960
1st   1963

Challenge Sedis (Yellow)
1st   1957
1st   1965

Challenge de L'A.I.O.C.C.
'Lifetime Achievement Award'

Prestige Pernod (French riders
only)
1st   1961
1st   1963
1st   1965

Plus numerous other awards
– regional, national and
international – during his
lifetime (including 1964 BBC
TV Sportsview 'International
Personality of the Year'), and
posthumously. He also won
honours in France, including
Légion d'Honneur.

Compiled by Richard Allchin

Publishers' Note:
We have tried to be as accurate and detailed as possible in the preparation of Jacques Anquetil's *palmarès*, but we are conscious that there may
well be omissions or errors. If any reader is aware of any, we would be
grateful if they would contact us so that the necessay corrections can be
made in any future edition.

Copies of any of Jeremy Mallard's cycling prints can be obtained by
contacting him at:
    The Pen & Think Publishing Company
    5 Station Road
    Stattesdon   Nr Kidderminster
    Worcestershire DY14 8TT